HELLCAT
OFTHE HAGUE

HELLCAT
OF THE HAGUE

THE NEL SLIS STORY
PIONEERING JOURNALIST

CAROLINE STUDDERT

Matador
Unit E2 Airfield Business Park,
Harrison Road, Market Harborough,
Leicestershire. LE16 7UL
Tel: 0116 2792299
Email: books@troubador.co.uk
Web: www.troubador.co.uk/matador
Twitter: @matadorbooks

ISBN 978 1803131 610

British Library Cataloguing in Publication Data.
A catalogue record for this book is available from the British Library.

Printed and bound by CPI Group (UK) Ltd, Croydon, CR0 4YY
Typeset in 11pt Minion Pro by Troubador Publishing Ltd, Leicester, UK

Matador is an imprint of Troubador Publishing Ltd

To Patrick and Isabella

BY THE SAME AUTHOR

Elizabeth Studdert, a life in carving
Matador, 2018

CONTENTS

FOREIGN CORRESPONDENT (1945–1962)

'LA SLIS' IN BRUSSELS (1963–73)

HELLCAT OF THE HAGUE (1973–2001)

INTRODUCTION
A QUEST AND A TRIBUTE

I was struck first by Nel's deep, smoky voice on the telephone. I was looking for a job, and the famous old pioneering Dutch journalist immediately gave me every conceivable contact in the Netherlands. She also told me to use her name. Thanks to Nel, in spring 1981, I started my first regular job as a journalist. I was even working in the Amsterdam office of her former Associated Press wire service, albeit on the affiliated AP-Dow Jones financial newswire.

I didn't actually meet Nel until August that year when she agreed to do a magazine interview, which took place in her apartment by the sea in The Hague. She was a surprisingly difficult interviewee, rattling happily through her dramatic life on her own terms but reticent to the point of obstinacy about more personally revealing matters.

Nel must have been sixty-eight then; thin, tough and weather-beaten with a dark complexion. She had a long, craggy face like a gloomy monkey, until it lit up with a dazzling smile. She was very smartly dressed in a chic tweed business skirt and top over a silk shirt, in colour-coordinated moss greens. This was an elegant woman. I was embarrassed when my editor headlined her interview 'Hellcat of The Hague', but Nel loved it. After the interview, I said I would look forward to her autobiography. She said yes, indeed, she must write one.

Some dozen years on, I asked Nel, what about your book? We were lingering amid empty white-clothed tables, about to be swept out with the crumbs after some press function in The Hague. She said immediately, we'll write it together – in short story form. I very much liked that idea. Just then, though, I was starting a new financial news bureau in Amsterdam, so I didn't get a chance to start visiting her regularly for several more years.

By then, Nel had lost her memory.

I didn't realise this immediately, as she could still churn out her oft-told life story on autopilot. But now I couldn't get her to pause and expand on any particular scene, or depart from her own script. I just kept on visiting and recording, and worked on a book plan starting with her island childhood.

Then came the final blow. I phoned as usual to tell her helper, Sonia, that I planned to visit, but Sonia said I couldn't come because Nel was going into a care home that day. I did visit her there a few times, but by then her memory had really gone. One of her minders, journalist Friso Endt, reckoned it lasted about six seconds. That's not even the length of a sentence.

So what was I to do next? I had no idea how to write this book on my own, but I still wanted to tell Nel's story. That is, if I could find out what it was. A long struggle followed, collecting anything I could find about her, and interviewing anyone who knew her. This was difficult too, as people kept dying on me – Nel was no spring chicken.

After I moved to Prague in summer 2001, I was shocked by the news of Nel's death at the end of that year. Facing a writing deadline, I had to miss Nel's funeral, a great sadness for me – though Nel would have understood the deadline. So I just went on slowly collecting pieces in the jigsaw puzzle of Nel's life and writing draft after draft of the book. Later, I put her story away for several years, before being irresistibly if nervously drawn back to it again.

I have asked myself, what is the point of it all now after such a long time? The point is Nel herself, her life and struggles as a groundbreaking woman journalist. It's her highly coloured personality, the impression she made on people and they on her. Her charm, rages, tiresomeness and reticence; all are part of Nel. The point is one woman's struggle and one woman's views on journalism, on women and feminism, on her country, on the EU at a formative time, and on the wider world. It wasn't an easy ride for her. There are sacrifices involved in breaking new ground. But she has left us a valuable legacy. She's left us a generous slice of twentieth-century history, seen through the eyes of someone who was *there*. After all, who could have foretold the future of this motherless child called Nel growing up on a tiny

Dutch island in the 1920s? An island that was only reachable once a day by boat. Lonely, neglected by her uninterested, absentee father, dependent on the care of a kindly maid; a young girl driven to seek solace and a surrogate family with her best friend's mother.

When I met Nel in 1981, she was a legend in her own time. That feisty, groundbreaking woman journalist with the smoky voice; that woman who stopped Molotov – blocking Stalin's 'Molotov cocktail' comrade from being made ambassador to the Netherlands. Correspondent in The Hague for the mighty American news service the Associated Press from the end of World War II, famed for her turbulent thirty-five-year career with the AP.

And famed for her coverage of the Dutch royals, starting with the old Queen Wilhelmina. Then chronicler of Queen Juliana, from her strange attachment to the Rasputin-like Greet Hofmans to the cataclysmic Lockheed bribery scandal involving her husband, Prince Bernhard. Meanwhile, Nel would follow the career of Beatrix, the last of the three queens, from princess to monarch. And far away in Libya in the 1950s, she claimed a unique interview with Queen Fatima, long before Gadaffi's coup.

In a completely different sphere, Nel broke new ground in initiating the Associated Press coverage of the EEC, during a formative period in the history of the European movement.

Nel became close to many leading figures around Europe and the US, straddling worlds of national and international politics, royalty, trade, developing Europe and culture. From Dutch premiers and monarchs to unusual people like British diplomat and maze-maker Randoll Coates, and in the music world, composer Leonard Bernstein and violinist Isaac Stein. She formed enduring friendships with other eminent women such as columnist and writer Flora Lewis, while also remaining loyal to her best friend from her island childhood.

She was much decorated. For services to journalism, one prime minister made her a knight and another promoted her to officer in the order of Oranje-Nassau. The French government awarded her with La Croix d'Officier de l'Ordre Nationale du Merit for services to France. And there were earlier decorations for her first career in nursing.

I wanted to know where all this came from, and how she had got to where she was when I met her. From that little island, out into the world she strode in 1932, traipsing around Europe collecting languages and making friends. White Russian post-Revolution refugees met in Paris and Rome, especially, were to feature right through her life. And languages opened many doors for her.

Then came her decision to become a nurse, collecting a diploma from a top-class school in Switzerland in 1938. Next, she wanted to study psychiatry in Vienna, a pioneering interest in itself, but Vienna was full of Nazis. On she went instead to Rome, learned Italian and did some shocked Mussolini-watching. Abruptly summoned home, she arrived in Holland in 1939 just as Germany invaded Poland, triggering World War II.

Even then, who could guess that by March 1940, she would be nursing war-wounded in Finland after the Russo-Finnish war? Another very handy attribute for a future journalist was her knack of always 'knowing someone'. This won her the Finnish nursing stint – during which the Nazis invaded Holland.

Then there was the quite dangerous merry-go-round to get to America, ending in a twenty-six-day boat trip from Finland to Baltimore. On went Nel to wartime Britain and a slightly longer nursing stint, until her languages got her into more rewarding war work, monitoring foreign radio stations for the BBC. From there, she joined the Associated Press, then a mighty news agency in America starting to make inroads in Europe.

She fell into journalism like a hair in the soup, said Nel. Almost accidentally, maybe? But she knew at once this was something that really interested her, more than nursing. With hindsight, though, I believe the earlier part of her life was a vital part of what formed her and laid the foundations for the journalistic battles to come.

And what battles they were. Not only was Nel breaking ground as a woman journalist; as well, in a country emerging from Nazi occupation, she was pioneering a more hard-hitting style of journalism. And then she fell in love with a young American journalist. Together, they had a huge influence on raising the standard of journalism in the Netherlands.

Then Dan Schorr left, lured back to a career in the US. So there was a tragedy to be lived through. After all her numerous rejected suitors, she did want to marry Dan, but it was not to be. Nel picked herself up, worked hard and travelled, a few years later plunging into the complicated and evolving world of the European Economic Community. After that, her last stint back in the Netherlands was to feature the enormous scandal of the Prince and the Aircraft-maker.

I should declare my own interest, which was further piqued by her suggestion that we write her story together. Of course it's that Nel *was* such a pioneering woman journalist, along with being a colourful character with an interesting story to tell. She was also a second-career journalist, and so was I. For both of us, I believe this international 'wire service' work was a good way of learning the trade, simply because one is thrown in the deep end and has to churn out lots of stories quickly, day after day.

There are obviously huge differences between the worlds of 1945 and 1981, just as there are between 1981 and 2022. Geopolitical changes will always be the lifeblood of reporting, and I'm sure Nel would have been just as engaged in the changes that happened after her time.

Technology changes have, however, accelerated since 1981, when the big tech revolution was only just beginning. For instance, at AP-Dow Jones financial news service, we used something then that looked like a computer, but when you wanted to send a story, it actually sent a ticker tape to the telex room and somebody had to physically put it on the telex. And we still had AP-DJ news pouring off a printer and piling up on the floor, which you collected, tore up and sorted through when you came into the office – rather like hanging up the washing, I thought. Nel would likewise have routinely done that with the AP's output right up until she retired in 1979.

Nel did progress from telex to fax, but not to computer, mobile phone or laptop. So she didn't have to face these big later changes. Enormous 'mobile' phones and very basic laptops arrived in the 1990s; the early laptops had a horrible habit of slurping up your story into some electronic black hole just as you were about to send it. Search engines to help you out with missing facts were also only just starting. Meanwhile, before all this new technology got properly established, all of us news service reporters still had to run like hell to the nearest fixed-line phone to report on a hot story – just as Nel was so adept at doing.

In that window in time when we overlapped, myself starting out and Nel winding down her career, neither of us could have anticipated the extent of the coming revolution with the internet, wifi, mobile phones and social media, the last being the worst to my mind for journalists. I was glad to become even more specialised in the noughties and to leave journalism altogether in 2013.

This was also the year when the first, archival edition of this book came out, marking the 100ᵗʰ anniversary of Nel's birth. It can be consulted at the Netherlands Institute for Sound and Vision in Hilversum, new home of the Netherlands Press Museum which housed Nel's archives, or via the author at crstuddert@gmail.com

It seems to me that trustworthy standards of journalism are more important than ever nowadays with this massive tidal wave of social media and citizen reporting, and particularly as a bulwark against 'fake news' and disinformation. There is also still much, much more work to be done around the world to ensure that the voices of women are heard and that they can follow the careers of their dreams in journalism as elsewhere. And there is still the European project, tracked by Nel at a fascinating and formative time. Finally, the Great Flood of 1953 stands out in my mind as a climacterical event – a crucial event, and a foreshadowing of today's biggest challenge of all: climate change.

I hope anyone interested in any or all of the above will enjoy reading Nel's story and what she had to say about the world and the people she encountered, just as I have enjoyed the challenge of discovering this story.

CONVERSATIONS WITH NEL'S FRIENDS

This tale of Nel and her views on the world has emerged from very many conversations and interviews (after all, another kind of conversation) with a wide gamut of people, from archivists in Nel's hometown to journalistic supremos, and from prime ministers to beauticians. A handful of these played a key role in shaping the whole conversation, so I'd like to give them a brief word of introduction.

Yolanda Frenkel Frank, a theatre producer in The Hague, was fascinated as a child by Nel, who was a close friend of her impresario parents, and knew her all of her life. I am also much indebted to her suggestions from reading various versions of the book.

Tyna Wynaendts, OECD librarian in Paris when I met her, was Nel's heir and the daughter of her best friend on the island where she grew up. She added a vital thread that runs through the book, as she knew all the families from the island and was in touch with Nel throughout her life.

Piet Wackie Eysten. I am also greatly indebted to Tyna's brother Piet, a lawyer in The Hague, and Nel's most important 'minder' in the last years of her life. I'm particularly grateful for his generosity in giving me access to his published 'Life Sketch' of Nel containing a quantity of valuable material about Nel's life.

Friso Endt (RIP), fellow journalist and another key 'minder', also provided quantities of information and helped me with access to Nel's archives.

Hans Nieuwenhuyzen (RIP), Nel's nephew in Rotterdam, talked to me at length about Nel and the Slis family and took a great interest in the book, as did his wife, Janny.

See also the acknowledgements at the end of the book.

BEGINNINGS
DISCOVERING EUROPE
(1913–1939)

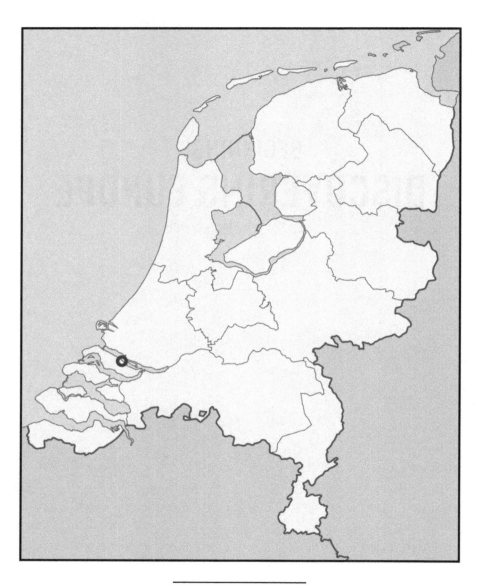

MAP OF THE NETHERLANDS

CHAPTER ONE

THE ISLANDER

Growing up on Goeree-Overflakkee

L ying off the foot of the Netherlands is the small island of Goeree-Overflakkee, separated from Rotterdam on the mainland by the wide Haringvliet channel. Back in 1913, the island could only be reached by boat, and seemed worlds away from the mainland.

On 2 September 1913 in the tiny village of Ooltgensplaat, Lena Koert, second wife of Johannes Aren Slis, gave birth to a baby girl. Christened Neeltje Adriana, she soon became Nel. Four years later, Lena died, and Johannes Slis moved back to the island's main town of Middelharnis where he had grown up. The forty-two-year-old widower did not turn out to be a very good father to his motherless child. Sometimes, I wonder whether he would have taken more of an interest in a son, but I doubt it.

Much has changed in Goeree-Overflakkee since then. Dyke-bridges have for many decades anchored the island to the mainland and to its companion island Schouwen-Duiveland, and Middelharnis is little more than half an hour's drive from the great port city of Rotterdam. But when Nel was a child, the island was still unconnected and isolated, and visiting Rotterdam was a major expedition into another world. In an interview near the end of her life, she remembered how it was at the beginning.

"You could go once a day over the Haringvliet, with the boat to Hellevoetsluis and then with a little tram to Rotterdam. That was my first impression of the big world," she told her interviewer. She remembered eating chicken soup in a restaurant called 'Wolf', considered *très chic*. "And then at four o'clock – that was already late because we had to go back with the tram – we had tea with *appelbollen* (apple dumplings)."

Going home was another marathon. "First with that little tram in the Rozenstraat to Hellevoetsluis. And then you went on this boat, sometimes in awful weather, that took three-quarters of an hour, or sometimes an hour… Then you went on a little tram again, to Middelharnis."

In Middelharnis, Nel's father, Johannes, who came from a prosperous family of 'gentleman farmers', bought himself a fine property on the corner of Stationsweg. Her nephew Hans Nieuwenhuyzen described it as a large and beautiful house, but it was later demolished to make way for undistinguished modern housing. As a matter of course, our 'gentleman farmer' also installed a farm manager to run his farm.

Middelharnis town council archivist Jan Both searched through the council's old records and discovered that Johannes Slis had a very substantial amount of land, and would have been considered quite wealthy. As Nel was fond of telling me, this was the best land in the Netherlands. Exactly how much land he had was difficult to work out from the archives, as farming families intermarried and there would be parcels of land in different areas. Inherited land was divided up between the family, making it a great advantage to have few or preferably no siblings. As far as I know, Johannes had none.

Jan Both was remarkably easy to locate when I asked for an archivist in Middelharnis' tidy modern town hall. He was a dark-haired young man, small and neat, and quite unlike my clichéd expectation of a dusty and reclusive ancient with a long beard. He would happily have spent all day talking about the island's history. As he rummaged in the archives and perused the spidery writing in huge old folders – which did *look* dusty – he kept up a running commentary.

"One married a farmer's daughter, and she had land too, so one married land actually, that was what they said then. Johannes' first wife also came from a farming family: Kadoek. I don't think that farm was so enormously big… The second wife also came from a good house, also with land.

"The third wife, the widow Mosselman, that was actually not a farming family, but in trading. But her previous husband, Overdorp, who was the mayor, was also from a farming family. So it was always in these farming circles that marriages took place. And they were always fighting about land…"

We shall hear more from Nel about that third wife, the widow Mosselman, who was to become the bane of Nel's life. And about the internecine state of warfare that existed between the families.

Most likely, Johannes' land ran to over a hundred hectares. The largest farmer at the time held 257 hectares, an impressive spread in Europe even by today's standards, and especially on a small island of around 160 square miles. As well as land, the Slis family shipping connections were a further source of wealth and status. The large collection of imposing Slis tombstones in Middelharnis graveyard bears witness to the prominence of the Slis clan: Nel told me the family could be traced back to 1545.

Johannes Slis himself was more interested in horses than in family or farming. He was "a gentleman farmer who never touched the soil," said Nel. "He more or less didn't need to. He was well padded, so to say, and he lived in a nice big house. He gave more to his horses than to the soil. He was totally oblivious to the difficulties of life, I suppose because he always had money, was born with money."

Nel described her father as "a dark man, with green eyes, not bad looking. He could be very charming, if you were not dependent on him." Unfortunately for her, he was always away buying and selling these tall carriage horses he was so interested in. He would travel all the way up the country to Groningen, where their breeding is still kept alive to this day by groups of enthusiasts.

"My father…" she mused, "I sometimes think, a kind of Bluebeard. His first wife died when my oldest sister was two. He remarried a woman who also died when I was two. Perhaps that is why I don't especially like horses. He was not what you'd call a father, not that interested, except to be told about when I came first at school. Then he was proud of me in a way. Then I got some attention from him."

I have seen these horses that so captivated Nel's father. One crisp autumn evening, twenty or more teams of handsome big-boned black horses appeared like a mirage from the past, snorting and clattering their way over a hump bridge across the canal in Amsterdam's historic Jordaan, passengers waving from the windows of beautifully preserved antique carriages. Then they were gone, like a dream. It seemed a romantic scene.

But for Nel, these horses were not at all romantic. She simply saw them as her distant, egotistical father's hobby, which took him away from home. "He was always on the go. He always found an excuse to go somewhere, especially to horse fairs. He travelled constantly back and forth to Groningen and Oldenburg, because there were these big, thick, heavy horses there."

While Johannes Slis was away from home indulging in his passion for carriage horses, his farm manager was in charge of a very different type of horse. These were powerful beasts for ploughing and tilling the island's fertile arable land.

Farmers in those days had special '*knechts*' or servants who had to get up early to take care of the horses and get everything ready for the arrival of the hordes of farm labourers. The *knechts* were socially closer to the household than the farm labourers, and were also expected to help out with other tasks. In high season, they stood by at the harbour to manage shipments of produce.

Isolated the island may have been, but when Nel was a child, it would have been much more populated than today and not necessarily quieter. Instead of cars and tractors, I imagine the rumble of carts and clopping of horses' hoofs, and busy scenes of loading and unloading at Middelharnis harbour, amid the rich aroma of the horse manure brought from Rotterdam to fertilise the crops.

Island society was headed by a small elite clan of wealthy farmers, a sprinkling of people in the shipping industry and a few 'notables', like the notary, the pharmacist, the doctor, the bank manager and the mayor – all very likely also from farming families. The most prosperous farmers were the large landowners on the big polders in the northwest part called Goeree, while holdings were small on the poorer land in the Overflakkee part. A polder is land reclaimed from the sea or river and protected by dykes.

Nel may have been neglected, lonely and often unhappy as a child, but she was also a child of the island elite. Perhaps this, along with her island toughness and strong democratic bent, helps explain why she would never be overawed by anyone in later life, including people in very powerful positions.

At the bottom of the island's social heap was the army of impoverished farm labourers, who had a terrible struggle getting through the winter. In the autumn, there would be hand threshing for a couple of weeks, and then virtually no work until it was time to plough again in the spring. A labourer's family would keep a pig, slaughter it and live off it all winter. The family would have a small patch of ground where they could grow some vegetables and thus struggle through to spring.

In the middle social stratum was a small group of artisans such as carpenters and shopkeepers. There was also a sizeable Jewish community, generally in retail trades such as clothes shops, but also often butchers and meat traders. Oddly enough, many people thought Nel was Jewish, though she wasn't. It did turn out, however, that the great love of her life was a Jewish man. I often wonder if she was a little fascinated as a child by such a distinctive group of people.

The Slis farmland, like the rest of the fertile Goeree land, was used for crops, mainly wheat and corn. Some sheep farming was seen from around 1900, but on the smaller farms outside the dykes. Before artificial fertilisers, the few cattle on the island were mainly valued for manure – but most of the manure had to be imported from Rotterdam. There, it was collected from the streets and shipped to the 'manure wharfs' in Middelharnis. The island cattle were looked after by herdsmen, who would have ten or twelve head and drive them up onto the dykes to graze, keeping a sharp eye out to make sure they didn't stray into the crops.

Nel's island was thus a remote, unmechanised farming world, based on manual labour. Small children generally take their social environment for granted, and I don't know what Nel thought of the many poor farm labourers, as I didn't find out about them myself until she was incommunicado. Nel did say that her mother was serious-minded and had 'social inclinations'. She used to talk about the poor and this was 'not done' at the time. I discovered there was a group of women in that period that formed a club called Dorcas, making clothes for the poor and running soup kitchens. This sounds like something Nel's mother might have done.

On top of the frequent absences of her father, Nel found herself cut off from her mother's family by the internecine family feuds. She maintained she never met any of them until she inherited some land when she was twenty-one. It seems a safe bet that land was a major cause of the friction; all those different plots scattered around must have been a rich source of border disputes. Even apart from the land, though, Nel's mother's family were against her father from the start and thought she should never have married him. They considered him a no-good spendthrift and were probably not shy about telling him so.

Nel often said she didn't remember her mother. "I'd just seen her in pictures and heard about her," she told me. Also, she would say Lena died when she was only two years old, whereas the records show that Nel was four. This seems odd, especially as she had a brilliant memory before she lost it. I have no explanation for it.

Another curiosity is Nel's completely non-religious upbringing. Archivist Both didn't find this as amazing as I did, because of a class difference in religious matters at the time. The big farmers took a liberal and quasi-agnostic stance, though this didn't stop some of them sitting on the church board as community leaders. The farm workers gravitated to the more extreme, strict orthodox 'Gereformeerd' pole. They probably complained vociferously about the libertine and godless elite. This elite was technically Reformed or 'Hervormd' and would be baptised, but was otherwise freethinking.

Still, Nel's case seems extreme. She claimed a completely areligious childhood: "I only understood the difference between God, Jesus and the whole club later, let's say when I was twelve or thirteen. Because no attention was paid to it. When I was eight, I asked my father, what's the difference between God and Jesus? He said, that you learn when you go to catechism." It seems a safe assumption that Nel never made it to catechism.

Nel's heir, Tyna Wynaendts, who was living in Paris when I met her, did remember that the well-heeled families of Middelharnis would never go to church or have anything to do with religion. But like me, she found it remarkable that Nel didn't even know the difference between God and Jesus.

"I mean, that's difficult to do, even for a non-believing family. I must say, my family still sent me to Sunday school because they thought I had to know a minimum even if they themselves only went to church at Christmas, because it was part of the general culture. But nobody ever told her anything – she was so lonely, she only talked to the maid."

Nel described herself as a serious, ambitious child, always very busy doing her homework, and very curious about life. She loved animals apart from horses, and owned a dog and a couple of cats. She led an active outdoor life, with plenty of skating in winter and swimming and tennis in summer. She learned to swim and ride a bicycle early, and drove a car at the age of ten. I wondered whether that was why she was such a terrible driver.

"We were one of the first to have a car on the island – and a radio," she said, adding irrelevantly, "but I have always needed the outdoors, throughout my life." She did like to emphasise her love of the outdoors, and it often seemed to me there was something breezy and outdoorsy about her slight, wiry body and in summer, her deeply tanned face and legs. I remember noticing her legs once, looking good without stockings well into her eighties, as they were tanned and slim and the inevitable veins didn't show up.

Nel was inclined to claim she was not unhappy and enjoyed the island as a child until her father remarried when she was ten. But Tyna said she was very lonely even before the remarriage, because of her father's lack of interest. Tyna put this down to his character, as well as a general lack of awareness of the importance of parenting at that time.

"I think her father was aloof and very egotistical. He looked after his horses and his pleasure, and he spent a lot of money apparently too. And he didn't really care what other people thought. Also, nowadays, parents know a little about the impact they have on their children by their own behaviour. Modern parents, well, they can't open a newspaper without reading about how it should be done, but in that generation, I don't think it occurred to people that it might not be good for their daughter if they were not more present, not more loving. In those days, they didn't even think about it, they just had their own lives, and if they weren't very interested in children, that was that."

At any rate, Nel certainly particularly hated the period after her father remarried. 'That widow' brought a younger stepsister, Trinette, to add to Nel's older half-sister, Jaan, from her father's first wife. As Nel liked to remind people, her 'Bluebeard' father's first wife had also died when her daughter was very young.

Jaan's son Hans Nieuwenhuzyen remembered that Nel could not get along with the widow, and there were always rows. Hans himself was clearly fond of Nel and got on very well with her. He and his wife, who was also from the island, kept in touch with her virtually all her life.

To my surprise, I found out later that the hated widow's daughter, Trinette, didn't die until 2000, apparently in Amsterdam, but Nel said nothing at all to me about her. Most likely they didn't get along either. Nel certainly complained vociferously about Trinette's mother:

"A woman I had absolutely nothing in common with. Alone with this strange woman, it was an unhappy time. I was stuck, the only one at home, as my father's eldest daughter [Jaan] was already married at that time."

In her loneliness, Nel clung to her Aagje, variously described as her father's 'housekeeper', charwoman or maid. "Aagje was the simplest woman you could think of, with a good heart. Really, I was brought up by the housekeeper. She was a sort of mother. Everyone was married, and I was left over with Aagje."

However, Nel did have one great friend: Tyna's mother, Jenneke. Two years older than Nel, Jenneke was the daughter of the island's notary, and in his big house on the Achterweg, Nel found the family cosiness and warmth she missed at home.

Tyna's brother, Piet, was to become a lifelong support for Nel too. Telling me sadly in our first interview that her friend Jenneke had eventually died, Nel said, "Her son is a lawyer with one of the biggest firms in the Netherlands, and if I was totally lost with anything, I always went to him, throughout my life."

This was the first time I heard about Piet Wackie Eysten. It was Piet who told me Nel kept a portrait of his grandmother, Jenneke's mother, beside her bed all her life. Nel was extremely grateful to this woman. Describing her as a very exceptional woman, she said: "She had us do handicrafts one evening a week, and then she read to us, preferably from books by Selma Lagerlof."

Thanks to Jenneke's mother, Nel found something of the warmth of family life that she was missing. Tyna said this was typical of her grandmother. "She once had Hungarian children staying with her when a whole trainful of Hungarian children was sent to Holland – I think they lived with her for more than a year. She was very much like that: 'Oh, if you don't have your mother, welcome, stay with us.' And a lot of Nel's generosity to all of us was based on that, I think."

Tyna herself also believes her grandmother was a remarkable woman. "A little bit like Nel in a way, my grandmother told people what was what, and if she liked or disliked somebody, you would know it in a few minutes. Very outspoken. And she loved Nel."

Tyna had a story about Nel and Jenneke as little girls skating, an activity in the lifeblood of the Dutch. "In Holland, that's what you do. Even when *I* was a child, the first day the ice was strong enough to go skating, the schools would close down for at least one afternoon, and the whole country was on skates."

Tyna said Nel needed to go to the toilet often, especially when it was cold. "So this happened when they were skating, and they wanted to hide, so they went under a bridge because getting on the land is difficult when you're skating. But of course the ice under a bridge is not so thick, so they both went through it, and they were completely wet and miserable going home, with everybody laughing at them."

When Jenneke grew up, she was originally engaged to a Mr Mijs on the island, Tyna explained. "Then my father came along and she married him, and years later, when my father died, she married the first, Mr Mijs. So they all knew each other and grew up together."

Looking at a photograph of her mother with Nel, Tyna reflected: "Here you see my mother, who really considered Nel one of the family, knowing she was so lonely and unhappy at home. So my mother and Nel were the closest friends, for more than seventy years."

I felt Nel's pleasure that they remained close friends virtually throughout Jenneke's life. "Our lives went in different directions, but later, circumstances brought us together again. Her husband died and she remarried later – I followed all of that."

She believed the lack of her own family in her childhood made her more inclined to strike up friendships. "I think you tend to make more friends when you have less family. I'm very lucky. I'm not so much extrovert but an easy mixer. Even if I feel immense dislike, it's with great gusto." This was certainly true, as later incidents will show.

Nel had several other extraordinarily long-lasting friendships spanning fifty or sixty years. Many were made when she lived and worked around Europe after leaving school. And for years after she retired, Nel did her 'Tour de France/Italy/Denmark/Spain/Portugal' and stayed with her friends in turn. But not for more than three days, she assured me.

"I believe the saying that 'guests are like fish and stink after three days'. Since I was freelance, I couldn't go away for three or four months. It was usually two to three weeks, country by country, sometimes combining Italy and Switzerland, or France; Spain and Portugal," staying with all her numerous friends in turn. While she also had friends in the Netherlands, Nel said, "In The Hague, they're mostly very good acquaintances – my friends are scattered all over Europe."

A recurring theme is Nel's insistence that she was a European first and foremost. She refused to be confined to the Netherlands, just as she had refused to be confined to her little island. As it happened, Nel didn't have to wait until she finished school to leave the island, because her father sent her to secondary school on the mainland, near Haarlem and not far from Amsterdam.

CHAPTER TWO
LEAVING GOEREE-OVERFLAKKEE
Secondary school at the Kennemer Lyceum

Before Nel left the island for a mainland school, she had attended the local R.S.G. Goeree-Overflakkee secondary school in Middelharnis. This school must have made a big impression on its pupils. In 1994, a local paper described the school's seventy-five-year jubilee reunion as attracting an estimated fifteen hundred former pupils to the town, including a seventy-eight-year-old man from Mexico City.

Nel also told me she met her first boyfriend on the island, though she was only thirteen when she left. "Very kindly, very nice, he wrote to me when I went away to school in Haarlem. He was the son of the mayor of the island."

What did Nel do, I wondered?

"It was all bicycling, going on the back of his bicycle. We just went to the beach, swimming, tennis, because there was nothing else to do. There were horses, but that horse business, it wasn't so fashionable then for women. But it never appealed to me. I was afraid of horses. Perhaps they reminded me of my father."

I once saw a photo of Nel when she might have been about thirteen, sitting sideways with her legs sticking out at an angle and her impish, inquisitive face staring cheekily straight out at the photographer. This photo reminded me of one I saw later of Anne Frank as a child; on the raised entrance next door to a good friend of mine on Amsterdam's Herengracht canal. I wanted to use that Nel photo as the book cover, but later I couldn't find it.

When she was thirteen, Nel was sent away to a school in Overveen, near Haarlem. As Nel put it: "The 'nobility' of the island, so to say, at that time sent their sons and daughters away as soon as they could walk, talk and be sensible to school in The Hague or Amsterdam."

Nel's father had big ideas and chose the Kennemer Lyceum because no school any nearer was good enough for him, she said. This was after being turned down by the Zeister Christelijk Lyceum, making me think perhaps they considered the family a little too non-religious.

In his sketch of Nel's life, her lawyer friend Piet Wackie Eysten did wonder if she was 'sent away' because she was hard to handle, as Piet's mother had sometimes implied, or whether it was because she was not doing well at the local school, which seems unlikely. His final suggestion that the village school was considered too limited for her talents rings true to me. It fits in with those big ideas of Johannes.

It turned out to be a good choice, and Nel was glad to get away from the hated widow. "I very much enjoyed it; I was very happy there," she said. Sometimes, she went back to the island for holidays, but she could also go to the home of one of the girls she met at the school.

It was a big move, she conceded. "From that island somewhere down there at the bottom of the Netherlands, to this chic school, the Kennemer Lyceum." Many of the pupils' parents were living in the Dutch colony of Indonesia, and their children were put up in the Kiho, apparently a special boarding establishment for these colonial kids.

Nel's adventurous and sometimes rebellious inclinations – especially regarding her father – came into play over her accommodation. She was initially boarded with a widow, whom she liked. But in her last year, she had to leave because the widow was sick. She decided to take a room, "as if I was a lone [university] student, with people who just gave me breakfast."

This was noticed. "I was called in to see the head of the Kennemer Lyceum, Mr De Vletter. He knew that I still had a father, and he said, does your father know that you are just living in a room? It was most unusual for someone at high school to be rooming already, not staying in a family. I said, yes, he does, he has my address, and I didn't want to say that he couldn't give a damn anyway."

Nel had high praise for the school's rector, De Vletter.

"He always stood by me," she said. "A big man, with a big personal interest. I have very good memories of the school. There I gradually grew up. I had no head for science, but languages spurred me on. For them, I really had a talent."

A similar story I came across was about Nel having a boyfriend. This gives a nice picture of the impression she made at the school.

"Friends later told her how she looked when she came to school. 'I talked back and I knew what I wanted.' And she had a boyfriend. An offence for which she was called up to see the rector: 'Did my father know? Of course my father knew. Naturally, I said. That was the first boy,' she says, 'and not the last, who I told I would never marry. I find affairs great fun, but I didn't want to marry. That is, I think, because of my father, he has coloured my picture of men.'"

Sometimes, I felt, the lady doth protest too much. There was at any rate going to be one man in her life she did want to marry. Still, 'I talked back and I knew what I wanted' was vintage Nel.

In April 1982, fifty years after leaving the school, Nel wrote a contribution for a class reunion, penned in Les Frères Charbonnel restaurant while on holiday in France's Dordogne. She complained that when she returned to the Netherlands after a stint in Brussels, she found Dutch journalists had a total lack of languages, especially as they had been "deprived of the entire Latin horizon," she said.

"Then I think nostalgically of our Kennemer Lyceum where we had to write, talk and read in at least three foreign languages every week." At the end of her piece, she wrote warmly: "On my many roads in the world, I have met many old-Kennemers and always with much pleasure."

Classmate Piet Schmal cited a survey showing a remarkable 72% would like to have their schooldays over again. But then, times were hard in 1932: "WE too fell… into the vacuum of an Economic Crisis… No place for school leavers… Delft engineers working as conductors on the trams… But WE had had the '*Umwertung aller Werte*' and economic lessons about Keynes… We were motivated and wrestled our way up, not to be held back… Youth always has the future and that has NOTHING to do with brains, knowledge or background but everything to do with the level and engagement of the education and the mentality thus formed."

Times *were* no doubt hard in 1932, but Nel was certainly motivated to wrestle her way up, and she did feel the school gave her a good foundation. She also believed her unusual, unhappy home life probably made her more enterprising and independent.

14

"I didn't really want to go back to the island, after the unhappy experience with my father's third wife. But I had enjoyed the life until then even though I lacked a mother figure – I suppose that made me more enterprising and aggressive. I think I'm a very independent person." With great satisfaction, she told me a story to prove this.

"It must be obvious: One time I drove from Brussels to Antwerp in a frightful fog. I couldn't see anything, and I stopped at a petrol station and there was a man filling his tank and he said, 'Are you ready to drive to Antwerp?' I said, is it possible and he said yes, if you follow me. So I followed him very slowly and when we got there, he invited me for coffee. While we were having it, he said: 'I'm sure that's the first time in your life that you've followed someone.' I never saw the man again, but the incident always stayed with me."

Nel was never again to live on Goeree-Overflakkee, but she was always proud of her island origins. Trying to understand Nel had me searching for something on an island. This is a phrase Swedish film actress Liv Ullmann also used in her book *Changing*. On the Swedish island of Faro, Ullmann found a people living close to the earth, close to the sea, characterised by simplicity. There is surely an echo of this feeling down the years from Nel's small, remote island of Goeree-Overflakkee.

Admittedly, Ullmann described her islanders as living in harmony with themselves, which doesn't sound much like Nel's islanders with all their squabbling over land and money. But Ullmann goes on:

'No outsiders could point at them and make them feel inferior. People who had trust in their place on earth. They were far from uncomplicated, nor without demands, hatreds and aggressions. But they had pride, a dignity which they allowed no one to crush'.

This seems to me a perfect description of Nel's islander character. When she left the island to go to the Haarlem school, Nel stood in front of her mirror, rolled up her sleeves and told herself that it would not matter what people said about her later, as long as it was not "That poor Slis." She, too, took pride and dignity with her from her island.

Ullmann goes on to say that old people and children are also islanders within our society: *'People who don't care to keep the mask and the facade in order. Who dare to show who they are'.* As Nel's friend, the renowned writer and columnist Flora Lewis said of her: "What you saw was what you got."

Origins foreshadow what is yet to come; later events take us back again to our origins. This is how the jigsaw puzzle of Nel's life is built up, though with many missing pieces.

CHAPTER THREE
A MOVEABLE FEAST: PARIS AND ONWARDS
Searching for a role

It is a fact that time seems to stretch out and almost stand still in childhood. But once we are grown up, it starts to accelerate. After Nel left school, I felt the pace hotting up as she set out eagerly into the world beyond the Netherlands, with all her senses on high alert.

Also in old age, people often go on remembering their earliest years when they can't remember what they had for breakfast. In Nel's case, it seemed to be the period after leaving the island that lingered most vividly. At first, I wondered whether this was because of her unhappy childhood, but eventually decided it was because she was speaking to an outsider. Tyna, whose mother Jenneke was Nel's great friend from Goeree-Overflakkee, found that even after her memory had gone, it could still be revived by showing her photos of those early years on the island with Jenneke's family.

For me, though, everything Nel told me about those 1930s years *felt* fresh and new, and painted in bright, bold brushstrokes. This was before the shadow of war fell, and before the postwar struggle to build her long career in journalism.

At the same time, the account she gave me of this chapter of her life was patchy and contradictory. Nor was it long on detailed descriptions of people and places. However many times she returned to the period with pleasure and great animation, she still insisted on swinging through it at breakneck speed. It was impossible to get her to pause and elaborate, or to fill out the picture at some interesting point. The brushstrokes remained entirely impressionistic: dramatic and significant from a distance, but dissolving into disconnected fragments on closer inspection.

The story began in Paris. Iman Slis, a pharmacist in Utrecht who had married the sister of Nel's mother, persuaded her father to let her go there after secondary school. This Uncle Iman was wont to keep an eye on Nel from afar and evidently had some influence with her father. He was presumably distantly related to Johannes.

Nel's stay in Paris sparked a lifelong love affair with the French language and culture. Some hints of an exotic Parisian lifestyle were picked up by Piet Wackie Eysten when he was a boy. He was also curious about a laconic telegram he saw from Uncle Iman summoning Nel home: *Viens – Slis*, it said. It was addressed to *mlle slis, rue tournefort, paris* and dated 27 June 1933. Its cause is unknown, but Nel did return soon after that.

Nel began her studies in Paris in autumn 1932 with a language course at the Alliance Française. She then took a '*cours de la civilisation française*' at the Sorbonne. "That was a very wonderful time," she said, her eyes lighting up. "I came there sort of wide-eyed, and *everything* was interesting to me. I liked the language, of course, and I liked the country. I always have."

And then there were the people she met, a tad more cosmopolitan than the population of her little Dutch island. "French, Russian or Yugoslav. They were a motley crowd. Some, very few, I may say, were Dutch. Then there were Yugoslav students and White Russian émigrés."

She shared a flat with one of these Russian émigrés, Tamara, who was also at the Sorbonne. Tamara was from a previously rich Russian family who lost all their money in the 1917 Revolution. Her father was described by Nel as 'pure Russian', while her mother was German. The family escaped to China after the Revolution, and Tamara was born in Harban, China. Later, Nel said, the family were 'all over the place', which was fortunate for her as she was able to stay at various stages with one or other sister in New York, Venice, Rome and London – and even with the mother in Munich.

Nel eventually met all five of Tamara's elder sisters, including the eldest, who became a lawyer in America. Another, called Dasha, a 'nice, handsome girl', wound up in Venice, and Veshti, the one she liked best, in Rome. Nel said she spent all her Christmases with Veshti for many years.

On Nel's bureau in her flat in The Hague, there was a striking photo of Veshti in a café in Rome, looking very Russian and theatrical. How I wish I had got a copy of that and many others when I had the chance. Nel had a couple of drawers in the flat full of photos, which we browsed through on one of my visits. But I hadn't realised that her memory was disappearing, let alone at what speed. There were many glamorous photos in the drawers of Nel as a young woman, which I couldn't find later either.

In Paris, Nel told me somewhat boastfully, "I forgot all about my first boyfriend on the island." Her second boyfriend was a Frenchman: "This son of the famous artist Royarts, he also wanted to marry me. He was a nice guy, Felix Conbruna. But I had to meet his parents and I thought, oh Christ, no. The parents were very bourgeois, and the only thing they thought of me was that I was 'une jeune Hollandaise'. But then they saw me and they thought, not too Hollandaise, perhaps, I don't know."

The bourgeois Parisians probably had a clichéd expectation of a bovine blonde in clogs and were quite surprised by the slim, chic young woman they met. Still, nothing came of it, prompting Nel's old refrain: "I think it's because I so hated my father, there was so little affection, that I couldn't face being married to a man."

After a year at the Sorbonne, Nel returned to the Netherlands for family reasons. Telling me about this visit prompted another rant about the sins of her father, as she at last met her mother's family and discovered their low opinion of Johannes.

"I had got a letter in a totally unknown hand, from my mother's sister, who I'd never met. She sent me a note to come back because she didn't want my father to get his hands on the property. I'd never seen my uncle and aunt because my father was damned by my mother's family because he spent too much."

Essentially, the message from her aunt was that her mother had left her land, and "if ever I needed it, I was welcome in Utrecht." This was to prove a real boon on Nel's final return to the Netherlands in 1973 after her stint in Brussels:

"It turned out I inherited eleven hectares from my mother, quite a lot, and I didn't realise the importance of it at the time, but later, I was able to sell the land and buy my flat in The Hague."

It was on this first visit to the Utrecht family that Nel discovered that the family had in fact done their best to discourage her mother from marrying Johannes, telling her that she was very foolish to do so because he was a spendthrift. "He had money of his own, but the LAND was very important on the island, because there's so little of it."

While Nel was staying with her aunt and uncle, a professor of pharmacology, he suggested she should study pharmacy at Utrecht University. Intriguingly, her uncle also decided after a few months that she should live on her own. This makes me wonder whether Uncle Iman found Nel a bit too hot to handle when she was actually staying with the family, fond though he was of her. She found a place with a widow, with two schoolteachers boarding with her. But by this stage, Nel was beginning to feel she needed to get out of Utrecht anyway.

The Utrecht family were meanwhile determined to make sure the land and its income would go to Nel and would not fall into the hands of her much-vilified father. "'Remember,' they said, 'that you must never sign anything that your father puts in front of you. He must not get hold of the land of your mother, because he will swallow it up.'"

Nel claimed that when her father eventually died, "there was nothing left, not of the money and not of the land. Everything was squandered." This may well be true, but to amend his overall record slightly, there is evidence that he did pay for Nel to do the nursing course she was to take in the 1930s. It also seems a reasonable assumption that he must have paid for the courses in Paris.

Nel's nephew Hans Nieuwenhuyzen also told me she did in fact occasionally return to Goeree-Overflakkee after she set out on her travels around Europe, even though she said she didn't. When he was a child of around ten or twelve, Nieuwenhuyzen remembered Nel's father giving her money:

"It struck me then, because it was a thousand guilders, at that time a very large amount of money."

Nel may have been a stickler for accuracy as a journalist, but she could be a pretty unreliable witness when it came to her own life, even before she lost her memory. She herself gave me the impression she never saw her father again after she left school, even though he died nearly a quarter of a century later, in May 1956.

Back in Utrecht in 1933, Nel only stuck it out in pharmacy for six months. "But then I got fed up with all those pills and I said I wasn't interested. The pills came out of my nose, I can tell you. So my uncle said, why don't you go to England for a year? 'So good for your character.'"

I love this Uncle Iman for that remark. So Nel did go to England. Unfortunately, this part of her tale was particularly fragmentary and opaque. Here is the arrival fragment, in Nel's own words.

"When I arrived off the boat, I went to Ilfrey Park in the neighbourhood of Harrow, a beautiful, enormous house. A sort of castle, which was then a guesthouse run by Ione Sherry, as British as they came. She came to meet me at Waterloo Station and I said to her, how did you know that I was Nel Slis? And she said, because you looked continental."

A good description, I imagined. What sort of clothes she would have been wearing about that time I don't know, but in the England of the 1930s I'm sure she would have stood out as an exotic continental visitor.

Nel then read English at Rhodes College, Oxford. Among others, she met a man from India who gave her riding lessons and some "very nice Irish people who sort of took to me." Then, she said, "I was billeted with people who actually washed their teeth using the crockery." This teeth-washing bit was one of Nel's more mystifying remarks that I never managed to clear up. This was followed by some random snippets about a couple more boyfriends she turned down for marriage, though the second one certainly sounded rather odd:

"I had a French boyfriend who was staying in the same house. He wanted to marry me too. We didn't sleep with boys in those days – that came later." This was useful information in a way, though I don't know exactly how much later sex arrived in Nel's life.

Then she met a Swiss woman who later became a famous doctor. "I went out with her brother and the brother wanted to marry me. I said, well, I don't want to marry – but he had said, of course, if I am going to marry you, then you have to get up early in the morning and take a cold shower. Extraordinary…" Indeed, very extraordinary.

Then, all of a sudden, Nel decided she wanted to be a nurse.

"I don't know why, but that often happens with girls. I lacked close relationships when I was young – girls want to make up for it themselves, I think. Maybe it was compensation for my lack of family ties. I was never part of a family – nobody knew what to do with me, sort of, and I was always moving from one place to another. Lack of affection is, I think, the reason I wanted to be a nurse."

Nel applied to a very well-known nursing school outside Paris, but it didn't work out. As she put it, "They were too Catholic and I was brought up not strictly but with the idea that the world consisted mostly of Protestants. The training was very famous, the director was a niece of the cardinal and I had to go to Mass at six in the morning. After twenty-four hours, I walked out of there with all my luggage…"

Then she had a letter from her White Russian friend Tamara, inviting her to join her in Munich. Back in their Paris days, Tamara often pressed Nel to come and stay with her mother in Munich during their vacations. Now Nel was off there like a shot for the winter. She went skiing in Garmisch and managed to study languages in Munich.

"So Paris had already proved to be my great opening to stay with families that were spread all over the world," especially this White Russian family, she remarked.

Tamara's mother was divorced. Apparently she had lost her husband in China. Reminiscing affectionately, Nel said: "She used to say, Nel, you're spending too much, because I did, too. Because, you see, I felt embarrassed, and I spent to give them something to repay their hospitality, because I didn't pay a *'pension'*, and I felt that being a guest in the house, I should bring them things…"

One thing Tamara's mother said made a big impression on Nel. "My German wasn't terrific, but we had all talked French, German and English at school and I had a knack for languages. The mother said to me, *'Nel, du wirdst nochmal mit dem naktenpopo an der Strasse kommen'* – One day, you'll land on the street on your bare behind. I never forgot that," she chortled with relish.

While Nel was taking German courses in Munich, she found an excellent nursing course in Lausanne, La Source, 'a very Protestant business'. She started the course at La Source in April 1935, and received her nursing diploma in November 1938.

"It was *très serieux,* La Source, *Premiere Ecole des gardes-malades independante et evangelique.* I found the evangelical part a silly business. You sung songs, *A toi Jésus toute ma jeunesse.* I thought: you won't get me, '*à toi Jésus*', never! But then we were sent out to work. I worked first in Lausanne, then a year in France in Metz and after that, a year in Geneva."

While she was doing this practical training, she could take long vacations and she started going to Italy. She took courses in Italian, first in Perugia and later in Florence.

"In Florence, I stayed with Florentine people, very nice, and they had a young man there and I was young too, not beautiful but I was young. He used to say, can you sing in Dutch and I said, I can't sing but I'll talk to you in Dutch. These boys used to say, "oh, it's like pulling the chain in the WC." Again, Nel gave one of her wicked cackles that I liked so much.

While in Lausanne on the nursing course, Nel shared a room with Inez Forel, daughter of a well-known psychiatrist, Auguste Forel. "A crazy but amusing person. Unfortunately, she had an affair with the gardener and had to leave the school."

That was a story I would have liked to hear more about, but had no luck there. However, Auguste Forel was significant because his influence made Nel want to study psychiatry in Vienna. Meanwhile, though, the Utrecht Slis family had already decided by 1938 that even though Vienna might be the cradle of psychiatry, it was also a viper's nest of Nazism, and put its collective foot down.

So Nel went to Rome instead and wound up staying there for a year. According to Piet Wackie Eysten, not much came of the psychiatry course there because she fell in love with an Italian doctor, from whom she learned Italian but not psychiatry. Nel did not enlighten me on such details, but she did give me a strong sense of how much she enjoyed Rome. As in Paris, this was also largely thanks to White Russian connections. I loved her obvious gusto about the Rome episode.

"I was staying with a White Russian family. They have played a great part in my life, these White Russians. This family was stranded in Rome in 1917, as the husband, Messoyedo, had been number two at the Russian Embassy before the Revolution. They managed by taking in paying guests… It was a wonderful year."

Nel did voluntary work for the forerunner of the UN Food and Agriculture Organisation, and continued to study Italian. She told me with some pride that she kept up the study of Italian all her life, right through the later decades back in The Hague.

In Rome, Messoyedo proved to be another 'very nice guy'. His wife, a Baltic baroness, had previously been very rich, and when they were stranded after the Russian Revolution, they managed to buy a large house with rooms to rent out to '*pensionaires* like myself when I came to Rome to learn Italian'. Nel was given the contact by Jonkheer van Panhuis, a Dutch diplomat who knew them from the pre-revolutionary era.

Apart from Messoyedo, Nel remembered the maid, Mikalina, who looked after the household because 'madame' liked her. And there was a resident cat. Other residents were a Spanish woman with a husband in Cuba, and some British women with husbands in the services.

There was also "a tremendous homosexual, very big, from Berlin, Combodel, who spoke with his hands when he recited poems, with ten big fingers on the table. His big hands were always on the table when he wanted to make a point. At that time, we didn't even quite know what homosexuals were. It was shady, sort of… So it was a strange mixture, a strange potpourri of people. And I thrive on that."

I have the impression that she called Combodel a 'tremendous' homosexual because he was overtly gay in a way that she had perhaps not encountered before. Her apparent ignorance about homosexuals does not strike me as surprising at that time.

Nel went on, by that time in full flight, her face lighting up with the memories. "And then the Russians themselves, there were many Russian contessas, numerous receptions and God knows what, and I quickly came across the name of a prince… I knew nothing about Russia – I came from Goeree and Haarlem. I learned much about these things. *Knowing* people, that was the thing, and since I never forgot names, I got to know a lot of people because I thought it was very fascinating. So different from my island – when you're young, all these characters with titles…"

Did they talk about the Revolution? I wondered.

"There was no talk of the Russian Revolution, but it was a kind of 'court-in-exile'. They were all refugees, some with lots of money. They talked a lot in Russian, but also in French, and they name-dropped like hell. I can't remember all the Russian princes and princesses that passed through my hands…

"There was a whole pecking order – at receptions, they were all there, dropping names. They didn't talk about the Communists, they only talked about have you seen the countess this, baroness that? *Terrible, très terrible.* A lot of the Russian aristocracy, of course, went to Paris, but lots also to Rome, because the wife of the last king, Victor Emmanuel, was something Montenegro and had been brought up at the Czar's court." This was Elena Montenegro, who went to secondary school in St Petersburg, where she attended the court.

When we were talking about that magnificent baroque photo of Veshti in a plush Roman café that I liked so much, this prompted Nel to recount an incident that clearly had deep significance for her.

"Yes, that photo of Veshti in the café – you WENT there to be seen! Veshti was a theatre woman. She did everything to do with the theatre. She was brought up very rich, but *il ne reste plus beaucoup…*

"I used to go and have a drink in the café on the Via Venezia, which was the Champs-Élysées of Rome, and that was always amusing because it was near the gardens of Rome where you walked. It was very chic. Messoyedo didn't want me to be late for lunch, as that would annoy the baroness, so he said: 'I come and get you at the Via Venezia.' Then he came with the taxi and I don't know what sort of nonsense we talked, but then he put his hand on my knee and said, '*Nel, vous avez l'âme d'un Slav*' – You have a Slav soul. And I think I have too, a little bit."

What does it mean, the soul of a Slav? I asked. "Generous, yes, and also not thinking about putting money in shares or this type of thing – not like the Germans, no, no, no. Yes, yes – for years, people used to say to me, are you Russian? I think it was the way the Russians talked, I started to talk like them."

After I discovered that Nel once had an unhappy affair with a Russian, I wondered whether this could have been Messoyedo. I don't think so, though, as she wouldn't have described the little incident in the taxi to me with such pride. Anyhow, she was so reticent about personal matters that she probably wouldn't have mentioned it if he was the one.

Nel also very much liked some of the Italians she met in Rome, though she never told me anything about her medical boyfriend. But Mussolini was now on the rise. "I got on fine with the Italians, I must say. But there was a big contrast between these White Russians living in Rome in an older world and the rise of Mussolini and his followers. With the Fascists in power, I listened to them – it was fascinating in a way. We saw the Mussolini rallies in Rome – we were mocking them at first."

Did they actually see Mussolini? "Certainly, yes, we used to go to the piazza to hear him expound. Everyone laughed then, but all the same… he was *pas très sympathique*, no, no, no. We went there to see the show. But Mussolini was starting to get louder and louder and there had been the Anschluss in Austria in 1938. Most of the instructors in Vienna were Jewish doctors, and I hadn't felt like going to that country with the Anschluss, so I had been quite stymied." The implication being that was why she went to Rome instead. But I already knew the Utrecht family had vetoed Vienna.

To fill in a bit of historical background, the Anschluss was the political union of Austria and Germany from 1938–45. Back in 1934, Hitler's plans for the union had been blocked when Mussolini sent troops to the Brenner Pass to safeguard Austria's independence. But by 1937, Mussolini was in the Axis camp and Hitler could put pressure on Chancellor Schuschnigg to legalise the Austrian Nazi party. The party stirred up unrest and in 1938,

Schuschnigg resigned and Nazi Arthur Seyss-Inquart became chancellor. He then invited the Germans to occupy the country and 'restore order'. After the occupation, Hitler held a plebiscite in which an overwhelming majority approved Austria's inclusion in 'Greater Germany', a turn of events that considerably embarrasses many Austrians to this day.

A sentence in an interview about Nel leaving Rome felt very evocative for me of those tense days, reminding me of the film *Tea with Mussolini*: "When the Jews in the tennis club started to flee to Brazil, it was time to get out…"

As Nel's images of those early years around Europe flashed by, I felt it was easy to see where Nel's abidingly elegant dress sense came from, between the influence of Paris and Rome and all these aristocratic White Russians she met along the way.

WAR

(1939–1945)

CHAPTER FOUR
TO THE FINLAND STATION:
NURSING, BALL BEARINGS AND THE BBC
'Like a hair in the soup'

In the summer of 1939, Nel's pharmacist uncle wrote to her in Rome, telling her: '*You can't stay, they're all fascists now. There's going to be a war – come back to Holland*'.

Nel told me she left Rome at the end of August and actually reached the Netherlands on 1 September. If so, this was the very day on which Germany invaded Poland, triggering the British and French declarations of war on Germany and thus the start of World War II. After that came the so-called 'phoney war', she reminded me. This was the protracted ominous lull following the Polish invasion, with little action except in Poland and at sea. It was to last until the German onslaught in the West the following year.

At this fateful point in history, Nel found herself once again staying with her uncle and aunt in Utrecht. She felt disoriented, partly because she hadn't been back in the country for some time. There was also the question of what exactly to do next, and meanwhile, "Utrecht was not the gayest place."

She volunteered for hospital work, but "in Holland, they're very snooty, they think the best of nursing is Dutch." If she wanted to work in a Dutch hospital, she would have had to do a refresher course for a year. Ridiculous, she felt, after doing such a high-level Swiss nursing course. So instead she did a shorthand and typing course and learned to drive. Despite the international tensions, she managed to have a wonderful winter, with lots of skating.

"Then there was this war in Finland…" Being Nel, she met someone. An enormous ball was held for the victims of the Finnish-Russian war in the Witte Brug, a smart, well-known hotel in The Hague. At the ball, she was chatting to one of her dancing partners:

"I said, I'm back here now after so many years and I'm ever so bored, and he said, well, I know something for you. He was the top man in the Red Cross. André de la Porte was his name, from a '*très grande famille*', and he knew I was a trained nurse – you know, La Source was a great school."

De la Porte told Nel the Red Cross was sending an ambulance team to Finland, and asked her if she would like to join it. The Finnish-Russian war had just ended, and "everyone was helping. Apparently it didn't matter there that I had a Swiss diploma. So I went to nurse war-wounded on the Finnish-Russian front."

On 21 March 1940, Nel left for Finland with the ambulance team, with nineteen nurses, six doctors, an interpreter and a driver. The team was cheered on its way from the Red Cross head office on Prinsessegracht in The Hague by Princess Juliana, chairwoman of the Dutch Red Cross.

Then, said Nel with a shudder, "we went by air to Copenhagen and Stockholm. It scared the wits out of me, I hated flying." This was the only time Nel ever flew. She also had a lifelong aversion to using lifts, which gave her claustrophobia.

From Stockholm, Nel insisted on taking a boat to Finland. As a result, she arrived via Helsingborg, "stuck on the Baltic Sea, virtually alone", because the others had flown the rest of the way. The team were stationed in Vierumaeki, about 150 kilometres northeast of Helsinki.

"That was really a magnificent building, which was originally meant as a training site for the Canada 1938 Olympics, but they never came off because of the war. There we had a contract for three months." As things turned out, it was to be over five years before Nel returned to the Netherlands – at the end of the Second World War.

A Dutch newspaper reported after their arrival that the ambulance team started work on 1 April in the sports school in Verumaeki, which had been converted into a surgical clinic and hospital:

"On that day, the operating room saw two operations, while the first six photos were made in the X-ray room. The ambulance functioned with all its own surgical and medical equipment, which, thanks to good packing, arrived completely undamaged after difficult transportation via plane, ship, rail and truck."

The number of war-wounded received and nursed by the Dutch Red Cross team in Verumaeki soon ran into hundreds. One of the doctors recounted his experiences in the Dutch *Magazine for Medicine*. It sounds like a Dickensian nightmare:

By weak lamplight, the patients lay cheerlessly staring in front of them, their eyes sunk deep in their exhausted faces, dyed green by the light. Visitors entering from the daylight suddenly found themselves plunged deep in immense distress. In one bed, a blind man was vegetating, no longer bothered by the half-light. Next door, a completely paralysed patient had quietly withdrawn in the dusky hell to die unnoticed, and a young farm boy with amputated arms tossed restlessly around and around.

On 10 May 1940, the Germans invaded Holland. Most of the doctors and nurses wanted to go back, and applied for visas, but there were three unmarried doctors who didn't want to ask the Germans for a visa. "They got away somehow with the aid of the Finns, in an aeroplane," Nel confided with a touch of asperity.

Nel herself had no wish to return to Holland. "I had no fiancé, no family and not even a canary. I wanted to go to England to do something against the Nazis. We were hearing this dreadful Blitzkrieg on London all the time on the radio… I did not want to go back to Holland, but the Finns were also not terribly funny."

From the end of June, the Vierumaeki sports school was no longer available and its entire medical inventory was transferred to Helsinki. A month later, when the last patients had been taken elsewhere, it was presented to the Finnish Red Cross. At the end of August, a message was received from Berlin that visas were approved for the ambulance team members. They travelled back to occupied Holland via Sweden and Germany, arriving there on 8 September 1940.

In a more acidic comment on the nursing team some years later, Nel fulminated: "Three of the seven doctors oiled themselves away like hares, without any discussion, when we heard the Krauts had occupied the Netherlands. The others went back to the Netherlands, also without any discussion… Dutch women were milksops then, they were always too late getting there. And now they still do nothing," she snarled, in a sudden flare of anger.

I find it difficult to imagine Nel in the frumpy Victorian uniform of the nurses in the photo of the Finland ambulance team on their return to the Netherlands. Despite the unflattering uniform, no doubt Nel still managed to look slim and trim and dashing. She was to don nursing gear once more later in the war after she reached England, in a more mundane last stint.

There can be no doubt that Nel would have been a practical and efficient nurse, with a 'no-nonsense' approach that very likely gave short shrift to petty malingerers and complainers. Her great curiosity and interest in what was going on would have stood her in good stead, and she would have been quite fearless and calm in the face of horrendous wounds or diseases. Her warmth, honesty and sympathy would then have come into play. She must have been a good person to have at your bedside if you were really in trouble.

I found no record of Nel speaking about nursing in Finland, nor did she talk about it with me. She was ever reticent about matters she regarded as private or did not wish to go into for whatever reason. Although it was not a lengthy period, it must have been a deeply affecting experience.

Nel and her fellow nurses were awarded the Finnish bronze Bravery Medal by General Mannerheim. There was also a handwritten statement to certify that '*Miss N.A. Sliss (sic) has been working as a diplomed nurse during the whole stay of the Dutch ambulance in Finland to the utmost content*'. This was signed by Dr J.A.C. Schepel, 1st surgeon of the Dutch Ambulance in Finland.

A few months later, a letter was sent from The Hague to inform her that she had been awarded a silver Red Cross medal for her services in Finland. The letter was addressed to Middelharnis, and it and the medal took years to reach Nel, at that time somewhere on the high seas between Finland and America.

After the other nurses left Finland, Nel and two other nurses camped out in the woods by the lakes, with reindeer wandering around the paths. They made fires to cook fish and even managed to smoke some, and they fetched bread by boat. "One was like me, a freebooter with practically no family. The other was Jewish, so she certainly had some reason to be afraid. So the Jew and I decided to try to get out some other way."

This was a lean and difficult period, I learned obliquely, with little to eat and great uncertainty about what to do. Plus, there was the fear of the ever-encroaching Nazis. Nel, however, managed to come up with more contacts, the first one taking them to the outskirts of Helsinki:

"The then chargé d'affaires, a very nice man, said he could take us and give us shelter with an old man who lived just outside Helsinki. So there we sat and played gin rummy, and I remember I even gave Dutch lessons to the Belgian ambassador's daughter. We were still trying to get out – the two nurses wanted to go to Indonesia, but I didn't – I wanted to go to England."

First, the three decided they would try to go to America via Sweden, but the Dutch ambassador to Sweden advised them to go via Russia. Apparently there was no feasible direct route, so rather mind-bogglingly, "we thought we would go via Russia and Japan to the States and then I could go to England and the others to Indonesia."

Even Nel conceded this wasn't easy. "For Russia, we needed to get a visa. For a visa, we had to go to Sweden. So we went to Sweden, the Jew and I, and I had one boyfriend there from Perugia University, who… I didn't feel very much like asking aid from him, because he wanted to marry me. He was a philology student, working on an English dictionary – not the most interesting thing… His mother was in a mental home and his father had shot himself. For several reasons, I didn't want to marry him, though he was a very nice man."

No wonder, I thought, with his family record.

Decades later, Piet Wackie Eysten discovered a telegram sent from Stockholm on 11 May 1940, the day after the Germans invaded Holland, and addressed to *Nel Slis, Dutch Ambulance, Vierumaeki*. It said:

'*Keep strong, stick to me, love Gustav Warburg*'.

Piet had no idea who this Gustav was, but he also found a letter from him kept by Nel among her papers and dating from nearly four years later. This was apparently written in reply to one sent by Nel from London at the end of 1943.

'*I am so glad you are all right, satisfied with your work and so on*', Gustav wrote. '*I am sorry you did not get my last letter of last summer where I told you that I am married since 17/7*'. Gustav had bought a house outside Stockholm, but was called up for military service.

'*Poor Finland and the Baltic States. Is there no other solution for Europe than the choice between brown and red barbarism? Please write me soon about yourself*', he went on. '*There are so many things I can't write in this letter, one has to think of the examiner*'. No doubt there was censorship. Whether this was the same former boyfriend as the depressive Swede from Perugia University, history does not relate, but she must have been fond of him, as she kept his letter.

Returning to her plight in 1940, Nel went on: "I sat there in Helsingborg and I went to see my embassy people and I said I'd like to go to America and the man said, well, we can arrange that… We got a visa for Japan, but not for Russia, so we had to go on, you know, standing in the queue."

Failure to get a visa for Russia was not for want of trying. Armed with an introduction to the Soviet Embassy from the Dutch ambassador to Sweden, Nel managed to speak to the Russian ambassadress, generally described as the 'famous' Aleksandra Kollontai, *La Kollontai*. She was famous for being Russia's first woman ambassador and according to Wikipedia, had been People's Commissar for Welfare in Vladimir Lenin's government in 1917–1918. So she was a very prominent woman in the Bolshevik party, and apparently the first woman in history to be a member of a governing cabinet.

Asked whether La Kollontai was charming, Nel said tolerantly: "She was at least human and she saw a possibility that I could get to America via Russia and Japan. From there, I could then get to England. Nonetheless, she did refuse the visa. La Kollontai accurately observed: 'Lady, your country has never recognised mine.'"

That somewhat circuitous route via Russia and Japan to America and England was now barred, but another epic journey soon took its place. "Suddenly we got news from a friend I'd made, a friend of the mayor of Helsinki, and he said come over, there's a boat going from Petsamo [then in northeast Finland, later in Russia] to Baltimore – quicker than all this circus. So we dropped all the Japanese and Russian part – we already had visas for America."

The voyage, on a 3,000-tonne freighter, took twenty-six days. At one point, it nearly sunk after hitting a submerged iceberg. Nel and her companions slept on the floor.

"The boat cavorted over the ocean and I was dead sick the whole journey," Nel recalled ruefully. The vessel was Finnish, and the Finns were neutral at that time. Also on board were two maids bound for the Finnish Embassy in Washington and two Jewish people, one from Czechoslovakia and one from Denmark. I couldn't make out whether those two were men or women, but am guessing men.

"We stopped in Tromso, in the extreme north of Norway. There the Krauts boarded the boat, and the Finns said, who have we got here? But then they let the Nazis through all the same. The captain said, I don't think that they will do anything, because they are people from the German Navy.

"They did leave the two Jewish people and the nurses alone. They also said – I actually heard one say – 'Ach, these Red Cross sisters are not interesting.' If he had just known how interesting we were!

"After that visit, there was not a drop of alcohol left for the rest of the trip, nearly a month... The radio on board also went on the blink then."

It must have been a terrifying encounter. In a later interview, Nel conceded that the boarding of the Germans was a risky moment, but claimed she was completely obsessed at the time with getting to America.

"Well, of course [risky]. But if you're twenty-six, then you only think of one thing, I must get to America as soon as possible... I only had one idea – that I must get away from these godforsaken Nazis. Nowadays, I would have shit my pants three times, probably. But at that time... But yes, I was very happy when I reached land."

In a foreshadowing of her excellent investigative nose as a reporter, Nel managed to talk with the captain during the trip. "Though that was a very difficult conversation. He knew a little bit of German and a little English. I knew no Finnish, so we just wormed our way around. Then I said, 'Will we ever get there?' And he said, 'Well, if only the load does not shift.' Because he had to go on to Japan. That was one of the few things [I learned] from our conversation..."

To her great credit, Nel managed to discover in this conversation that the ship was carrying ball bearings from Sweden for the Japanese. "Which I promptly reported to the British Naval attaché in New York – I don't think the boat ever got to Japan."

Altogether, it was a gruelling trip. "That Finnish boat, the *Britta Thorden* – I shall never forget it. It was stormy all the time, I was sick as a dog, and when I stepped onto the quay green in the face, still in this lovely Carl Denig [nurse's] outfit, along with the stateless Jews, the maids for the Finnish Embassy in Washington and two fellow nurses, there were these rich American ladies on the quay saying, 'How interesting – refugees from Europe.'"

Nel arrived in the US in November 1940. It would then take her until the following May to get to England. Once in New York, she stayed with her Russian friend Tamara, who had married an American diplomat. It sounded as though this proved a little awkward, though Tamara did her best to help Nel out.

"But they were just married, you know... Since I had only my uniform, she gave me clothes for New York. I was applying for jobs, I was a graduate nurse, so I was going round all the agencies. I spoke Dutch, German, French, Italian, English, but I wasn't at my best after Finland, there was very little to eat there, so they told me at last they were really looking for a blonde receptionist, something like that."

This indignity merited a big snort of disgust. Also here was one of the few indications Nel let slip as to what a gruelling and hungry time it had been skulking in Finland looking for a way to get out and reach the US.

Eventually, Nel ended up working at the Netherlands Purchasing Commission of the Dutch government-in-exile. There, she translated pilots' handbooks for the Brewster fighter aircraft they were optimistically hoping to buy to defend Dutch Indonesia from the Japanese. Nel said they never got the planes. She went on wearily:

"But I got so tired of America – it was not at war, it was before Pearl Harbour, and I felt out of place and uncomfy... I was going mad from these Americans, who just did not want to participate in the war, and from these American wives, who hadn't got anything better to do than knit socks for those poor Europeans..."

Nel had been nagging her consulate in New York to get her to England, and eventually she got herself onto the second Canadian naval division convoy, which left for the UK in May 1941. The passengers sailed on a Union Castle Line ship, which docked in Scotland. Setting foot in the UK, Nel faced the reality of a country at war. The Finnish war with Russia had been over when she was nursing its victims.

"There I got a night train – I had never seen a blacked-out train before... I was accompanied, because they didn't really trust me much – that woman not in uniform, who is she? So I was under escort by a man and a woman, obviously from the Brits, to see if I was kosher and not a spy. If the English hear that you speak two or three languages, then they think, hmm, suspicious."

After thus arousing some suspicion on her arrival, Nel was subject to a two-hour screening in London. Her inquisitor was the 'already famous' Colonel Oreste Pinto. She described him as a British security officer of Amsterdam-Portuguese origins who had "put a rope around the neck of many a spy."

Pinto's work with MI5 during the war interrogating refugees did in fact result in the capture of eight spies, and I discovered that he interviewed over 30,000 immigrants at the euphemistically named 'London Reception Centre' in the Royal Victoria Patriotic Building in Wandsworth. The 1961

BBC TV series *Spycatcher* was based on two books he wrote: *Spycatcher* and *Friend or Foe?*

Afterwards, Slis complained vociferously about the screening to the prime minister of the London-based Dutch government-in-exile, Pieter Gerbrandy, but finally admitted, "I did find him [Pinto] a nice guy." After all, she repeated, "I was the only one not in uniform. [The rest] were American (sic) girls, all in nice uniforms, and all kinds of uniformed boys, who had come from far and near."

Having got through her interrogation by Pinto, Nel found nursing work from August as part of the Netherlands Voluntary Red Cross in New Cross Hospital in Wolverhampton, where the Princess Irene Brigade was stationed.

She was inclined to be dismissive of this job, describing it as nursing a colony of Dutch exiles. "Anyway, these colonies are always uninteresting," she groused. "They were not sick, of course, it was just ingrown toenails and blackheads, and there'd be a great feast if someone got appendicitis."

Her nursing work was nevertheless appreciated. Miss F. Cain, the hospital's matron, gave her a reference on her departure, which said Miss Adriana N. Slis had acquired '*very valuable experience in the up-to-date surgical technique and treatment of acute surgical and accident patients*'. The document also wished her every success in her future career, little knowing that Nel was then about to leave the nursing profession for ever.

The nursing stint did produce one invaluable contact for Nel's future life. In Wolverhampton, she nursed Cees Fock, then working in London with the government in exile. Fock, who also became a lifelong friend, would prove a staunch ally and advisor in The Hague after the war during Nel's first years as a journalist. He also became an excellent contact for her when he was appointed Secretary-General of the General Affairs Ministry. In UK terms, this ministry approximates to the Prime Minister's Office.

Whereas Nel evidently felt sidelined in Wolverhampton after battling so hard to get to England to do something about the Nazis, her next move would definitely make her part of the war effort. After leaving Wolverhampton, she went to London to stay with another of the Russian sisters she got to know from Paris, this time, Lottie. This sister had married an Englishman in Singapore, "and she was happy to take me in," said Nel.

In January 1943, she got a job with the BBC monitoring service, by taking a test. Created in 1939 at the outset of WW2, the purpose of the service was to gather and interpret international news as rapidly and economically as possible. The BBC website notes that Churchill was an avid customer of the service and would ring up in the middle of the night and ask, of Hitler, 'What's that fellow been saying?'

Nel monitored various languages for the BBC, in the first place Dutch and Flemish. "I found the food horrifying," she suddenly remarked with typical bluntness while talking about this period. "We were sitting in the country in Evesham, later in Reading and Cavendish."

There were monitors from all over the world – Swedes, Kenyans, Arabs, a Dutch woman with a Kenyan background, a whole slew of Czechs and Slovakians, a contingent of Danes and other northerners. As well as Dutch and Flemish, Nel's linguistic talents meant she could also fill in on monitoring French and Italian broadcasts.

Everything was monitored and translated, from military business to rationing of bread, Nel recalled. For example, if a monitor heard about bread rationing, this information went straight to the economic affairs ministry, while reports of potato disease went to the agriculture ministry. Though the Dutch official broadcasting station was censored by the Germans, Nel said she assumed that the information about food and suchlike details was reliable.

"But of course you also heard this gigantic propaganda. Mr Max Blokzijl was one of the lads I always had to listen to. Another was Anton Musset…" Unknown names to me, but this was probably quite creepy listening for the freedom-loving Dutchwoman.

Nel's acute powers of observation must have been much valued by the BBC. "There could be clues everywhere: '*Die Deutsche Soldaten sind braun verbrannt heimgekehrt*' (the German soldiers have returned home tanned) meant they'd been in the tropics."

Nel's annual salary at the BBC was £300 plus cost-of-living bonus, and she worked there for nearly two years. It was also possible on request to avail oneself of 'Corporation bicycles' for free transport, but this carried a warning:

Users of Corporation bicycles are not permitted to use the bus service to and from Wood Norton [where the Monitoring Service of the Overseas Division was based at that point] unless it is found there is room in the bus for such people when all passengers entitled to priority have been accommodated.

Citing these regulations, Nel's lawyer friend Piet Wackie Eysten remarked that the BBC did not leave much to chance.

In 1944, when Nel was again staying with her White Russian friend Lottie in London, she met a friend of Lottie's who was working for the

Associated Press. She told Nel that she was doing similar work to the BBC monitoring and making more money, and that the AP were desperately looking for people in London. "The BBC did not pay so well, because it was government work," Nel remarked.

It was a very different set-up, as the BBC operation was vast, with 2,000 people listening in to every conceivable news service. The AP had a tiny staff compared with this, and was 'only for spot news'.

What happened next sounded a familiar Nel Slis process by then: "I met a journalist at a party about then, given by the White Russians [Lottie]. He was an Associated Press director and he asked, just to keep the conversation going, who was I actually? So I told him that I was Dutch and what had happened to me, and then he said, 'What are you doing now?' I said, 'Well, I'm monitoring, for the BBC.' Then he said, 'We have no correspondent in occupied Europe and we also have a monitoring service, but with us all these details about bread and things are not important. We have to know what they're up to. Would you like to work with us? We pay better, but you do have to work at night a lot. But shorter hours and well paid.'"

As a result of this encounter with the AP director, whose name was Bob Bunnelle, Nel then did another test, and after obtaining the approval of the Ministry of Labour and National Service, she joined the AP in Fleet Street, at a salary of seven pounds and seven shillings a week or about £382 a year.

Money was not the only consideration. Nel's letter accepting the appointment showed that she was looking for opportunities to get back to the Netherlands, and calculated her chances of being sent to an as yet still occupied country were greater at an international press agency than at the BBC.

'*I feel sure I shall be happy working for your organisation and look forward to the day when it will be possible for you to transfer me to your office in Holland*', she wrote to Bunnelle from Wargrave, Berkshire on 16 October 1944. I'm not sure what she was doing in Berkshire, but Nel always liked to move around. Possibly she was visiting yet another White Russian, or some other friend.

She began work on 25 October, initially on the day desk "until we get you worked into the organisation," said Bunnelle. And thus began Nel's long journalistic career.

"I sat in a closet with all sorts of other Europeans, who each had an occupied area to cover and write pieces about." The job also meant living in London again, "where these V-1s and V-2s were descending."

Here again, as with her encounter with the Nazis on the boat from Finland to Baltimore, Nel initially claimed that "at that time, you found nothing scary, nor can I remember that anyone ever went into the cellars in Fleet Street when there was an air-raid warning." Fleet Street, then still the nation's press headquarters, was quite colourful, though.

"God, and they drank, these young guys, I'll never forget that in my life." Because they were scared, too, she finally admits. "You heard the V-2s that flew over your head in Fleet Street. There was one that was really a big boozer. He was so queasy sometimes that he didn't know what to do. Then he opened the drawer and then, *roetsch*, he shut it again…" Wondering whether to throw up in it, I surmised.

Marking the big change from the BBC monitoring service into actual journalism, Nel explained that at the AP, "it was all about news and not reports about potato disease," adding with satisfaction, "That was a good deal more interesting. I didn't do badly because I knew many people, you see, and I had my ears quite open.

"I often gave them a piece of news, for instance, that Queen Wilhelmina was going to ride in a Jeep through Walcheren [the peninsula in the southwest of the Netherlands on which the port of Vlissingen or Flushing is located], or about the Dutch planes for Indonesia. Or the Dutch plans for emigration. Because Holland was badly hit by the war, they were talking about emigration for the first time for many centuries.

"I had a couple of nice scoops there – I knew, for example, twenty minutes before the rest of the world that the Americans and Russians had met on the Elbe and that went straight into the papers."

A complimentary note from Bunnelle on 28 April 1945 confirmed that Nel was already doing excellent reporting work. That meeting on the Elbe was a particularly important scoop.

Nice work on the linkup today! As you see from New York's message, your report was about twenty minutes ahead of all others, which is very nice indeed, and which will go into your personal file as another evidence of the capabilities of Miss Nel Slis. RB

Nel had picked up on French radio the news that the Russians and the Americans made contact on 25 April at Torgau, not far from Berlin. The telegram from New York that Bunnelle refers to reads:

Thanks, fine rapid work Paris radio on linkup, putting us approximately twenty minutes ahead both oppositions

'Both oppositions' are the competing international press agencies Reuters and UPI. The telegram marked Nel's definitive arrival in the world of international journalism, and was a sign of her potential as a world-class journalist.

Nel ended her account modestly: "Anyway, I was trying hard to do that job when the war ended." She had also kept her sights on getting back to Holland with the AP after the war, and an opportunity was then emerging. "By that time, the AP was saying listen, before the war, only Reuters sold news in Europe, but now the AP will be in competition – we're going to sell the American news service, because it's become much more important now in Europe."

Nel was immediately onto the case. "At a certain point, I heard [and it was actually fairly secret] that the AP were going to Holland. I told that to Burne, Chief of Bureau, and he said, 'If that is true, will you go to Holland too?' I said. 'Well, I will go and see if that rich clay is still lying in Goeree and Overflakkee and if there are still a few cents there.' And then he said, 'We are going to set up a bureau there. Will you work for us?' So then I said, 'Yes, I'll go back.'"

So, as Nel was fond of saying, "I fell into journalism like a hair in the soup."

Halfway through a 1990s radio interview, when Nel was talking about how the English found her suspicious because she spoke two or three languages, the interviewer thoughtfully repeated 'suspicious' and remarked that she had a colourful life as a girl. Were there others like her at that time? he asked.

It was undoubtedly unusual then for a young woman to travel, study and work her way around Europe on her own, and even to be allowed to do so, as Nel duly conceded. A certain predisposition was necessary for this, she remarked, attributing hers to the fact that she had, in a manner of speaking, brought herself up.

Were other girls not jealous of what you had done at that time? the interviewer asked. Nel snapped back, "I don't trouble myself much with other girls," possibly irritated by the interviewer's repeated use of the term 'girl'. After all, by the time she reached London, she was a seasoned traveller with a first-rate nursing diploma, experience of nursing the war-wounded in Finland and five languages under her belt. And she was twenty-nine.

But did she 'trouble herself with young men'? To this, Nel replied frankly, despite or perhaps because of the series of rejected suitors she had already chalked up, "I was more involved with myself. How I could get from here to there, what would I do then, etcetera." Then, relenting about her 'girls' jibe, she added, "No, I have always had very good women friends. Few, but very good."

Taking up the interviewer's point about few women travelling and studying independently at the time, Nel said, "Few Dutch women perhaps. Because look, Dutch girls did go abroad and so on, but they had everything nicely arranged for them, and I just had to wait and see. Yes, I was not *comme les autres*. An odd one out? Yes, but I was really not stuck-up about it. I had to keep swimming."

Life up to and through the war may have been a big adventure for the curious islander, but it had not been particularly easy for Nel to 'keep swimming'. This may explain why she often repeated the phrase about falling into journalism like a hair in the soup. At last, this was something that really engaged and challenged her, something to get her teeth into, more than nursing.

All the same, I do feel that nursing was an important part of Nel's life. Though she talked very little about it, she did say she enjoyed it and wouldn't have missed it for anything. Between her three years' training, Finland experience and about two years in Wolverhampton, it had taken up half of her adult life between leaving school and the end of the war. We cannot have Nel without her nursing. It, too, was part of her even though she went on to pursue a very different career.

As well as the Red Cross medal for Bravery, Skill and Dedication and the Finnish decoration for her work nursing the war-wounded in Finland, she also received a bronze plaque from the Princess Irene Brigade for her nursing in Wolverhampton.

Pondering Nel's early adventures around Europe, Tyna Wynaendts felt her attraction to languages was in itself unusual. "Usually, people who are very good at languages already have one parent of a different nationality, or have been exposed at a very early age to a different language, but Nel wasn't at all. She never met foreigners; she'd never travelled abroad before she went to Paris. Why did she want to go? For a Dutch girl to go to a Swiss [nursing] school was also outrageous – you would go to a Dutch school."

There were obvious forces propelling Nel out of the country – her unhappiness and her problematic father – but she also had good friends there. Tyna recalled that as well as her close friendship with Tyna's mother, "she had lots of boyfriends, even [when she was still] in Middelharnis."

The key to Nel, Tyna concluded, was her strong desire to be independent. "That's what she kept repeating: that it's a good thing for a girl to know that it's always better when you can be completely independent financially."

This was very unusual at that time. Tyna said when she was sent to university in Leiden, "it was never said, of course, but it was more to find the right husband than to really do something academic. But Nel always insisted, make sure you can look after yourself."

After joining the AP in London, Nel was now about to embark on a new battle of independence to build her career back in Holland.

FOREIGN
CORRESPONDENT

(1945–1962)

CHAPTER FIVE
THE AP'S SLIS
"Who are you, actually?"

Nel moved to Amsterdam in summer 1945, soon after the liberation of the Netherlands. The initial months back in the country passed in a whirlwind at the AP's new bureau at Nieuwezijds Achterburgwal 225, in central Amsterdam. The AP and Reuters had shared an office in the capital before the war, but after it ended, the AP set up its own office, with Henk Kersting as Bureau Chief.

Under Kersting's tutelage, Nel went on learning the trade of journalism, as well as acting as general factotum. "I was doing everything, selling photos, news, translating, getting news. Amsterdam, and the AP bureau there, was a witches' cauldron then," she said in an enigmatic aside. I'm guessing it must have been tough facing all the chauvinistic young males in the office after the war, and she was fortunate that Kersting was so supportive. There were still a few of those guys around when I worked in the AP office in the 1980s.

Kersting taught Nel the basic 'tricks of the trade', and became her supportive and appreciative bureau chief for the bulk of her AP career. He himself was already a well-known journalist, and had been in the resistance during the war.

Although she was still relatively new to journalism, Nel had chalked up considerable experience of the wider world since leaving school thanks to her travels, nursing training and practice and wartime adventures. When she visited her old friend Dr De Vletter, rector of her secondary school, on her return to Holland, he invited her to tell the higher classes and the teachers something about her travels, her impressions of Finland, her voyage from Finland to America, relations between Russians and Finns. As that chapter of her life closed and she faced fresh challenges in her home country, it must have been rewarding for her to have a chance to review those years back at her much-loved old school.

Among events covered by the AP soon after Nel started work in Amsterdam were the odd combination of a world cycle race and the first Ecumenical World Congress, in August and September. The Congress was held in Amsterdam's Concertgebouw, home of the world-renowned Royal Concertgebouw Orchestra. Nel was unimpressed by the American AP specialists parachuted in for these events.

"Our American religious correspondent couldn't manage to say anything other than 'Concertgebouw' in a week. Another American colleague fainted in a tourist boat at the end of the festivities because of the large quantities of *jonge jenever* (Dutch gin)."

Nel gave me the impression that the Amsterdam-based period was relatively brief. She said an AP bigwig was touring Europe after only six months to see how things were going and told her the AP needed someone in The Hague: "The news had come that the International Court of Justice was being based there, and then, the Dutch were losing Indonesia." The decolonisation of Indonesia and the opening of the International Court of Justice, along with Marshall Aid and Dutch postwar reconstruction, were all big news for the Americans.

The senior AP visitor was very surprised to find that there was a bureau in Amsterdam (the capital) but no correspondent in The Hague, the seat of government. So Nel was in due course invited to be the AP's first correspondent in The Hague. Kersting, who recommended her for the post, received a typically succinct telegram from New York: '*We'll send Slis to The Hague*'. This was an important post: all the big international newspapers had a correspondent in The Hague in those postwar days.

In The Hague, Nel set up home and office in a flat in 11 Javastraat. She told me she was on two months' trial in The Hague from April 1946, but according to her archives, the official appointment was from July 1950. Still, this big time difference is less significant than it might seem, as she would probably have started working the beat there anyway soon after that visitation from the AP bigwig, and the AP may have been slow to make the appointment official. I wouldn't be surprised if there was resistance in New York to installing a woman correspondent.

There was one intriguing detail about Amsterdam. Tina Wynaendts told me Nel shared a flat there with a young woman called Puk Gukov. Puk had a rich, thrice-married father; Puk's mother was his second wife. The Gukovs were the richest family in Holland and owned the Catshuis, which later became the official residence for Dutch prime ministers.

Tyna said this was the only time Nel ever shared a flat with a woman. She speculated that perhaps because there was no loving relationship at her home when she was growing up, that was why she didn't want to share with anyone – apart from this one attempt with Puk. "And they didn't stay friends."

Once installed in The Hague, Nel needed to get her teeth into the nitty-gritty of Dutch politics, a new area for her. As she put it, "I had to make my way in the small world of The Hague and of parliament, which was beginning to operate again. Well, I'd never sat in parliament before, so I ran hell for leather – Slis in The Hague." After two months, Nel beamed, Kersting wrote to New York and said: '*Slis has done a workmanlike job*'.

"That's how I started in the Netherlands with the AP, and I was with them until 1979."

Thus was 'AP's Slis' born.

Nel set up her office in the front of the flat, and the AP paid her rent of 50 *guilders* a month. She furnished it with a telex, a filing cabinet and a desk with a typewriter. This, along with piles of notebooks and newspapers, would remain her total journalistic equipment for her entire life, apart from the later addition of a fax machine. Fortunately for her, she would not have to face the switch to computers, which would probably have driven her crazy.

Material for much of this book was mined from that same filing cabinet, by then aged and battered. Fellow journalist Friso Endt thoughtfully tipped me off to go and root in the filing cabinet before it went off to the Press Museum, which was to house Nel's archives. "You won't be able to access it for at least two years after that," he warned me. So I took as much as I could, photocopied it and hastily returned it. I was very grateful for that tip-off.

In general, Friso helped me somewhat sporadically. Sometimes I had the feeling he thought that I, an outsider and a foreigner, shouldn't be writing Nel's book. Eventually, I asked whether he wouldn't like to write the book himself. No, he said, he didn't have time. Friso was a small, temperamentally bristly man with a well-developed ego, and often seemed most forthcoming to me with stories about Nel that also shone a bit of glory on his own journalistic career. On the other hand, he remained a great admirer of Nel, whom he had witnessed at the height of her powers, and he loyally played a key part in helping to look after her towards the end of her life.

Back in those days in The Hague, Nel found herself fighting her way into an unreceptive, often hostile male world as well as into a new reporting area. She described her initial difficulties at great length in many interviews. "It wasn't easy," she told me. "I had to work hard to get to know the unknown parliamentary and diplomatic world of The Hague. Right away I plunged into my books – especially political science – from the Kennemer Lyceum, which someone had luckily kept for me."

In a city emerging from occupation, life in The Hague could also still be chaotic. "I had been away for so long… I worked hard and undressed in the dark, because there were no curtains when I moved into Javastraat 11… I had nothing, how did you find a pillow, a towel? That alone was a problem already. I had no bicycle. I walked and walked. I walked the soles off my shoes. I sent my shoes to England to have them cobbled, it couldn't be done here. It was chaos in the Netherlands just after the war – anyone… got a job regardless." Nel complained vociferously of hindrance by authorities and press information people "who couldn't inform, never knew anything and only sat there because they had been so good in the war." She often had to carry on working when she was mad with rage. There was no doubt in her mind that she encountered hindrance *because* she was a woman. She was virtually the only female around at the time.

Nel certainly wasn't shy about describing her battles, making quite an impression on her various interviewers. "There were bastards sitting there," she told one of them. Sometimes she came home crying from rage and frustration. "Then she goes to the bathroom, rolls up her sleeves, showers her streaming eyes, looks at herself in the mirror and says: 'Slis, they will NOT make you small.'"

"I was a tough one," she said. "You must be very strong physically and mentally. Everywhere I went, I had to explain first who I was and then, what the AP was. A female correspondent at that time was a freak of nature – I was the one and only in the Netherlands and there was no precedent for this. They didn't want to take you seriously. I could have stuffed them…"

The civil servants, the politicians and the spokesmen all got up her nose. "In the beginning, a woman in this work was of course a novelty, but with all these spokesmen, just out of the resistance, it was difficult. Who is that broad, where does she come from? If there's one thing I never want to hear again, it's *'who are you actually?'* That's what they always said, these godforsaken Dutch. It still rings in my ears.

"Ha, who are you actually! I will write a book about it one of these days, and this chapter will be called: *'Who are you, actually?'* I'll never forget it my whole life! Condescending? Yes…"

Fortunately, they weren't all like that. General Affairs Ministry secretary-general Cees Fock, whom she had nursed in Wolverhampton during the war, helped her greatly and gave her much-needed good advice. And through him, she met other people, gradually building up contacts that often became good friends as well as valuable sources.

Meanwhile, Nel was having little joy with her fellow journalists. As one of her interviewers wrote, *'All the male journalists and reporters were urbane and scrubbed clean. But they swaggered with indignation if they heard the word CAO [collective labour agreement]. They all wore ties – preferably bow ties. At press conferences, they made a small bow and addressed ministers as* "excellentie".

Another interviewer was equally scathing: "Drab, grey three-piece suits who bowed and scraped to every minister like jackknives and then asked obvious questions."

Not, of course, the AP's correspondent, the first interviewer hastened to add. After a few routine questions by other journalists, she was more likely to ask the minister, "But Mr… tell us now, without beating about the bush, exactly how things stand."

Nel said she got scoops for the AP because she dared to ask the authorities proper questions, unlike her male colleagues. "If it was about news, I trampled them all into the corner," she said with a touch of pride, adding; "But I was a woman, I was young, I was a lot more beautiful than I am now and I gave as good as I got." Nel herself reckoned her early experiences in The Hague made her more aggressive. "And it gave me a bigger gob, definitely. They found it really strange, actually. That broad that's walking around… who is that broad?"

Her approach was not always appreciated, especially her habit of phoning ministers after they had gone to bed. Apparently it never occurred to her that they might consider her a bit of a nuisance, because she herself was so busy working hard from dawn to dusk and then 'pounding away until deep in the night'.

She was once banned for three weeks from the foreign affairs ministry, because Foreign Minister Eelco van Kleffens found her too impertinent. A fellow journalist told the story. "Nel Slis was sitting in the press spokesman's office. When he went out for a minute to fetch a document, the minister came into the room just then, whereupon Nel Slis immediately shot at him, 'Well, Mr Van Kleffens, now you can tell me something directly...' So that ended badly. It was the period when the average journalist licked the backside of the minister and not yet the other way round, like now."

Quite apart from all the difficulties she was encountering in the Netherlands, Nel's ambitions still stretched beyond her native country. At a fairly early stage, she tried to get a transfer to Paris, but there was no vacancy. Undeterred, Nel approached Paris Bureau Chief Preston Grover directly. He saw no opportunities for Nel there either, transparently confirming Nel's experience of prejudice against women in this male profession when he wrote to her around Christmas 1951:

'You know of course that you are rowing against a fast tide. You are practically the only woman reporter abroad in the AP. The reason is of course that most jobs seem to call for men. I don't know why this is necessarily true, but that is the prevailing idea. Nevertheless, of all Europe, Paris is the most likely place for a woman reporter to find something to keep her busy'. Doubtless, Grover meant writing about haute couture and the like.

Nel's boss Kersting also approached Wes Gallagher, AP's General Manager in New York, on her behalf to try to get her some training in the US. But Gallagher at that time saw no post where Nel's many talents could be better used by the AP than in Holland. Even a visit by Kersting to New York failed to produce any results. One of the directors, Lloyd Stratton, remarked that "she seems to be a fabulous woman," but said this was all the more reason to keep her in The Hague.

So Nel just had to go on 'finding something to keep her busy' in the Netherlands, amid her dreary, nit-picking male fellow journalists. However, things gradually improved, and Nel even found a few compatible souls in the press fraternity. She described a kind of camaraderie that developed:

"After all, in time, I became a sort of *copain* and there were very good lads there who also helped you. You had Jaap Hoek of Trouw there, first class. And Dries Ekker of *Het Parool*, a deranged boy, sometimes a bit jealous if you got something before him, but very able and a good reporter, Louis Metzemakers of course (later, editor of the Dutch financial newspaper,

Het Financieele Dagblad) and Marcus van Blankenstein, who also did not treat me like old rubbish. The nicest were Jaap Hoek and Metzemakers. Jaap Hoek was my first real friend among my colleagues, and later Marcus van Blankenstein. With Blankenstein, you could see very well that he had travelled the whole world before the war. That man was well read."

Nel was quick to differentiate herself as a press agency reporter from newspapermen like Blankenstein, saying she was 'no soul-searcher', and had 'no time for dissertations' or getting into digging out why people behaved as they did. I would say Nel was not doing herself justice here, as she was, in fact, very interested in sniffing out what was going on below the surface.

She was nevertheless crystal clear about her top priority. "I was a simple agency reporter with a good nose for news, and I am paid for that nose." She once said her nose got longer during her career as a journalist, which I reckon it did, literally as well as figuratively.

Oddly enough, towards the end of her long career at the AP, Nel found herself feeling a certain homesickness for the postwar period, "the fighting with spokesmen, plucked out of the resistance, who didn't know what they should do with a journalist, looked askance at this skirted Argus and on top of this had never heard of the AP."

It is obvious that Nel was not just breaking the mould of Dutch journalism by her sex, but also by her direct, persistent and aggressive approach, in contrast to the often mealy-mouthed, sycophantic post-occupation reporters of the day. Friso Endt described Slis among the press corps of the day:

"They were all big shots, the Dutch and the foreigners. And Nel came there among them as the only woman. She worked day and night, she never stopped. She went to every cocktail party. Not for her pleasure but to hear and to feel what was going on."

Describing what was unique about working for a press agency, Nel said: "You always have to phone in your first paragraph. This is the great difference [from newspaper work]. You must always be the first one at the telephone. In the Vredespaleis [Peace Palace] with those damned slippery floors and stairs, I took off my shoes and stockings under the table to get to the godforsaken telephone first without slipping, and the phone was always damn well downstairs." She said she was never tempted to switch to newspaper reporting. "I found it much too interesting working for an international press agency. It was much more world-oriented. As well, I learned so much with AP... I learned the five w's – who, what, where, why and when. That's what America brought to Dutch journalism."

When she interviewed Colonial Minister Jan Jonkman about the Indonesian crisis, New York immediately telexed that she must also have the opinion of an Indonesian. "I learned that early on: if there is an issue, then I have to interview not only A but also B." Another aspect of being a good press agency reporter was the importance of pinning down the facts. "Facts. Facts I must have. Checking and then checking again, you learn that at an agency. Otherwise, I get a query...

"Ach, this whole business of journalism, there are just three golden rules, and I question whether you learn that anywhere at a school for journalism. I know for sure not. These rules are: you must have done your homework, you must have a tremendous interest in the subject and finally, you must possess tenacious stamina. And on top of this, I had the good luck that I also have a nose for news."

The Jonkman interview was a breakthrough for Slis. It was widely picked up by international newspapers, and she was taken a little more seriously. However, "distrust remained, and that was partly based on my being a woman. Luckily, I could fall back on Henk Kersting in Amsterdam and on Dan Schorr. I learned a lot from them, but I had to fight hard for it." We shall hear more about Dan Schorr shortly.

An anecdote about the early years in a 1963 interview in *Het Parool* showed Slis at her most combative. In 1948, she was sent to Margraten, near Maastricht, where the Netherlands American Cemetery and Memorial is located, and managed to hitch a lift in the car of the Polish chargé d'affaires. On the way back, Nel asked him to stop at a pub called Tante Sophie so that she could go to the toilet. Three drunken men and a drunken landlady were sitting together in the pub. When she was finished, one of the drunken men pushed into the booth, shouting, "You are a spy." Slis then 'valiantly struck him away from her' and a regular battle ensued. The Polish diplomat, who had been waiting outside, appeared, shocked, in the doorway. "Call the police," shouted Nel. To her relief, he did so, and a Black Maria arrived and took everyone to the police station.

"I was furious. I phoned Premier Beel and I said, 'What sort of country is this? A land of wild beasts?' After that, I gave a press conference in bed, beaten all black and blue, and the *NRC* had a column on the front page, headlined '*Cherchez la femme*'. I still haven't forgiven them yet for that. The fellows were up in court and given a two months' sentence. I got 27 *guilders* for my torn-to-pieces only black suit."

The most atmospheric photo of Nel that I found from this period is on the cover, showing her back in the AP office after the coronation of Queen Juliana. Still in party frock and hat, she is seated at an antediluvian typewriter, surrounded by male colleagues in top hats. One of the prettiest catches her on her own at the Winter Olympics in 1949. But in virtually every other photo throughout her life where she is in action as a journalist, it is striking that Nel always manages to be right next to the key person of the moment.

In 1955, after ten years with the AP in the Netherlands, Nel wrote a surprisingly polite and decorous article for the Foreign Press Association's 30th anniversary magazine, which still managed to give a vivid picture of her gruelling working life as a journalist. But she admitted that the hustle and bustle of press agency reporting could be quite addictive as well: "If things get too quiet, you would start missing them."

In her article, there are some sly digs at 'working' and cocktail-partying wives, carefully muted so as not to alienate them or their husbands. She also talks about the need for women journalists to dress up and the extra expense they incur. This is less of a problem nowadays, at least in the Netherlands. But on another of her gripes, I can vouch for the fact that it can still be hard to get first names out of the Dutch, as required by international but not necessarily by Dutch media. A Dutch company chief once told an exasperated agency reporter, "I'll give you my first name if you promise not to use it."

One story from the initial postwar years demonstrates Nel's determination and effectiveness when she got wind of something of which she did not approve. Weekly newspaper *Vrij Nederland*'s reporter Igor Cornelissen, writing in 1982 and remarking that Nel was known for years in The Hague as '*that difficult bitch*', declared: "It would be nicer and more appropriate if she went down in history as 'that woman who stopped Molotov'."

In 1957, Nel Slis got hold of the news that the former comrade-in-arms of Joseph Stalin, after whom the Molotov cocktail was named, was to be foisted onto the Netherlands as ambassador. That same evening, she phoned Cees Fock, by then secretary-general in the prime minister's office and close to Premier Willem Drees.

"I told him that these Russians wanted to appoint Molotov here and I said: 'Cees, that really can't be allowed, goddamit.' Cees asked if I knew it for sure and when I confirmed that, he said, 'No, of course we cannot have that man here.'" That was naturally, said Nel, *front-page news*. Ending his article, Cornelissen wrote: '*If we remember correctly, Molotov, foreign minister under Stalin, then became ambassador to Outer Mongolia.*'

Considering all the hours she worked, it seemed to me almost impossible that Nel could have any life outside her work. But she always found time for her friends and for cultural events, which were often woven into her work as well. Conversely, many of her contacts also become good friends outside work.

An advantage of being posted to The Hague was that her childhood friend from the island, Jenneke, was now living there with her husband and three children, and Nel became a frequent visitor. Jenneke's daughter Tyna Wynaendts found this long-lasting friendship remarkable considering they were so different. "My mother was really a *femme au famille*, who looked after her family and for whom her family always came first. And Nel, so ambitious, and a feminist also, supporting women's rights; my mother was not interested in that. But they got on very well." At the same time, Tyna felt it was not a very intimate friendship, perhaps because they were so different.

Tyna was about ten years old when Nel started stopping by in The Hague, and she felt fortunate to be speedily adopted by Nel as a sort of goddaughter. As a journalist, Nel would get two tickets for nearly all the performances at the annual Holland Festival cultural jamboree, for example. She often took Tyna with her, because she felt she had to learn about good quality ballet and other performance arts. After the ballet, she took Tyna behind the scenes and introduced her to the performers.

"She knew everybody, violinist Isaac Stern and Nora Kay, prima ballerina of the New York City ballet and married for a period to Isaac Stern. Nel was friends with the whole Stern family, and I was then a ballet fan. We would be invited to cocktails after the performance – it was absolutely wonderful, especially meeting and knowing Isaac Stern." Stern became another of Nel's lifelong friends, writing her long letters every Christmas.

Nel also liked to take Tyna for a walk in the seaside resort of Scheveningen every Sunday, telling her that she had to get out of the house for health and beauty, and 'you need some wind.' In fact, Nel wanted somebody to walk with, but Tyna was always happy to go out with her. She also sometimes visited Nel's flat on the first floor in Javastraat, and remembered her cat, 'just like mine, tabby, a normal cat'.

"Nel was also very generous to me, taking me on little trips and holidays and buying me gifts," she added.

Tyna also remembered the faithful Aagje from the island, who cooked for Nel and looked after her. "She did everything for her. Aagje would have died for her." Aagje worked for Nel until she went to Brussels, and later on, when she couldn't work anymore, she went to Tyna's mother to polish the silver and do small jobs so that she could still 'make her own living'.

Ever Nel's loyal defender, on one occasion, Aagje even made sure Nel got some of her own family's silver. Tyna told me: "When one of Nel's aunts on her mother's side died, Nel went there to give a helping hand and Aagje went with her on her own initiative to defend her interests. They went through the house and Aagje said you must take this and you must take that – and you can take the silver, nobody wants it. And Nel said afterwards she was very grateful, because at that moment she had not thought about it."

Nel often dropped into Tyna's home at around 'borrel time', the Dutch cocktail hour between six and seven, fascinating Tyna by her un-ladylike habit of drinking *jenever*. "She was one of the first women ever to drink *jenever*. At that time, women were supposed to drink sherry or port, but not *jenever*, that wasn't done. And my mother frowned on it."

Throughout the period when Tyna was at secondary school, Nel was around several times a week. She gave a lot of advice, for instance, telling Tyna she didn't keep her shoulders straight and should see a specialist, and naturally knowing the right person to see. Or later, telling her she must stop ballet because her feet were getting knobbly.

"She interfered a lot, but I liked that, because she mainly had a different opinion than my mother's and it often happened that this would be more what I wanted to do."

Surprisingly, Tyna said her mother only occasionally seemed to mind Nel's interference. "I think she rather liked this friendship." Perhaps for a woman immersed in home and family, it was refreshing to have such an exotic friend as Nel.

A bonus for Nel at that time was that she could get things off her chest with her surrogate family when life infuriated her too much. "She would also come in when she was upset about things, when somebody didn't want to talk to her. And she had enemies too, people who couldn't stand her. She would come for a borrel, fuming, and would talk to my parents, who didn't quite understand the whole atmosphere and what she was talking about, but just knew she had to let off steam." Nel also sometimes joined the family for Christmas, as she was often on her own and was 'more or less one of the family' as of old on the island.

Nel was close to Tyna's brother Piet as well, but spent less time with him than Tyna, as it wasn't so easy to take a boy shopping, for example. She did, however, also take Piet to concerts. He was equally fascinated by her. In the beginning, Piet said, they called her Auntie, but that annoyed her. He remembered vividly her strange parking habits with her little Renault 4 car.

"To our secret amazement, completely ignoring traffic signs, she would park on any random street corner. Her unrestrained use of language, the foreign cigarettes she smoked, the *jenever* she drank made an indelible impression on my brother, my sister and myself."

Nel often took Piet, a young music lover, to concerts in the Kurhaus or K&W with her free press cards. Like Tyna, Piet was introduced by Nel to many famous people, including Leonard Bernstein, "with whom she withdrew to the Kurhaus bar after the concert, where Bernstein then after some time took Sandor Vidak's place behind the piano."

Many of Nel's contacts with famous musicians stemmed from her friendship with Johanna Beek, who with her husband formed an impresario team that brought many of these leading musicians to the Netherlands. Piet remembered Nel telling stories of a weekend with Mstislav Rostropovitch in the Beeks' weekend cottage, for example. The odd surviving photo shows Nel with such international figures, including Arthur Rubenstein and Igor Stravinsky.

As a child, Johanna's daughter Yolanda was similarly impressed by Nel. "She was so much not a conventional person. I was brought up very properly and loved her out-of-the-ordinary swearing and screaming, and my parents were great friends of hers."

Nel could, however, also be extremely unreasonable, and there were a number of stories of violent rows with people, including close friends. Nor was she in the least prepared to make up with someone once they had fallen out. Yolanda told me of one such incident, which she found quite upsetting:

"My parents had a little cottage in Brabant. My father didn't like company, but he loved Nel very much. She was one of my parents' few friends. I would see her there sometimes during the holidays. One day, she had a row with a mutual lady friend – she never wanted to talk about it, but from that moment, my parents couldn't have them in the house together.

"My father died a long time ago, when I was twenty-seven, but my poor mother on her deathbed wanted Nel to make peace with this mutual friend. I tried desperately, but Nel is so stubborn. That was an example of her total stubbornness. Why could she not even pretend, for the last wish of my mother? But there was no way, it was against her principles."

Nel talked about disliking people with gusto, but sometimes this seemed far too mild a term, so perhaps it is no surprise that Nel was by no means universally liked.

"'That horrible woman' – I'm sure there are people who really disliked her, because she could be so violent when she talked about someone she disliked," Tyna said. She herself had also faced an explosion from Nel, though in her case, she felt it was justified. She had to meet her at the entrance to the Holland Festival for a concert, and she was late. Nel left the ticket for her. Afterwards, Tyna said, "it's 'why were you late? That's the last time, you can forget it.' She was FURIOUS."

Tyna reckoned she was too dependent then on her mother telling her it was time to go, and Mum wasn't around that evening. "Nel was really shouting at me and I was very, very upset and went two or three days later to apologise. She said, you know, in life, when you do that, when you're not respectful, that's one of the first rules, and you'd better learn it. And she was right, of course."

Nel also got on well with Tyna's father, though they did have fights from time to time because he considered she interfered too much with the family. She had less contact with Tyna's elder brother, who was less amenable to Nel's rules, once getting up her nose by cleaning his pipe and blowing tobacco all over her carpet. They were still friends but not close.

When Tyna was about thirteen, Nel started getting her to do her filing. Tyna was thrilled, as she was paying her for an hour or two of work. She presented Tyna with a great pile of newspapers, gave her subjects and told her to make cuttings.

"She would say, for instance, make cuttings of Wilhelmina, and I said why? 'Because when she dies, the AP will want a story, and I want it right there, now. I want to go through my own drawers and pull out what's important.'" Everything had to be classified chronologically as well. Tyna cut out the pieces and wrote the date on them. She loved doing it. "It was a way to get out in the evening somewhere my parents would allow me to go."

At the end of Nel's stint in The Hague, just before she went to Brussels, Tyna was impressed by one of Nel's holiday jaunts with Johanna Beek,

Yolanda's mother. When they set off from Paris where Tyna was living at the time, she went with them for the first day. "They had no plan at all, they were just in Nel's car – she was a terrible driver – going south somewhere, and we had dinner in front of this hotel near Paris, and the next day they put me on a train. I thought it was so nice to go on a holiday like that without any plans, and just stop at a nice restaurant if you see one. And they were really enjoying themselves."

Johanna was complaining that she had just discovered Nel in The Hague and now she was leaving. "There are so few women I really get on with who have cultural interests and who have a little creativity in their way of living. Now I have a real friend, and now she's going to Brussels," she groused.

But this lies in the future. Back in the early years in The Hague, Slis was acutely aware of her journalistic learning process, and she undoubtedly learned fast – especially, she told me, from foreign reporters. "More and more people used to come here reporting for American and British papers on what was happening in Holland after the war. I learned a lot about journalism from the Americans, working for the AP. I had to, it was my education.

"There was a Jewish American journalist who worked for the Christian Science Monitor, Dan Schorr, he taught me a lot about journalism."

And she fell in love with him.

Note: Nel's salary when she started working for the AP is not known, but by 1953, it was 671.65 *guilders*, which translates into 304.78 euros.

CHAPTER SIX

AN AMERICAN LOVE

Slis with Schorr

The story of the Dutch losing their huge Indonesian colony brought Slis and Schorr together. Daniel Schorr, a young American journalist, turned up in The Hague in 1946, demanding to know who this woman Slis was. He was complaining that the news service he was working for, Aneta, was constantly being beaten by the Associated Press on the Indonesia news. Apparently Nel overheard this, whereupon he started the ball rolling with the not terribly immortal words:

"Are you Slis? We must have a drink!"

Nel herself didn't consider she was playing such a major role in this big loss-of-colony story. She thought it was the reports from the AP's correspondent in Jakarta that were influencing opinion in America. It was, however, a very big story. As Nel put it, the Dutch had held sway for 300 years over a country a thousand times bigger than Holland, "and we got rich as shit from it." Wassenaar, for instance, a super-rich leafy suburb full of big colonial villas, is a product of the old planters in Indonesia. But after the Second World War was over, the Americans and, Nel believed, also the British, wanted the Dutch out of Indonesia.

Given the Indonesian question as their initial meeting ground, I subsequently received largely oblique fragments of information from Nel about her relationship with Dan Schorr. Schorr himself did speak about it to me, as did Nel's heir, Tyna Wynaerts, but it would be Nel's great friend Flora Lewis who ultimately conveyed the full significance of the relationship for Nel.

In 2000, Dan Schorr told me his version of this period in a lengthy phone conversation from Washington, where he was just finishing his autobiography.

When he met Nel, Schorr had been working in New York for Aneta, the news agency of what was then still called the Dutch East Indies but would soon become Indonesia. During the war, Aneta took over from the Netherlands-based ANP's Dutch news service following the Nazi occupation of Holland, as the ANP came under German control and was no longer an independent service.

Schorr had started working with Aneta before the war. He joined the army when war broke out, but after it was over, he wanted to go into mainstream journalism. The ANP persuaded him to go to Holland first for a year to reorganise its service, emasculated by occupation. This proved quite difficult, with the service just emerging from the war and five years of Nazism.

"They had lost their sense of what was news and what was propaganda, and they had no independence from government. In New York, agencies like the AP and UPS were using the ANP and it was often pretty bad, useless."

There was a lot of opposition, too, "particularly from a guy called Lambooy, who had played a questionable role during the occupation. So it was very, very tense, with me coming along with my free American ideas – back to free journalism."

Lambooy certainly sounds a nasty piece of work and Nel also ran up against him. She was delighted to be able to irritate him a few years later by provoking his curiosity when sitting opposite him the only time she was wearing her Red Cross silver medal and Finnish decoration.

"He couldn't contain himself, and said, 'Miss Slis, what is that?' I got what I wanted. That man had actually told press chiefs earlier, 'You must not say anything to Miss Slis, she is not serious.' And that sort of thing, Slis does not take, you see." Yes, knowing Nel a little by that time, I did indeed see.

Back in those postwar years, Schorr struggled with the ANP but the arrangement didn't work very well, and having done his stint, he went back to the US at the end of 1947. "I concluded I no longer wanted to work for a Dutch or any other news service, but I did want to work in Holland."

Schorr returned to the Netherlands as a stringer, first for the Christian Science Monitor, and then in due course for *Life* and *Time* magazines. "Later, I worked for ABC Radio, which became CBS, and eventually this led to a career with CBS."

Schorr said that when he got to know Nel, the two of them had the idea they could help each other. "She had a profound acquaintance with things in Holland, while I could help her with my knowledge of American journalism."

They shared an office in Nel's apartment. "I even remember the address, Javastraat 11. I had a separate room with a desk and a telephone. That was from 1948, for three or four years." Schorr rather quaintly added, "I will not disguise the fact that our relationship was not just professional."

There were many very big stories Nel was able to break to the AP with Dan's help, he told me. He could do this because his clients were newspapers and magazines with later deadlines. For example, when things were going badly in Indonesia soon after the war, the Dutch resumed police action against Sukarno, the country's first president. Schorr heard from someone in the US Embassy that the Truman government took a dim view of the Dutch behaviour:

"They were ready to threaten, if the Dutch didn't show more accommodation to the nationalist parties, that they would suspend the Marshall Plan aid. I realised I could do this for Nel – the news would be out in a couple of hours for one of my clients. I gave the story to Nel and there was an AP bulletin, also for their clients in the Netherlands – they learned of the threat to suspend aid because of the refractory attitude of the Dutch in Indonesia."

Schorr could also look at Nel's copy and show her how to simplify it. "She was a great, great journalist. She knew a news story, she knew how to interview people. But writing for an American news service, she needed help and I gave it to her."

Conversely, Schorr was generous in his praise of all the help Nel was giving him. At the start, he didn't know any Dutch and she could help him read the newspapers. She also helped him in many other ways, he said, waxing enthusiastic.

"It was a fruitful cooperation, most fruitful. Nel had enormous enthusiasm, looking into whatever she was looking into. She was better at 'did you notice what he said there?' She had a better feeling of what was under the surface. I don't mean to be sexist, but as a woman, she had more sensitivity, intuition. I was more on the surface. She frequently gave a sense of nuance I didn't have."

And Schorr was much impressed by her fiery temper in the cause of justice. "She had a great sense of justice and if this was offended, she got very angry, storming around, *Godverdomme...* (Goddamit). A temper, but attached to her sense of justice, not just angry.

"For example, in the early days, there was still rationing, and when we went to see some government official for lunch, the officials were able to work their way round the rationing, and she didn't think that was fair. She was very truly a democratic, egalitarian person and that sort of thing made her very angry. Mostly at the establishment, pretentious establishment people."

Schorr was also impressed by Nel's pride in the island she came from: "She was very proud, by the way, of her beginnings, coming from the island. She would talk quite often about that Goeree..."

He did manage to get in a dig about the Dutch art of mutual disapproval. "Holland's so small, but there are still differences... between Friesland, North Holland, the Hoge Veluwe... The Dutch manage to find ways of disapproving of everyone else. Nowadays, not anymore, but before, the Catholic south was not highly regarded."

They took vacations together. Schorr remembered a trip to Brittany in 1948, for instance, and a trip to Austria together on another occasion. "We were very close... I found it remarkable, with her good looks and talent, that she had never been married."

Perhaps she wanted to marry you, I suggested.

"I suppose so. I have to admit I did not treat her fairly. It was all wonderful, free together. Then in 1953 there was the Great Flood, and after that, I got lots of work and lots of attention back in the States, and the CBS offered a job working in the States, so I left Holland. In the way people can do, selfish, egotistical. Back in the States, she was out of my life. Then I felt ashamed, I didn't write, didn't contact her..."

Later, Schorr said, he did go back, with a delegation of journalists in 1955. "There was a reception at Hotel des Indes and Nel was there. Typical, she walked over and said, 'You bastard, you never tried to get in touch...'"

He came back again once more in the early 1980s, married with two children. "Really a question of taking my wife around Amsterdam. I didn't get in touch with Nel, but I did with Henk Kersting, who said gently you'd like to know how Nel is, she's doing fine."

Schorr sounded choked at the end of the phone conversation, perhaps affected by his memories.

There is a bit more to the end of the affair. Nel, who had met Schorr's mother, did tell me that the mother wrote him that if he married a goy, she'd kill him. However, Nel admitted elsewhere that the mother threatened suicide in the letter, which feels a more virulent threat. After all, "I'll kill you if you do such-and-such" doesn't normally sound so serious. According to fellow journalist Friso Endt, Schorr also left the letter lying around and Nel found it and was convinced he did this on purpose. Not the nicest way to end an affair. To me, Nel said dismissively:

"He didn't want to marry me, but there were other friends... I've always been a loner, so it didn't matter to me – I've always had a lot of friends."

It's true that Nel always had a lot of friends, but Dan was the only man Nel actually did want to marry, and that had to be painful when it didn't work out. That remark was a transparent cover-up. I felt it only revealed just how much it did matter to her. I noticed her almost brusque dismissiveness and how she looked away from me as she said it.

Some time later, at the beginning of the 1960s, Nel had her handwriting analysed. Among elements in the analysis, freely translated by me, it found:

Good logical intelligence present with a sharp understanding. Via strong sensory perception and an adequate processing of impressions, an extensive experience has been built up.

The analysis continued in the same professional vein:

Dealings are characterised by exceptional vitality, diligence and perseverance. A plan, once adopted, will be brought to fruition at any price. Often, an impulsive motive is at the bottom of this, which, however, if considered important, pushes aside all other matters. The writer is by nature pretty hasty and sometimes too unbridled...

The way of operating is very accurate; committed and carried out with dogged tenacity... Due to experience, great confidence in [the subject's] own capacity has been developed in relation to specific matters.

There is, however, a remarkable feeling of dissatisfaction in relation to life in general, which can lead to painful severity both against the own self and the environment. The self feels besieged by the oblivious outside world and is always ready to spring into defence. Often a counter-attack is launched before there is any question of a real attack.

65

Character: strong, honest, faithful to conviction and very decisive.
Great pugnacity is coupled with this, which is passionately indulged.
A great drive to expression gives form to the unbridled energy, whereby
the manner of behaviour can often be very 'original'.

Accommodation is not innate and only present if the writer herself
considers this necessary. She takes little account of the interests and
feelings of others, and can also easily hurt someone without consciously
intending to do so. Right is, however, right and there is no person in the
world who can convince the writer otherwise. She readily takes on another
in conscious opposition, and is then aggressive and quite uncontrolled.

It does not cause the writer the least difficulty to make her way into
a community; she is often able to push through into pretty closed circles.
There is a strong desire for love, but the writer is very idiosyncratic
in this. She rejects the ordinary and is actually disappointed by the
community in her affection.

The last sentences, though I'm not sure what he meant, made me think of
the affair with Schorr. Possibly nobody else measured up to him in Nel's
eyes, so she was disappointed in love and to an extent, also in life.

Piet Wackie Eysten, who selected the handwriting analysis, remarked
that Nel did not easily share her innermost feelings, even with her most
intimate friend, Piet's mother. Only rarely did she entrust a sentence or two
about her feelings to a black daybook:

It looks as if a great part of my life is being spent by feeling persecuted.
God help me to be humble, brave, wise.

Reading these few words from Nel's vulnerable core reduced me to tears,
especially after that startlingly perceptive handwriting analysis.

Piet concluded that Nel was perhaps unsuitable for a long-term
relationship with a life partner. Her temperament, he felt, would have
severely tested it. Whether he is right or not, one thing is certain: Nel did not
want to divulge how much she cared about breaking up with Schorr. And
perhaps Schorr never truly had any idea of the depth of her need for affection.
Superficially, perhaps, this seemed such an un-Nel-like characteristic, but it
is one that makes so much sense looking back at her lonely childhood. Or
perhaps he did perceive it, and this scared him off.

Nel's and Dan's friend Louis Metzemakers told me, as did several others, including, by inference, Dan himself, that 'Danny' Schorr broke off the affair when he went back to America. American writer and columnist Flora Lewis, who became another lifelong friend of Nel's, said this was not true and explained at some length what really happened. This immediately made perfect sense to me.

"It was Nel who broke off, as I understand it, because there came a point where she said, make up your mind, I'm not going to hang around. Either we get married or we break up. Because she was beginning to feel too much hurt by this. And then he left Holland in any case.

"She wanted to marry Dan. But for a very, very long time, not only with Nel but long after, Dan simply absolutely refused to consider marrying anybody. The reason he always gave was that he was afraid he would upset his mother. Whatever Nel may have said [*about the letter*], I think that Dan for his own reasons just didn't want to marry. He was afraid of marriage, why I don't know. Nel really loved him and they got on very well."

I was saddened that I didn't have more to record about the happy and fruitful times the two did share together, as I felt this was the high point of Nel's emotional life, when she was in a fulfilling relationship with a man she truly loved. Looking at that character analysis, it makes so much sense that she sought to cover up her deep hurt and pass the end of the affair off dismissively.

As for Schorr, Flora said his behaviour with other girlfriends was for a long time the same: "When he left Holland and took up with other women, it was the same behaviour. And I think he exaggerated, and to a certain extent, invented in his own mind his fear of offending his mother as his own shield. So he could say, oh, sorry, dear, I adore you, but I can't possibly marry you, my mother…

"I gave him lectures later, long after Nel, in other countries, saying it's all very well, you're having a great time as a bachelor, but there'll come a time when it's Thanksgiving or Christmas and you'll be all alone. You won't like that. He did marry a Jew in the end, but a long time later, and apparently the mother was enchanted."

Tyna was very surprised by Flora's account, as Nel had always given her to understand that Dan did want to marry her but was prevented by his mother. It would make sense, however, that Nel simply found this less wounding; it was her way of passing off the end of the affair more lightly.

Tyna also pointed out that it was still considered quite outrageous in Holland in those days for an unmarried woman to be openly living with her boyfriend. "They were very close, but we didn't talk about that at home, because they were living together and they were not married, and my mother didn't really approve. So that is typically Dutch, everybody knows it but we just don't mention it. I only learned later that there had been this period in Nel's life, because in my family, it was ignored."

Tyna knew Flora quite well. "She was a wonderful person, in a way like Nel, but more brilliant. I mean, Flora is one of the most brilliant minds I've met."

I wanted to get to know Flora better, as she was such an important person in Nel's life, but my first attempt to interview her was a dismal failure. While I was visiting Dublin in April 1999, I was tipped off by Yolanda that Flora was in Holland to do a TV interview. I phoned her at her Amsterdam hotel, and she sounded friendly and invited me to have dinner with her there on my return. But Flora had to change this, as the television people wanted to take her out to dinner.

I joined them at a restaurant called Zuid Zeeland on a canal near Amsterdam's iconic Flower Market. I had met Flora once before in Nel's flat some years earlier and I found her quite alarming then, even meeting her while under Nel's wing as a newcomer to journalism. I hardly expected her to remember me.

This time around, she was in an extremely bad temper and neither the young Dutchman who had interviewed her nor the young woman, presumably a TV executive, seemed to be having much luck in putting her into a better mood. Worse still, the restaurant was cramped and bourgeois and produced indifferent pretentious food it imagined to be 'French cuisine'.

Flora talked grumpily with the television people. They discussed Iris Murdoch, how extremely difficult Alzheimer's disease makes people, and what a hard time was had by Iris' husband. Nel was never diagnosed as having Alzheimer's, but many people believed it was the cause of her loss of memory and sometimes raging moods.

Suddenly Flora turned to me at the table and said, you can ask your questions now. But I passed on this uncomfortable offer and wrote down her details in Paris to arrange a meeting there later. Unfortunately, Flora didn't reply to letters. I also complained to a fellow journalist in Paris, Alan Tillier, that I found her intimidating, and he emailed back:

Yes, Flora is intimidating. I shall never forget inviting her when I went to live in Paris in the 1970s. She grabbed a bottle of Scotch and proceeded to down it. She can also be snooty – later when I needed a job and asked her about the chances at the NY Times, *she replied haughtily, "We cannot all be stars, Alan." She looked like Bette Davis crossed with Joan Crawford that day.*

That was a perfect description of her at that Amsterdam restaurant.

Eventually, I phoned Flora up, as I had to go to Paris for a wedding, and she kindly agreed to see me between the wedding and the reception. She talked to me about Nel in her charming flat in Paris overlooking the Seine, full of antique furniture collected from around the world. This was in January 2001, nearly two years after the previous debacle. She was subdued and patient – in fact, like a lamb, as Nel once improbably described herself. Flora let slip that she had been quite ill that year.

Flora, who certainly understood how much Nel cared about Dan Schorr, told me she actually first met Nel through Schorr. Flora arrived in the Netherlands from Berlin in 1949 when she was working for the *New York Times*.

"Nel was the girlfriend. She was more or less shacked up with Dan Schorr, who was an old friend from New York. Because of Dan, we met Nel and saw quite a lot of her. She came up into the house and I became very fond of her. When they broke up, that was after we moved away, but whenever I was in the area, I always went to see her. And she visited me once in a while."

A final twist to the tale of Schorr's departure came from Friso Endt, who found out that Dan was actually sacked by Paris bureau chief Frank White before he left. Apparently Schorr had to do a story for *Life* magazine about the first Marshall Aid goods arriving in Holland, and when he was told *Life* had postponed the story for a couple of weeks, he sold it behind their backs to the *Daily Mail*.

"Nel used to say, 'Oh, he was so eager for money, after I warned him, don't do it for a couple of pounds,'" Friso said. But she never told anyone about Dan being sacked, "and he went away with the Oranje Nassau order [*a Dutch decoration*] and a big party," he added.

"Dan said Nel told him he was a bastard? He was, but Nel learned the trade of journalism from him. It was Dan Schorr who made her. He said he learned a lot from Nel? Oh well, that's nice. Of course, what she said always, he had no manners, he was a boy from Brooklyn, and she taught him how to handle a knife and fork…"

"I always saw him when I was in Washington, and he always asked about Nel. So that's a fact. But it was Dan Schorr who taught her the American way of asking questions. That was very unusual in this country. I was the young reporter from *Het Parool*, and I was interested in English and American journalism… it was quite different, and much more interesting, the way to put a story together. So I became a stringer for London dailies."

"Nel used to live here, on the Javastraat. It's on the first floor, near the corner. She had a big terrace at the back. I went there – I was a young boy, and I looked on Nel as a mighty journalist. She was the only woman, and they were all afraid of her, because she had a big mouth. In the days of Nel, and before, in the days of Henk Kerstens and Herman Bleich, the Foreign Press Association was powerful. Oh yes, they built up the FPA."

Though their personal partnership was doomed, the Slis and Schorr combine did indeed make a huge impression in those years. As *Het Parool* newspaper observed: '*Those were the years that Schorr and Slis had the news from The Hague in their hands*'.

The touching, blurry photos of Nel and Dan in relaxed and intimate mood show their closeness, counterpointed by a rather fierce photo I found of them looking like two peas in a pod in full professional mode at some press conference or reception.

As a footnote, nestling next to each other in the Foreign Press Association archives, I found Nel and Dan's acceptance of an invitation to meet Juliana, Queen of the Netherlands, on 19 March 1952.

Schorr went on to become a top reporter for CBS, until he got into a big fight with them for broadcasting something they didn't approve of. This information came from Flora Lewis, who told me that was when he left and went to CNN. "He was one of the first at CNN."

When Schorr was involved in a court case in the US some years later for refusing to name a source who had given him a secret report on the CIA, Nel followed the reports about this affair closely. And finally, on her seventy-fifth birthday, he did write to her, saying:

Lives drift apart in these decades. You might not recognize me as a family man with a son at Yale and a daughter at Harvard. Yet, the Dutch years are not to be forgotten. Nor you at the centre of them.

CHAPTER SEVEN
THE GREAT FLOOD OF 1953
A climacterical event

As Indonesia brought Dan Schorr into Nel's life, the Great Flood in a manner of speaking swept him out of it again, as the bylines, fame and job offers it brought him in the US were to tempt him to go back to America. This cataclysmic event therefore marked a watershed in Nel's own personal life as well as in the life of her country.

The Great Flood of 1953 was the country's worst natural disaster in Nel's lifetime, and her island was in the front line. Goeree-Overflakkee and neighbouring Zeeland were among the areas that suffered most.

In practice, I found Nel didn't like to talk about it all that much to me, possibly because she associated it with her last days with Dan. About that time, though, I came across some evocative writing by the novelist Hammond Innes about Holland and the Great Flood.

Writing at the end of the 1950s, Innes described how he first saw the Netherlands, sailing into the Hook of Holland:

A vast expanse of sea and sky with only the spire of a church or the sails of a windmill to show that we were coming into land. We sailed up to Rotterdam, past oil refineries and cranes and miles of warehouses; it was hard to realise that this, the greatest port in the world, was all built on piles in a quaking land of bog.

And then down through the rivers and canals to Flushing – locks and bridges and barges everywhere, and from the deck no land visible except the dykes on either side, their green tops in silhouette against the cloud-spattered sky. But when I climbed the mast, I could see all the rich land of Holland laid out below the level of the water on which we sailed – way, way below it, as much as twenty feet.

Innes wrote movingly of the 1953 flood disaster. '*Saturday evening, January 31, 1953 – I remember listening to the radio with that sense of disaster that both fascinates and appals. Gale warnings, tide warnings... all the coasts of the North Sea were threatened.*'

Innes quotes Jean Ingelow's *The High Tide on the Coast of Lincolnshire* (1571):

'Men say it was a stolen tyde
The Lord that sent it, He knows all.'

A stolen tide! It swept in over England's east coast... and Holland stood in the direct path of the storm. Wind force close on a hundred knots, and almost one quarter of that country below sea level – five million people, half the population, with no protection against the elements but the dykes they themselves had erected over the centuries...

In that first onslaught, the sea did not breach the protecting dykes; it swept in over the top of them. In places a twelve-foot wall of water rampaged through farm and village. And in that and succeeding nights, 1,800 people lost their lives; 10,000 farms and houses were destroyed, a further 40,000 damaged.

Recalling the apocryphal story of the boy sticking his finger into the sea dyke to save Haarlem, Hammond Innes wrote:

A ludicrous story for anybody who has actually seen a dyke, but it captured the world's imagination as a symbol... But on the night of January 31, 1953, a group of men did in fact what the little boy did in fiction... All that night they lay shoulder to shoulder against their crumbling dyke at Kalijnsplaat, supporting it and holding back the waters by the sheer weight of their bodies.

They were not heroes. Or if they were heroes, then half Holland was heroic that night, for they were just one of many groups who did

what they could in a desperate situation and fought the flood tide the
way their fathers had fought it before them.

When this happened, Nel had already been a working journalist for nearly a decade and was well established as the first Associated Press correspondent in The Hague. While it must have been harrowing for her to cover, it was a big story, and she knew the character of the people on her island.

"I was born on Goeree-Overflakkee. I knew the country and the mentality. I reported that people on Tholen island were sitting in black skirts on the roof waiting to be saved, and when a German boat came along that wanted to help them, they shouted, 'Oh, no, no Germans!' They stayed sitting on the roof."

Goeree-Overflakkee's archivist Jan Both told me many Germans came to help. "Yes, they came from far and near, even from America, Sweden, Belgium... because the Netherlands only had one helicopter. Fishermen came from other places, even from north Netherlands. There was also a Bavarian pilot who was immediately involved when he heard about it on the radio, and he was able to pick up a lot of people from the rooftops."

He added some more details. "Goeree-Overflakkee was one of the worst affected areas, especially under Oude Tonge... A large number of people drowned – over 300 in Oude Tonge alone. In Middelharnis, it was a bit less. The outer dykes were flooded, but some of the inner ones held."

It was a bleak story. "The flood happened in the middle of the night and took most people by surprise, for they were sleeping. It was in the middle of winter, it snowed and the water was ice-cold. So if you just fell in, you quickly drowned. And such an enormous flood, you couldn't escape – you just had to grab something, and you had to be rescued quickly, because if you're not dressed, you are freezing... There are gruelling stories of people on a roof... at a certain moment, one after the other lets go from the cold... a whole family. And you could see nothing, of course. It was extremely dark, because all the lights were out."

*

I didn't really know why I decided to give this tragic climacterical event a chapter to itself, even though I had a very scanty record of Nel's own reporting involvement. It just seemed so important for Holland. It suddenly took on a wider significance in November 2021, when the COP26 climate conference was going on in Glasgow, Scotland. After the 1953 flood, the Netherlands, which has forgotten more about managing water than the rest of the world ever knew, took action to prevent a recurrence, in the shape of the innovative Great Storm Surge Barrier. This made the Great Flood and the Dutch reaction to it seem to me a kind of foreshadowing of today's climate challenge. By the time of COP26, the Netherlands, with so much of the country below sea level, was itself already deeply occupied with planning ahead to combat climate change. This is for others to write about, but it made me feel a glimmer of optimism: The Dutch have solved so many of their own problems over the centuries that I feel sure they can make a key contribution to the global climate battle.

CHAPTER EIGHT
LIFE AFTER SCHORR
Indonesia to Staphorst: scoops and schnabbeltjes

After Schorr left, Slis simply carried on with her reporting. Most likely, plunging deeply into work provided some distraction and even solace, as I have also found at times of personal crisis.

On the decolonisation of Indonesia, Nel and Flora Lewis had both closely followed the process from the start and continued to track its results after Dan left. As I knew so little about this period, and wasn't even aware that Indonesia had been occupied by the Japanese, I found Flora's account quite enlightening, especially as I hadn't managed to find any substantial examples of Nel's reporting. It gives a flavour of the major story that Nel followed.

"We spent a lot of time with the Indonesians," Flora said. "The Dutch hated the Americans, because the Americans were pushing very hard for Holland to decolonise, and the Dutch, at first, had the same reaction as the French. There was a great deal of resistance."

It looked as though there was going to be a war, like the French in Algeria, but before reaching the final confrontation, "they finally came around and said okay, we make a deal." Once they had decided on independence for their huge colony, Flora considered the Dutch handled this decently and thoughtfully.

"They were extremely generous, both with the people from Indonesia and later, the Surinamese colony, in solving issues," such as allowing people to choose between staying on as citizens of the ex-colony or coming to the Netherlands.

Losing Indonesia was hard for the Dutch after so long a period of colonialism. "Decolonising necessarily broke a lot of patterns. Everybody had some kind of problem. Like coming off communism, whenever you have a big social change."

Nevertheless, "with a great deal of push from the United States – which was resented – they made an agreement. Otherwise, there really would have been a war. And you can imagine, with maybe 150 million in Indonesia in those days and ten million in Holland – if they had had a war like the French and Indochina, I wonder whether they would have survived at all."

Just to join the dots here in terms of timing, the Netherlands eventually recognised the country's independence at the end of 1949. It had first been declared by the shaky new republic's President Sukarno on 17 August 1945, two days after the surrender of Indonesia's Japanese occupiers.

Unexpectedly, as Nel was personally in favour of decolonisation, an interview with a Dutch fellow journalist a few years after decolonisation revealed that she had a slightly jaundiced view of its effect on the Dutch themselves, however desirable in itself. Indonesia, the interviewer remarked, was world news at the time, the story of a small country losing its empire, with Britain, America and the East Bloc all arrayed against it.

"And still," said Nel, "and still I believe that we have withered since then. Not that I believe we should or could have held onto Indonesia, but still, you had more people before with a broader spirit, people that had looked over the border. Because what are we now all in all in the Netherlands? Fifteen million nitpickers. We don't have anything else apart from that gas to sell, and that is diminishing. The French are right when they say that we must be the 'transporteurs' [hauliers] of Europe."

A 1963 report in *Het Parool* newspaper, which was largely focused on saluting Nel on her departure to Brussels, also hinted at how raw, uncomfortable and sometimes hypocritical the new relationship still remained with Indonesia even fourteen years after the original Round Table Conference. The end of the piece is vintage Slis.

Everyone who was anyone was at the lavish reception, given by the Indonesian chargé d'affaires Mohammed Sjarif in Oud Wassenaar Castle to celebrate Indonesian National Day. '*Out in the chill autumn evening, people stood for twenty minutes in the queue that swung from the driveway via the hall to the reception hall. There a broadly smiling Sjarif shook hands*', the reporter wrote. *'Remarking on the number of businessmen, the hacks whispered: "Are we the Chinese of Europe, or aren't we?"'*

Many who had said only a few years ago that there was nothing to talk about with these *'peloppers'* (an untranslatable denigrating term) suddenly had *'friendly and (yes) flattering smiles for the Indonesian diplomats'*, our reporter complained. One such turncoat had *'written "exclusively" from New Guinea fighting slogans about the fatherland's forces against these miserable and nasty Indonesian paratroopers. This was the same man who wrote a year later from the palace of Sukarno (and again, very exclusively) about how completely charming the Indonesian president actually could be...'*

At the end of his piece, remarking that this would be the last time people could see the Associated Press correspondent in The Hague at work, he wrote: *'As the guests were departing, we were standing next to AP bureau chief Henk Kersting. Nel Slis stepped over to Sjarif to say goodbye. Kersting said: "It wouldn't surprise me if Nel is on kissing terms." And yes indeed, she laid a hand most warmly on the shoulder of the chargé d'affaires and kissed him goodbye on both cheeks, saluting him on the success of this reception'.*

Nel also wrote about the effects of Marshall Aid and how the Netherlands got off the ground again and became industrialised. As she said: "That was a story! Don't forget that before the war, the Netherlands was a country of farmers and fishermen. There were no industries, only agriculture. We lived off Indonesia. And then the discovery of gas. That has been our biggest salvation."

It is perhaps not widely known or remembered today that this nation of farmers and fishermen was starving in the 1944–45 'hunger winter', due to the German blockade of food and fuel. Someone once told me that all the trees in Amsterdam were burned for fuel in that bitterly cold winter, and estimates of deaths from starvation ranged from 18,000 to 22,000. I will never forget a bond dealer in Amsterdam reminiscing about how delicious tulip bulbs tasted when you were starving. To eat one's income, that is desperate indeed.

There was a lot of reconstruction to be done in those difficult postwar years. In a feature on Sicco Mansholt, architect of the EEC's Common Agricultural Policy written after her move to Brussels (see Chapter 14), Nel recalled Manshold's key role in the vital Dutch postwar reconstruction of agriculture after that terrible winter. I particularly enjoyed the vignette of Manshold and the pope:

"At the age of thirty-seven, Mansholt was picked by socialist Premier Willem Schermerhorn as Holland's first agricultural minister to reorganise Holland's ruined agriculture and the food distribution for a starving population. Mansholt made Dutch agricultural produce competitive again on the world market while improving the structure of agriculture and raising farm incomes.

"Farming is in his blood. On a clear sunny day, he is apt to sniff the air and say, 'Good day to plough'... When Mansholt was visiting the late Pope John XXIII in Rome, the two were found 'talking like two farmers, with Pope John slapping his thighs and shouting 'bravo, bravo.'"

Nel also quickly started doing what the Dutch call 'schnabbeltjes', freelance assignments for other media ranging from the Religious News Service in New York to *Ladies' Home Journal* as well as the more prestigious *New York Times* and *Newsweek*, under pen names like Adriana Dykes or Len Koert.

She also began providing summaries of Dutch press reports for the EEC information service in The Hague. In 1960, a freelance relationship was formed which was to endure virtually as long as she could still write. Through Dries Ekker of *Het Parool*, she contacted and started to write for the EEC daily news bulletin *Europe*, headed by Italian journalist Emmanuel Grasso. She always did get on well with Italians.

Newsweek took news stories from Nel on, for instance, the loss of Holland's New Guinea colony and the death of Princess Wilhelmina, the old queen who had abdicated in favour of her daughter, Juliana. The magazine also took features including the fiftieth birthday of George Szell, at the time a regular conductor of the Concertgebouw Orchestra; a Leiden professor's experiments with underwater breathing of dogs and mice (*'the mice died upon return to the air, but the dogs survived'*); and Princess Marijke's name-switch to Christina.

An important staple remained feature writing for her own AP, which valued her 'human touch' and 'feel and flavour.' "Humanized story-telling is needed day to day," New York instructed its foreign bureaus, and this was one of Nel's strengths. Her reporting on a gathering of royalty in Amsterdam for the silver wedding celebrations of Queen Juliana and Prince Bernhard, for example, was singled out for praise. In fact, her reporting on royalty was so much appreciated throughout her career that this is explored in more detail in Chapter 11.

On a quite different tack, in the depths of rural Holland, Nel sniffed out an offbeat tale of adultery and its mediaeval treatment in the village of Staphorst. It was a minor classic of extreme Calvinism and superstition in a country village that will probably live on forever, much to the chagrin of the village dignitaries.

It is not hard to imagine that Nel was herself underwhelmed by the behaviour of the Staporstians but still relished making a good story out of it. The main incident – the parading by the young men of the village of an adulterous couple through the town in a pig-pen on a cart amid much shouting and singing – was creepy enough, but there was also a reference to the public humiliation of another poor unfortunate girl who simply failed to get pregnant.

However, it was Nel's investigation of Staphorst's marital customs that so much impressed one of her numerous fascinating friends, the former British diplomat and distinguished garden mazes creator Randoll Coate, that he wrote especially to tell me this story in his own words:

'I arrived to take up my post at the British Embassy in The Hague in the autumn of 1953. I soon heard from colleagues that the most renowned and feared journalist in the whole of the Press Corps was the AP correspondent, Nel Slis. When I met her I enjoyed her frankness, her plain speaking and her sense of humour and we became firm friends'.

Nel gave Randoll a copy of Dykes and Bykes, a satirical book of short, pithy pieces she had written about her country, which had a chapter on the marital customs of the village of Staphorst. The mayor of Staphorst took exception to her colourful account of the proceedings and invited her to visit to show her that the old custom no longer applied.

As I was very interested in the folklore of Holland, Nel invited me to accompany her and I accepted with alacrity. We arrived in Staphorst on a Sunday and were invited to join in the Sunday service. Once all the congregation was in church, the doors were locked for two hours, and the Verger tapped with his staff anyone who fell asleep during the very long sermon.

The main argument between Nel and the mayor was her description of the Opkamertje (literally, little room) still being used for its original purpose: when a daughter reached marriageable age, a golden heart was placed over the lock of the front door and this *signified that the suitor might climb through the diamond-shaped window of the Opkamertje and press his suit. The mayor asserted that this practice had long been discontinued and invited us into one of the houses decorated with a golden heart on the door.*

During the visit Nel managed to slip away into the Opkamertje and on her return she winked at me and whispered that the bed was quite rumpled and had obviously been slept in that night. This fact coupled with the presence of the golden heart made her feel that she had won her point!

Randoll was to renew his friendship with Nel nearly ten years later when en poste in Brussels. It greatly amused him that when he mentioned that Nel Slis was a good friend of his, he claimed that "journalists would blanch and exclaim 'But she is the most feared journalist in Brussels!'"

Also in the early years after Schorr left the Netherlands and quite a while before Nel herself left for Brussels, she was to have an unexpectedly eventful voyage to the US, as we shall see in the next chapter.

CHAPTER NINE
SLIS GOES TO AMERICA
A far country

On a windy day in spring 1957, 312 Hungarian refugees and 500 Dutch emigrants set sail from Rotterdam on the *SS Waterman*. Altogether 1,050 people were crowded on board the 9,117-tonne transport ship, bound for Halifax and New York. Nel was on board, on her way to a four-month stint in the AP's New York and Washington bureaus and a trip around America.

Her aversion to flying was about to provide her with another scoop – and a narrow escape from disaster. Luckily, I stumbled across a large cache of Nel's reporting on this event, so I've sometimes felt as though I was actually on the trip myself.

This US trip followed another bout of persistent lobbying of the AP by Nel, this time successful. I doubt she had any wish to see Dan Schorr in the US at this point, having bluntly told him he was a bastard for not keeping in touch when he visited Holland in 1955. Nel's itchy feet and yearning for wider horizons would have been more important. Besides, after working for the AP for over a decade, she felt it owed her something. And last but by no means least, she wanted to lobby head office in person to secure a pension. I do think the desire for a change of scenery was perhaps exacerbated by the break-up with Schorr, as covering the home beat might have been feeling slightly flat.

Nel's lobbying efforts did not succeed at first, but after she contacted AP's New York heavyweight Lloyd Stratton and asked him to press her suit within the AP, he set the wheels in motion, suggesting: "Nel could produce her worth at both the world desks in New York and Washington." But he also cheekily asked Kersting whether the Amsterdam bureau could cough up the costs of her stay.

After some haggling, a complicated compromise was reached on a four-month stay. Nel would have to pay for her travel and accommodation. Part of her salary could be charged to 'Foreign News Collection' and part to 'AP World Service', while AP Amsterdam would have to pay for her replacement in The Hague. Nel also gave up some holiday entitlement, on condition that she would be able to make a trip around the US after finishing her stints. The upshot was that Nel, who refused to fly, found herself sailing from Rotterdam on the SS Waterman on that fateful Monday on 11 March.

Three days later, the Waterman collided in mid-Atlantic with an Italian freighter. Nel the reporter instantly sprang into action. The initial telegram after the incident shows how quickly she managed to get access to the ship's facilities to contact her AP office. Her eyewitness account was in all the Dutch newspapers and winging its way around the world the next day.

I imagine Nel racing around pestering the ship's officers for information and for the means to send her telegram and reports, and buttonholing stewardesses, crew and passengers for their reactions and stories. Here is the first instalment of her report as it went out:

MID-ATLANTIC COLLISION, 14 MARCH

In the early hours of Thursday 14 March, stewardesses Anneke van Riel from Hilversum and Riet Muller from Amerongen were taking a morning walk on the deck when the Waterman collided with the 7,174-tonne Italian freighter SS Merit. There was a dense fog, preventing them from seeing the Merit until it struck. The impact and clanging alarm bells a few seconds later jarred most Waterman passengers from their sleep, and lifeboat stations were manned.

In assorted attire, some 850 life-belted emigrants – including 250 small children and babies – with the 200 crew including about one hundred Indonesians, gathered at the lifeboat stations in superb order when the alarm sounded. There was no panic during the 45 minutes passengers waited at the lifeboat stations, under a light cloudy sky. At 9.20 GMT, the lifeboats were swung free but not lowered. Most of the passengers were unaware just what had happened, except for the two stewardesses. The collision had ripped a hole in the Waterman's hull plating 15 feet above the waterline, but passengers were assured there was no danger.

When 54-year-old Captain J.C. Flag calmly called off the alarm and shipboard life returned to normal, normal routine meals resumed in four shifts, and several people appeared at the breakfast table still wondering what had happened. Canada-bound 51-year-old Dutchman, Reverend Willem Wilman from Friesland, sat quietly at breakfast unaware of the alarm, listening to the tales of his table-mates about how they went to the lifeboats in hastily picked up garments, some with shaving soap still on their cheeks...

About noon GMT, loudspeakers told the passengers that the Waterman was returning to Europe. The migrants, especially the 300 Canada-bound Hungarians, appeared confused and disappointed. Most Hungarians had never seen the sea before. They heard the news in Hungarian from an interpreter. The 500 Dutch emigrants, of whom 200 were going to Canada and 300 U.S.-bound under the Refugee Relief Act 1, were deeply depressed at the idea they were returning, because they had 'burned their boats' behind them.

Having delivered her first reports, Nel started looking into the condition the boat was in, and what was going to happen next. The operating company, Royal Rotterdam Lloyd, had ordered Captain Flach to head for the French port of Brest for repairs to the ripped-open hull plating. Another Dutch government ship, the *Zuiderkruis*, was to meet the *Waterman* at Brest to take the passengers on to their destination. Some Dutch passengers told emigration officer Berend Kosters they would refuse a further sea trip and insist on air transport. Others joked about going back: "Now we can pick up our forgotten umbrellas."

Next day, the *Waterman* was sailing in a moderate wind after a fairly rough night. Some Dutch emigrants were busy trying to send reassuring cables to their relatives, while other passengers were drowsy after the high drama of the collision and retired to their cabins to sleep. Some passengers stayed on deck to watch the colliding vessel, the *Merit*. The Italian vessel, owned by Lofario di Giovanni of Genoa, was hit on her bow but was able to resume her journey to Hamburg. A 6,067-tonne German freighter, *Eibe Oldendorff*, which was en route for Amsterdam, was meanwhile making for the *Waterman* to stand by in case of further difficulties.

In the evening, the Dutch and Hungarian emigrants started fraternising, playing card games and chess. The Hungarian refugees had fled Hungary after the bloody Soviet crushing of the October 1956 uprising.

Nel was impressed by the positive atmosphere from the start of the trip, which at first seemed to be reinforced by the camaraderie of surviving a potentially dangerous incident. Later, she saw a reaction setting in, with a kind of 'snake-pit atmosphere' developing on the ship that night.

Afraid to go to their cabins in case of any further disasters, many Hungarians would 'huddle on the chilly and wet decks during the bleak nights' for the rest of the trip. Each day, they carefully measured the distance separating them from terra firma on the ship's maps. Rumours were rife, as they couldn't follow what was going on, having only recently arrived in Dutch transit camps from Austria. Even after some brief Hungarian announcements by an interpreter, they still felt nervous about returning to Europe.

The Dutch emigrants were not too happy either. After days of seasickness, some wanted to fly to the US or Canada. A couple with three grown-up children were determined to leave the ship and let their children go on alone. A Dutch immigration officer spent all night persuading them to stay with the ship.

Within the largely male Hungarian group, Nel said about seventy percent were young labourers and thirty percent 'intellectuals' or artists. Among the latter, with his wife and three daughters, was Budapest's most famous photographer, who had connections with Budapest Opera. Apparently their son was an active revolutionary and had to stay behind – making me wonder whether he could actually still be alive after the uprising. Others included engineers, a bookkeeper and a printer. Many had friends or relations in Canada they hoped would help them.

Many Hungarians spent time studying grammar books provided by the Canadian authorities. An orthodox Jewish group, including some six children and a rabbi, were the only Hungarians to have a religious service. Our linguistically adept reporter couldn't resist a sly dig at the Dutch migrants, who 'seem to rely on their often inadequate smattering of English'.

On Saturday 16 March, the *Waterman* limped into Brest with its cargo of dejected emigrants and refugees. The passengers were to be taken onto the SS *Zuiderkruis*, due to arrive from Rotterdam that night. The Dutch consul in Brest, Robert de la Menardiere, arrived early in the morning with boxes of sweets for the 250 small children and babies aboard the ship.

A surveyor from Lloyds of London then boarded the ship to assess the damage from the collision, followed by Dutch government shipping department representatives in the evening. Nel now managed to discover how disastrous the collision might have been but for some nifty steering of the *Waterman* at the crucial moment, and how much the crew had to do to keep the ship going after the collision.

The *Merit*'s anchor had ripped open the carpenters' and plumbers' room, right behind the vulnerable wheelhouse. If a last-minute steering manoeuvre had not swept the *Waterman* around, the *Merit* could have ripped the Dutch ship open right in the middle, inevitably sinking her.

Wooden and iron plates and sailing cloths were used to shield the wheelhouse and water and oil pumped out to lift the poop deck and reduce the risk of water running into it. After the collision, the *Waterman* sailed at nine miles an hour instead of its normal seventeen miles, as the crew worked feverishly to partition off the undamaged wheelhouse and screw-axle.

In the evening, the SS *Zuiderkruis* duly arrived in Brest and collected its passengers. On the following Friday, 22 March, she sailed into the Canadian port of Halifax, and the 311 Hungarian refugees and 200 of the Dutch emigrants went on shore to start their new life. The Hungarians were especially relieved to quit the rough Atlantic after their 'agonising' first encounter with the sea. This was the first group to sail to Canada, out of some 2,000 waiting in Dutch transit camps.

Under an agreement between Canada and the Netherlands, the Dutch provided food and accommodation for the Hungarians in the Dutch transit camps, and the Canadians paid their passage. At the camps, they were 'exhaustively' prepared for their new lives. It certainly sounds that way. Seventeen Canadian teachers and two social workers were on hand to give the new arrivals intensive courses in basic English and orient them for their life in Canada. They were even given dolls to show how they and their children would dress, and visited miniature supermarkets to be shown how they would shop.

Nel concluded that the transportation was extremely well organised, thanks to over a decade of experience. With an extraordinarily high birth rate and one of the lowest death rates anywhere, the Netherlands had adopted a policy of full employment after the war, requiring the government to encourage emigration as well as industrialisation. Between 1945 and 1957, about 120,000 Dutch migrants moved to Canada out of a total of 277,000 emigrants. The *Waterman* was the first joint shipment of Dutch and Hungarians.

Immigration procedures in Halifax were a pleasant surprise, contradicting tales of 'gruff and abrupt immigration officers' Nel had heard earlier. Halifax had handled some 28,000 immigrants over the past eleven weeks, with arrivals from countries including Greece, Italy, Germany, Holland and Hungary over the past weekend alone.

After the migrants disembarked, they entered a large assembly hall and then went through a medical examination if necessary. Screening was rapid, at one minute per person. A civil examination followed, and the Hungarian refugees were given railway tickets and money. In the next hall were representatives of churches, the Salvation Army and social services. Parents could see to their luggage in the baggage room, and there was a Red Cross nursery for the children.

Finally, the new arrivals entered the last hall, where they could have a hot meal and buy food in a special low-priced government-run food store, before boarding their trains. The Dutch migrants collected large stocks of food, as many faced a four-day journey. There was a small hospital and surgery, and for any migrants who had to wait if their papers were unsatisfactory, a dormitory, recreation hall with television, and cafeteria. It seems they thought of everything in Halifax.

On 27 March, as the *Zuiderkruis* pulled into New York Harbor to unload her last 260 migrants for the New World, Nel sounded off about the effect of government policy on the crew, who complained they never got to go home. The Dutch government operated three of its own Victory ships refurbished for shipping people instead of cargo: the *Grote Beer* as well as the *Waterman* and the *Zuiderkruis*. It chartered a fourth, the *MS Johan van Oldenbarneveldt*.

The three Dutch ships were designed to ply tropical waters with a heavy cargo. Without the stability of such a cargo, a commander responsible for hundreds of lives could not keep to a regular schedule across the storm-prone Atlantic. So the crew ran out of home leave on practically every crossing, our sympathetic reporter told her readers.

To me, this whole emigration tale and all the organisation involved has a very strong wartime flavour of people being shifted around in bulk, like troops. Similarly, Nel was critical of 'emigration' as almost coercive government policy rather than a genuine individual decision.

Nonetheless, she concluded that morale on the trip had been good. The ship quickly turned into a little floating Holland – complete with its home-grown religious differences: "The ships are so much Dutch territory that... Reverend Willem Wilman said differences between Nederlandse Hervormd (Reformed), Gereformeerd (the more Calvanistic branch) and another offshoot known as Article 31 persisted even through the collision and frightening storms." At the last dinner aboard, the Hungarian rabbi toasted the health of Queen Juliana and the Dutch people, 'who gave us such a warm and friendly reception in Dutch transit camps'.

Once in the US, the working part of Nel's trip proved successful. On her return to the Netherlands at the end of July, she found a short personal note from Stanley Swinton, General News Editor of the AP World Service: *'Just a welcome home note to say how much we appreciated having you here'*. Kersting was pleased, too, pronouncing Nel's visit 'very useful, looking at it from this end, both to herself and the Amsterdam bureau operations'. All of Nel's American stories were picked up by AP subscribers, and her style and English improved. And the knowledge of the US she acquired would benefit her work back in the Netherlands. Stratton was equally positive, writing that Nel left her mark on the AP staffs, both in Washington and New York. "She gave a very good account of herself as a workman (sic) and also as a person." And her English improved, thanks to "the hardboiled training and criticism she got and admirably took from the Washington news desk and from Swinton in New York." Nel herself also referred to this training in a letter to Stratton: *'Even the criticism was welcome and refreshing, as well as useful, of course. I figure I learned about as much during my four months in the US as I have in the last four years in The Hague. Let's hope it will result in a heavier flow of feature material from The Hague.'*

Higher up the AP echelons, Wes Gallagher was impressed, too: *'We were delighted to have you and you made a real contribution to the service and a personality hit in the Feature department'*.

Among a few bread-and-butter AP reports I found with Nel's byline from New York, I sensed from one that Nel did not think much of the wife of the new American ambassador to the Netherlands. Said wife must have been less than thrilled by how she was described. But Nel had had enough of diplomatic wives back in the Netherlands. The ambassador also sounds pretty odious to me and possibly also to Nel, but perhaps that just reflects my prejudice against jutting, forceful jaws.

To paraphrase the interview, Nel described the forty-seven-year-old new ambassador, Philip Young, as tall, dark and handsome. Oh dear. Worse still, "he radiates energy, while his jutting, forceful lower jaw speaks of considerable willpower." His wife is "lively, prematurely grey (sic), blue-eyed." Later, "short and plump (sic) Mrs Young" is said to be active in the Red Cross, Girl Scouts and Republican Party. No, I doubt the greying Mrs Young would have been over the moon about those descriptions.

We learn that the ambassador is 6 feet, 2 inches tall, weighs 190 pounds and parts his hair in the middle. His athletic appearance is deceptive, as he is not interested in sport. His hobby is woodworking: He makes some of his own furniture – and *pipes*.

I'm guessing Nel wasn't happy that he was an avid pipe smoker. She had been very annoyed by that pipe-smoking brother of her friend Piet Wackie Eysten back in Holland.

Finally, Nel sounded Young out on politics and royalty and obtained suitable responses for her readership: '*Ambassador Young said he was very appreciative of 'the role the Netherlands plays as a promoter of West European unity and of NATO'*, but he refused to commit himself on such touchy issues as West New Guinea, or landing rights on the US western seaboard for Royal Dutch Airlines.

'*He visited Europe in 1951, but has never been in the Netherlands. Young said he is a great admirer of Queen Juliana. He met the Dutch queen, as a princess, at a family supper given by the late President and Mrs Roosevelt during World War II.*'

A second report, on the construction of nuclear shelters, is a grim reminder of the Cold War days. For me, it evokes memories of a massive nuclear shelter I saw under a mansion-sized 'cottage' in New Hampshire a dozen or so years later. This was built by a rich matriarch who spent the last twenty years of her life corresponding with the Pentagon about bomb shelters. A well-concealed entrance led to a complex of small underground rooms, completely sealed off by a protective layer of lead. One room had twelve camp beds, while others were stuffed with provisions, including a cupboard full of silver polish and another with prunes in brandy.

About the time Nel was writing her nuclear item in America, one in three English schools were given talks on what to do in case of a nuclear attack.

The advice included whitewashing the windows and filling up the bath (if you had one) before the bomb fell, which sounded difficult in the likely time available. You could also make a singularly useless-looking primitive heater, using a flowerpot and a candle. Those were paranoid days, when the threat of a nuclear holocaust hung palpably over the world.

Nel's nuke report featured an interview with West German interior minister Dr Gerhard Schroeder, who had come to study the US civil defence system – and graciously concluded that it was 'adequate'. "We have similar requirements in our Ruhr area, which is also densely populated, and heavily industrialised," he told her.

Another report on a South African bishop recalls the early years of the anti-apartheid struggle. The Anglican bishop of Johannesburg, Richard Ambrose Reeves, described as an outspoken foe of segregation laws, was in the US on a fundraising tour to aid the dependants of 156 South Africans on trial for opposing the government. Speaking in St Ann's Church in Brooklyn, New York, Bishop Reeves said optimistically that if the racial struggle in South Africa ever led to open conflict between church and state, the whole of the Anglican communion would be ranged behind the church in South Africa. He concluded:

"As a church, we have no choice but to resist to the end, at whatever cost, any attempt to divide us from our brethren in Christ." It would have been nice if all Anglicans had indeed done so, but at any rate this particular branch of Christianity did produce Archbishop Desmond Tutu, who was to play such a key role in the battle against apartheid and in promoting reconciliation after its end.

The only New York culture report I found with Nel's byline (though there must have been many more considering all her friends and contacts such as Isaac Stern and Leonard Bernstein) was about an international experimental film competition proposed by a Belgian film librarian. He certainly didn't lack ambition about the people he wanted to get on his jury: '*Such people as Hemmingway, Faulkner and Picasso*'.

In May, actually in the middle of her AP stint, Nel embarked on her tour of the US. The Dutch version of her journal for the folks back home was sometimes a little unsatisfactory, whetting the appetite for more and leaving me wondering what Nel thought but did not write, to paraphrase Brecht. It seemed a dutiful rather than enthusiastic record, but still invaluable as her snapshot of the country in 1957. Even the AP gave it the low-key title of '*Daily Notes*'.

Headlined 'Vacation journey through America', it told readers that 'Miss Nel Slis, Associated Press correspondent in The Hague, who is working for a few months in New York, has made a three-week vacation trip through America. Here are some of her daily notes.'

Nel started with some statistics on money, an ever-fascinating subject for her Dutch readership, and I guess for most of us. She found it possible to visit twenty-one states in America by train in three weeks, covering 12,000 kilometres, for less than 1,900 guilders (500 dollars at that time). The train cost about 750 guilders, and 'per day, I spent on average slightly less than 40 guilders for hotels and meals.' She also advised travelling in May rather than the holiday months, when hotels raised their rates.

Europe may have its 'charm or inconvenience' of frequent changes in language, money and habits, but there are some changes too when travelling around the US, she discovered.

'The time does change in nearly every state, and one has to put one's watch one hour back or forward. The laws also change. In some states, one cannot get any alcoholic drink on the train; in others again, one can. That can be annoying for those who are fond of alcoholic drinks, especially if one considers that the train sometimes travels through three states in one day.' Also perhaps including Nel, who liked her glass of whisky of an evening.

Nel considered the journey along the Hudson between New York and Chicago as beautiful as a trip along the Rhine. She was amused to discover that 'although the Americans can't say that this is where Charles the Great stayed, and there, Napoleon, one hears people saying "here is the Ford family's castle," and "Roosevelt lived there."'

Chicago she found an impressive city with an enormous mixture of races – and the biggest abattoirs in the US. Here she met the vice-president of chemical company Union Carbide:

'To my surprise, this man, whose name is Lloyd Cooke, was a Negro, who told me that he would not hold this job if he had not been ten times more brilliant than his white competitor. He was a man in his forties, recently divorced from his Canadian wife and engaged to one of his employees. She was a young American engineer, born in Germany. He also told me that he is president of the Chemical Society in Chicago, but that he will never succeed in becoming a member of Chicago's golf and country club.' A comment that made it into Nel's widely published English-language report of her tour.

As well as a magnificent collection of modern contemporary European paintings in the Museum of Art, Nel noted that Chicago was famous for its beefsteak: '*Which one can best eat in Stockyard Inn, a very snobbish and luxurious restaurant, next to the abattoirs and near the building where the Democrats hold their conventions. All the furniture is upholstered with splendid shiny cowhides, and the drawings on the wall look dubiously much like those of the French grottoes of Lascaux.*'

Via Nebraska, Nel arrived in Colorado's 'mile-high city' of Denver, where an unusual 20-centimetre snowfall cost her a pair of galoshes. Here she first noticed the feeling of the frontier, constantly shifted to the west by the American pioneers. '*Which makes travelling through America so fascinating for Europeans. One begins to realise better what courage these pioneers had in those days.*'

Nel was impressed by the modern facilities in the American hotels. '*Even in the modest hotels with rooms for five dollars, one finds all the comforts which people in the better hotels in the Netherlands look for in vain, like Kleenex in all the bathrooms, a telephone, enough lights, the facility of having your clothes pressed à la minute and in most cases, radios and televisions.*'

The journey from Denver to Salt Lake City was spectacular, though a somewhat robotic stewardess was a disappointment. '*Sitting in a special train on the upper deck in the "vista dome", with a completely transparent roof, one can marvel at the Rocky Mountains, this year still completely covered with snow. The stewardess on the train uses the loudspeaker to give a continuous commentary on the landscape and the history of the construction of the railway. This history is an epic in itself. But when I met the same stewardess later in the bar, I discovered to my great surprise that she herself scarcely understood the text she read, and could not give any further supplementary information at all. Apart from this, she looked very attractive and elegant, and had a perfect broadcasting voice.*'

Salt Lake City in the Mormon state of Utah was a city of broad streets and much greenery, unique for its prevailing Mormon atmosphere as well as the biggest American open copper mine, Kennecott, and the Great Salt Lake itself. Sitting in the lake, Nel was next to a middle-aged Parisian on vacation in America with his wife. He said to her, piqued, "One thing I do not understand. Taxi drivers in Paris have a very good wage. But here, every taxi driver actually has his own car. France is a rich country, after all. How is it that America is so prosperous?"

Nel rated the train journey after Salt Lake City the most beautiful in America. Travelling along the ravine of the Feather River, 'with its virgin forests [it offers], fantastic natural beauty for a whole day, nearly all the way to San Francisco.'

She was now arriving in a completely different part of America. 'After Denver, "the west" begins, and the subject of conversation of the ever-garrulous Americans changes. Before Denver, there was much more talk of stomach ulcers and psychiatrists. After Denver, you come across a great naive interest in everything that is foreign, and nobody appears to have an ulcer.' I myself once stayed at a ranch in North Dakota run by a cowboy with an ulcer, but I did assume he was pretty unusual, even in 1971.

Although Nel did visit San Francisco, which I imagined she would love, I found only one reference to this 'beautiful cosmopolitan city'. Then on to Los Angeles, Hollywood and Beverly Hills, with the rich film stars' residences she found 'reminiscent of Bloemendaal before the war'. Bloemendaal is a plush, verdant little town in a pretty seaside area west of Amsterdam.

Nel was quick to report that not everyone in Los Angeles was rich. 'The Fairfax "farmers' market" (expensive) and the downtown "central market" (cheap) give visitors an impression of the enormous wealth of the film world and the modest existence of the toiling other inhabitants. There is also a large Dutch colony.' Both those markets apparently still existed well into the twenty-first century.

From Los Angeles, Nel travelled to Phoenix, Arizona, in fashion as a 'health state'. 'Since this [status] has been generally accepted, the value of the land has multiplied tenfold. It is indeed very pleasant here, warm and dry, and recently, superb hotels have mushroomed.' Nel's visit was recorded, along with one of her favourite photos of herself with two cats, in the June 6 edition of a delightful local Arizona news rag called SAGE. I love its report:

VISITOR. Recent visitor to Cactus, friend of Mrs. Rosella Oelke, was Nel Slis, the only woman Associated Press Correspondent overseas. Miss Slis, author and newspaperwoman in her own country, is a native of Holland and lives at The Hague. She is touring America on vacation and is seriously considering buying a residence.

I feel sure that this 'buying a residence' business was tongue in cheek, with Nel unable to resist the hospitable but naive acceptance of such an unlikely thing for her to do.

The pocket-sized publication also had a splendid front-page slogan:

EVERYBODY IS READING SAGE

The only newspaper you can open up in a high wind – or read on a horse.

Next came New Mexico, also with a reputation for health, and El Paso in Texas with its bridge into Mexico over the Rio Grande. '*In Ciudad Juarez, the biggest town on the border, people can eat beefsteak for one-third of the price in America, if they pay in dollars. Juarez, with its many shops, is completely built up on American tourism.*'

Nel discovered that Texans had a strong vein of patriotism about their state. '*People returning from Mexico over the Rio Grande have to give their nationality. There, one hears as well as "American", people saying "Texan", mightily irritating customs and immigration.*'

Heading through the desert from El Paso to San Antonio, still in Texas, it suddenly became pitch-dark at three o'clock in the afternoon, when huge rain, hail and a thunderstorm broke out.

'*The area through which we were travelling is completely empty desert where one virtually does not see a single living soul. Once or twice there was a hamlet where I saw stranded drivers standing around.*'

In San Antonio, Nel noted its well-preserved history, '*including the "Alamo" building which is the symbol of the liberation of Texas from the Mexicans, and the house where the Spanish governor lived, who was Philip V's representative. Here you can see the weapons of the House of Habsburg, unique in America. There is a very Spanish-American atmosphere in San Antonio with its many former missionary houses now visited as museums.*'

The train from San Antonio to New Orleans in Louisiana ran through a swampy area of thick forests with a humid and sultry atmosphere. New Orleans Nel found 'French' and 'touristic'. '*Everyone goes to visit "le Vieux Carré" where the French-Canadian Bienville (governor of French Louisiana, 1701–1743) once kept house and held orgies with Creole beauties. "Creole" is a complimentary term in New Orleans,*' Nel informed her Dutch readers. '*It has nothing to do with mulattos or half-breeds, but rather with the Americans of French-Spanish origin. Thirty percent of the population here are Negroes, and for the first time since New York I encountered racial discrimination here, which continued throughout the entire South to Washington.*'

At this point in her travels, Nel was 'hijacked' by a 'larger-than-life' rich woman: '*An oil trader, widowed and divorced, with all force insisting that I should see her indeed beautiful house in Laurel, Mississippi.'* She was recently divorced from her second husband, whose family practically owned the little town: *'Lumberjacks who had made their fortune two generations earlier from the wood from the forests in Mississippi.'*

The woman found Laurel boring, but was energetically planning to create her own environment. *'She has a good library, a splendid collection of gramophone records, two beautiful dogs, a lovely house and her own forest. She advised me to visit one of the plantations, which have been described so many times by Tennessee Williams. I would then see that nothing is further from the truth than that everyone living there is depraved and degenerate. The plantation owners, who sometimes own three or four aircraft with which they fly to New York to go to the theatre of an evening, she called "very entertaining" and "good chess players".'*

Nel was probably underwhelmed by this bored, rich woman, and would have disapproved of all that ostentatious wealth and flitting off by plane to New York, quite apart from the undercurrent of racism, though she may have admired her American energy.

A large number of local American newspapers picked up Nel's English post-vacation report of her tour of America. A version in the Tampa *Sunday Tribune* featured a charming photo of Nel interviewing a young black lift operator.

By the time of this visit to America, Nel had been reporting from Holland for the AP for some twelve years, with another six to come before her move to Brussels. She was an AP 'name' in America and according to some, even better known in New York than in Holland. But Yolanda Frenkel Frank says Nel did not really like America or the Americans, and this seeped through here and there in her travel notes.

Pondering Nel's feelings about Americans, Tyna Wynaendts said, "I think it was a love-hate relationship at first – no, I think she hated them more than she loved them. She appreciated many things, especially people like Isaac Stern. And she realised that they could be the people they were because of America, with all the opportunities of that country. But I think deep down, she never had a very good relationship with her bosses in the States, and they were not very nice to her. No, I think she did not really like Americans."

Nel's negative feelings very likely stemmed to a great extent from her long battle to extract a pension from the AP, making her more and more irate – especially in the period before she went to the US. "She was shouting about the Americans every time we met her," Tyna recalled, "because they wouldn't give her any pension after all those years. And then she went to America. She didn't really want to go, not so much that she didn't like the country, but because of the voyage. She wouldn't fly so she had to take a boat. But she felt she had to go, to talk about her pension. In the end, they promised her a pension – she said it wasn't good enough, but she got something. Certainly, there was a period of her life when she could have wrung the necks of every single one of them."

CHAPTER TEN
THE LAST QUEEN OF LIBYA
Fatima the Beautiful

A s well as her much-applauded coverage of the Dutch royals which we will
home in on in the next chapter, I discovered that Nel had visited Libya in
1954 and interviewed yet another, rather exotic, queen: Fatima, wife of King
Idris. This was particularly fascinating for me, as I lived in Tobruk a couple of
decades after Nel's visit. Fatima was destined to be both the first and the last
queen of Libya, as Idris was deposed by Gaddafi in a bloodless coup in 1969.

Nel probably saw more of Libya on her visit in 1954 than I did when
I was actually living there in 1973–74. She talked about trips to Sabrata,
Leptis Magna with the Turkish ambassador, to Benghazi, and with the
Italian consul to Surinaika. In Surinaika, to Nel's surprise, "we stayed in a
hotel run by the Brits!"

I found out about the visit in that 1981 interview, when she was musing
about Africa. "There's a whole new Africa, very important, I think, for
Europe to keep pace with developments in Africa – with characters like
Gaddafi around," she remarked. Neither of us had any idea how Gaddafi
would eventually turn out.

A Persian friend of Nel's had married an American diplomat, and she
visited them in Tripoli in the winter of 1954. During the visit, Nel met King
Idris and interviewed his queen, Fatima, who she described as 'all done up
in wonderful Dior dresses'.

When I eventually got to visit Tripoli, it was a surprise, as it looked like
a regular Mediterranean city with many arcades and flower stalls. Benghazi,

where I first arrived, seemed more exotic, with its huge jumble of pastel-coloured buildings, often topped by forests of spikes where the buildings awaited more stories. And then going to the marketplace to find a 'taxi for Tobruk' – shades of the old war film of the same name. We shared the big taxi with three or four friendly Libyans in their red-checked *keffiyeh* headgear – and a goat.

The Turkish ambassador and Italian consul showing Nel around were perhaps more culturally inclined than our Libyan friends, who hurtled us all too rapidly through the impressive Roman site of Leptis Magna. We never made it to the other sites.

In any case, Libya was very different when Nel visited in those pre-oil days when the Libyans were, as she put it, 'as poor as rats'. She found the Libyans she met "a very nice, thin upper crowd, a delightful and handsome people… but now rather Muslim, Gaddafi, anyway, I think religion is rather poisoning the atmosphere – it has done more harm than good… Religious wars…"

Sadly, this now sounds only too prophetic. Libya seems to have got stuck in deep trouble in the twenty-first century. In the doomed Arab spring of 2011, I watched Libyan demonstrations on TV with amazement. Bustling Tobruk was unrecognisable from the sleepy overgrown village I remembered, with goats munching cardboard boxes on the corner by our apartment and donkeys pulling carts everywhere.

At the beginning of the Gaddafi era, the students at the Higher Petroleum Institute in Tobruk all had friends on the revolutionary committee or were on it themselves, and felt quite free to criticise their leader. Tobruk had been an Idris stronghold, so Gaddafi may have located the HPI in Tobruk as a gesture of goodwill. The HPI, where my husband worked, was a new third-level institute set up to train the Libyans to run their oil industry, which Gaddafi had just nationalised.

An old tourist book I found from the pre-World War II era of Italian colonisation described an extremely odd sole tourist 'sight' in Tobruk: a 1,000-metre-long barbed wire fence. It didn't say what it was for. This curious sightseeing object was superceded by the German, French and British cemeteries resulting from the many World War II battles fought in the area.

Italy renounced all claims to Libya after the war and the United Kingdom of Libya was created, ruled by Idris until 1969. He was overthrown in the Gaddafi-led coup while he was visiting Turkey for medical treatment. As far as I have been able to discover, he was a reasonably popular king in those pre-oil days.

As this is rather a unique interview, I am reproducing it just as I found it in Nel's files.

The Queen of Libya

====(by Nel Slis, Associated Press correspondent, who became the first western journalist to be received by the queen in her palace)

------Benghazi, Libya (Ass.Press)----Fatima-al-Sjifa, queen of Libya, is one of the most elegant queens, but perhaps the least known. She is married to Idris, the first king of Libya, who is 20 years older and a first cousin of hers. Both belong to the tribe of the Senoessi, a religious sect which has followers in every country in North Africa.

The 43-year-old Queen Fatima was brought up in Arabic-speaking countries, mostly in Egypt. She does not speak any foreign languages, but understands a little English.

Before her marriage, she had a role dealing informally with men, and scores of British officers remember how she played tennis in shorts. Since she became queen of Libya, however, she has led the life of the typical Libyan woman, strictly separated from all men.

"It will be a slow and gradual process before the Libyan women attain emancipation", she told me, "But the Libyan girls are very much longing to learn and to win their freedom."

Queen Fatima, small and elegant in her black clothes, which were made for her by Christian Dior, spoke Arabic, which was translated by her lady-in-waiting, the beautiful 24-year-old Mrs Selma Dajani, a Palestinian, whose husband was one of King Idris' advisors.

Queen Fatima spends the greatest part of her time in the small palace just outside the war-battered city of Benghazi, and one of the two capitals of Libya. King Idris, who himself comes from the province of Cyrenica, prefers to live here than in the more cosmopolitan co-capital, Tripoli.

Queen Fatima, who was receiving a journalist from the west for the first time, said she was pleased that there was interest abroad for her poor country, which had suffered so much from the war.

It is hard for one to imagine that the elegant queen, who would attract attention in any society and would command respect, is a descendant of raw (sic) Arabs who, like the forefathers of her consort, whose fourth spouse she is, were in the habit of roaming through the desert.

Tranquil and smiling, Queen Fatima told via her lady-in-waiting of the journey she had recently made through Europe and during which she visited Germany, France and Spain. Her eyes began to shine when she spoke of her visit to southern Spain, Andalusia, where she found the Arab influence very striking.

She spoke of the future possibilities for the emancipation of Libyan women. Instead of playing tennis in shorts, she is currently obliged by her royal rank to go back many centuries and live the life of seclusion... of 99 percent of Libyan women.

The women of Libya live a more concealed life than their sisters in other Arab countries. They are dressed in the barracan, a hand-woven wool or silk cloth – the material depends on their circumstances – in which they wrap themselves up in such a way that only one eye is visible.

Only if she goes abroad does the queen live like a western woman, dressed in European clothes, and then a visit to a fashion show or to the Folies Bergère in Paris – where she has indeed been – fascinates her just as much as any other woman in the world.

Having to dress in the barracan is perhaps harder for her than for all her Libyan sisters, in view of the fact that she knows the freedom of the west.

The wife of the leading statesman in Libya, premier Mahmoed Moentasser, for example, never comes in contact with the world.

But this is simply the Mohammeden law, which in its most orthodox form forbids the woman to be seen by a man other than her husband, and concerning the husband – the woman sees him for the first time after the elaborate marriage ceremony, which lasts a week.

Queen Fatima however believes that Libyan women will make important progress in a subsequent generation on the road to freedom. They will be able to study and go abroad.

While a Sudanese, dressed like a European butler, served exquisite, sweet and creamy cakes, she said "we have many good American friends and one of my greatest wishes is to visit the U.S. one day".

"If I were to go to the United States", Queen Fatima went on, "I would dearly like to fly, but" – as she added here – "the king won't fly".

King Idris does not like either flying or sailing, but he has still accepted an official invitation to himself and the queen to make a visit to Turkey this spring, a country with which Libya is linked by many historic, religious and emotional bonds.

*

Fatima did not die until 2009, many years after Idris. She was a very beautiful woman, and given to good works. From her obituaries, it emerged that Egypt's Gamal Abdel Nasser provided a home for the couple and treated them quite well, though they did lose all their possessions in the coup. A small palace was restored to Fatima just before she died, aged ninety-seven or ninety-eight. Just two years later, Gaddafi himself was killed by his captors and paraded before a mob in his home town of Sirte.

The completely swathed women with just one eye visible described by Nel in her interview with the queen hadn't changed a bit in Tobruk by 1973. Still, Gaddafi himself had a kind of bodyguard of dashing if somewhat fierce-looking women in modern dress, and the schoolgirls of Tobruk wore snappy navy blue trouser suits. But those Tobruk girls all still disappeared into the all-enveloping barracan after they left school.

In Benghazi and Tripoli, it was already different by the mid-1970s. Women were certainly out and about in western-style clothes in those cities when I was living in Tobruk. They were going to university and holding jobs, so Fatima was right up to a point in her optimism on emancipation.

Nel's interview with Fatima now seems to me a fascinating piece of time travel to a country which was partly but not altogether changed when I lived there twenty years later. And it's a glimpse of a world remote indeed from the twenty-first century.

CHAPTER ELEVEN

THREE DUTCH QUEENS: JULIANA'S 'RASPUTIN' AFFAIR

Wilhelmina, Juliana and Beatrix

The AP greatly appreciated Nel's coverage of the Dutch royal family, ever popular in the US, to such an extent that at the end of her AP career, she would even be kept on for a few months past her retirement age in case Queen Juliana abdicated.

Nel's coverage started with the old Queen Wilhelmina during her very first months as a reporter with the AP in London in the war, when Wilhelmina was living in exile in the UK. Wilhelmina had become queen in 1890 at the age of ten, initially under the regency of her mother, Queen Emma. During the war, the queen broadcast frequently to the Dutch people, and came to be seen as a symbol of resistance to the Nazi occupation.

Wilhelmina once wrote a book, *Eenzaam maar niet alleen*, meaning 'lonely but not alone'. "A bit like me," Nel remarked. Wilhelmina disliked and got rid of much of the pomp and ceremony of the court, deciding she should be addressed simply as Mevrouw Van Oranje, like calling Queen Elizabeth of the UK Mrs Windsor.

She was also a very 'Protestant' queen. A wartime incident Nel got hold of had her asking the Dutch prime minister in exile, Pieter Gerbrandy, to find her a quiet, strict Protestant church. All the churches he produced were too 'Roman' for her. Eventually, he found one she liked, but then it turned out that there were only footstools to kneel on, or standing room. Said Wilhelmina, "Kneeling I do not do."

Nel said she began covering Queen Wilhelmina in what was *called* her democratic period. But this didn't apply to the press, which were kept at a safe distance. There were no interviews or talks with chief editors, or drinking coffee with members of parliament, as her daughter, Juliana, did later. But Wilhelmina was far easier for photos. In her day, the royal family were mad about dressing up and were much photographed, often in national and historic costumes. Juliana, on the other hand, had a great aversion to photographers.

The Wilhelmina story I like best is about her abdication, in 1948. For this and Juliana's coronation, Nel's all-male American colleagues hired top hats and tails, but at the last minute decided not to go into the Amsterdam church. Nel herself, in party dress, hat and gloves, refused to stick around staring at the pillars in the church on her own for three hours. So they spent those three hours together, all dressed up to the nines, in a café on Nieuwezijds Voorburgwal. Then the 'really fun and spontaneous moment' came when Juliana and Wilhelmina appeared on the balcony of the palace on Dam Square.

"The old queen clapped Juliana hard on the shoulder and shouted loudly, 'Long live the queen,' then promptly disappeared for good. Some people said her teeth fell out when she shouted."

There were no riots in those September days of Juliana's accession, nor were any expected, Nel reported. An image stuck in her mind of two communist MPs with small children on their shoulders, waving flags. "But I still ran foul of a policeman, who tried to keep me behind a barrier until he, incredulously, saw my press card," she grumbled.

In 1980, when Wilhelmina's daughter, Juliana, abdicated and her granddaughter Beatrix was crowned queen, there were indeed riots in traditionally socialist Amsterdam, much to my surprise as a newly arrived resident. On Rozengracht, around the corner from the Nieuwe Kerk on Dam Square where Beatrix was being crowned, a street party was in full swing with food and drink stalls, music and festive decorations. Suddenly a series of Black Maria police vans whistled ominously past, heading towards invisible demonstrations.

In the evening, we tried to find a fireworks display by Central Station, but only saw a busload of military gents in dress uniforms and cockatoos, looking like life-sized toy soldiers. The rest of the evening was spent running away from tear gas, water cannons and hordes of riot police, who eventually totally surrounded us. We took refuge in a café until things quietened down. We never found the demonstrations.

Fourteen years earlier, Beatrix and Claus' wedding had sparked more serious riots. This was partly because Claus was German and was rumoured to have been in the Hitler Youth. People were also affronted by Beatrix's lavish spending plans for her residence. After the wedding ceremony, Nel reported that smoke bombs sent black plumes into the sky as they paraded through Amsterdam in the Golden Coach.

When Beatrix's eldest son Crown Prince Willem-Alexander married the Argentine Maxima in February 2002, twenty-two years after his mother's coronation and thirty-six years after her wedding, footage was shown on TV of that earlier wedding with those black smoke clouds billowing away over the Golden Coach.

Maxima's wedding, however, turned out to be a popular affair, despite a tricky run-up. Her father had been junior agriculture minister in the notorious Videla military junta. There was considerable political concern about the marriage, for which Dutch parliamentary approval was required. Eventually, a solution was found. Her parents were not invited to the wedding and watched it on Dutch television in Brussels, just as I was simultaneously watching it in Prague. Maxima's parents also remained absent for Beatrix's abdication and Willem-Alexander's investiture in 2013.

As things turned out, Maxima, an attractive young woman with long blonde hair, quickly managed to win the hearts of the Dutch via a television interview with the couple, plus a timely tour of the country. This was thanks to her pleasant personality and successful efforts to learn Dutch, helped by the fact that she was obviously in love with the amiable prince. The Dutch even apparently forgave her somewhat naive remark that she believed her father when he said he knew nothing of all the disappearances in Argentina, saying, "Why should he lie to me?" Many were probably touched by her tears at the wedding, when *Adiós* Meu *Meniño* was played on a bandoneon.

After that very quick flip through some of the abdications, weddings and coronations of the three queens, we return to Juliana. After Wilhelmina abdicated back in 1948, it would be Queen Juliana and her husband, Prince Bernhard, who were to provide Nel with so many meaty royal reporting stints, in Juliana's case particularly on the Hofmans affair.

The first thing I came across in Nel's Juliana files was nothing to do with the Hofmans affair. It was just a snippet on the queen's first state visit to

France in 1950. Apparently the press were told at the last minute that they were expected at an Élysée reception.

"Thanks to our fashion reporter in Paris, Pierre Balmain then lent me an impressive evening gown which, a bit musty, had already been shown many times by one of his top mannequins."

However, odd things were already happening by then with Juliana, but to get to their roots, it is necessary to backtrack a few years. In 1947, there had been the eventful birth of Juliana's fourth and last daughter, Marijke. (She later switched to Christina.) Nel described the frenetically expectant atmosphere, as it was thought that it might be a boy.

"We camped for a week or more with about one hundred journalists in a hotel in Baarn, in a cold and snowy January. We bivouacked daily in front of the gates of the palace in Soestdijk, very cold. Finally, it happened. It was a girl."

The AP was competing with the Dutch ANP press service in the national papers, so the ANP telex room was practically sealed up.

"I remember the competition was terrific – because it might be a prince. An American colleague working for Aneta at the time was sacked on the spot by the late Van der Pol of the ANP because Van der Pol thought he'd passed on news to me, the AP!"

A few years after Marijke was born, news began to leak out about Juliana having rubella or German measles while pregnant with her. Simultaneously, the first rumours started to circulate about Greet Hofmans. She was a faith healer of dubious provenance who became a kind of Rasputin figure vis-à-vis Juliana. The queen's husband, Bernard, along with Dutch MPs and other leading figures, feared Hofmans was exercising an undue and undesirable influence on Juliana. As a result, "a small number of journalists, among them Henk Kersting and myself, were put in the picture by worried MPs." It was a code of honour at that time not to publish that information; something that would be impossible later, Nel acknowledged.

Both Dan Schorr and Friso Endt also said they talked with Prince Bernhard about Hofmans. Nobody revealed their sources. Nel said her own main informant was her old friend Cees Fock, Prime Minister Willem Drees' chief aide. Fock considered Nel an important link, as she was from the AP. "He told me everything about the history of Greet Hofmans," Nel whispered to one interviewer. No, they never took advantage of her, she said confidently. "They never gave me misleading information. I was, after all, too slippery for that."

Nel discussed the Hofmans story with Kersting, but he felt it was too sensitive for the AP to break the news. But when they discovered that German magazine *Der Spiegel* was about to publish, they got ready to run with the story. They were tipped off on this when the AP in Amsterdam was asked for a photo of Greet Hofmans for *Der Spiegel*, a photo client of the bureau in Bonn.

The AP knew which day *Der Spiegel* would publish. "For days, we were busy getting the story completely ready to put on the telex the moment *Der Spiegel* hit the streets. I remember vividly how I, scarcely recovered from this publication, was phoned in bed in the morning before daybreak and dew. AP New York had sent a short message: '*Slis must have séance with Hofmans*'."

At the crack of dawn, Nel set off for Nassaukade in Amsterdam, where Greet received her clients. She sat in the waiting room on a beautiful warm summer morning amid a colourful crowd, with people from all walks of life. Women with dogs, and some men as well. "They lapped it up, what she said, they were really serious. They animatedly swapped their experiences with Greet. I must have looked rather bewildered, because they cheered me on with 'she is terrific', or 'I have benefitted a lot from it'."

Nel was racking her brains about what she could actually ask her. "I was as fit as a fiddle, and did not suffer from depressions." Then her turn came to go behind a curtain into a little room to face Greet. "A sort of severe, tall, thin and dark schoolmistress. Black skirt and high-necked white blouse. She had piercing eyes."

In the end, she told Hofmans a true story about a friend whose husband was sick. "She buried her face in her hands. After what seemed a very long time, she said, 'I see that this man is going through a very long, dark tunnel, and it does not end well.' She was right, too. He did die, as a matter of fact, of cancer."

Nel's impression was that Hofmans believed in herself. "But on the other hand, a fake, a real fake. I found her a totally creepy person, completely gruesome. I don't know… I found it creepy. She eventually vanished like snow in the sun."

How Hofmans gained her influence over the queen went back to Juliana's pregnancy with Marijke. The queen's doctor warned her not to visit some sick soldiers who had returned from Indonesia, because she was pregnant. But Nel said Juliana wanted to 'do good' so she visited them anyway, and caught German measles. As a result, Marijke was born nearly blind. "That was, of course, a tragedy." In her anxiety about her baby's blindness, Queen Juliana sought help from Greet Hofmans. Fortunately, Marijke's condition ultimately responded reasonably well to normal medical treatment.

"There were things that we didn't write about in those days, and now we would." In the Hofmans period, Juliana was scheduled to go on a state visit to America and was to address Congress. At that time, Nel said Holland was trying to get weapons out of America for New Guinea, the disputed Papua region of Indonesia. But under Greet's influence, Juliana wanted to write her speech herself and say in it that all weapons should be thrown into the sea. Foreign Minister Dirk Stikker, who was to accompany her, tried to dissuade her. Juliana got angry and then made a truly bizarre remark: "What I would like to write is *'beer is best again'*." Only much later was this story used by journalists, says Nel.

I was mystified by Juliana's remark until Yolanda explained that the Dutch brewers ran a joint advertising campaign in 1950 to promote beer drinking, under the uninspiring slogan *'Het bier is weer best'* (Beer is best again). Stikker himself actually resigned over that New Guinea question, becoming NATO Secretary General ten years later. Dutch New Guinea became independent, but not until 1961; it joined Indonesia soon afterwards.

Much later, in a *Newsweek* article on Juliana's daughter Beatrix, Nel revealed that the less-than-regal publicity about Juliana resulting from her mystical attachment to Hofmans had a sequel in her attachment to a Polish-American, George Adamski, "who claims to have talked with creatures from the planet Venus."

As Nel hinted, Juliana's mother, Wilhelmina, had been pretty much out of touch with reality well before she abdicated, and Juliana and her strange vagaries became more and more worrying to Dutch MPs. So the down-to-earth and emphatically normal Beatrix's arrival on the public stage and later on the throne must have come as a relief to the politicians.

All the same, Juliana enjoyed wide popularity among ordinary Dutch citizens, similar to that of Elizabeth, the Queen Mother, in Britain. Whereas the British 'Queen Mum' managed to keep her public charm intact even when she was over one hundred, Juliana seemed to win Dutch hearts by being seen as 'everybody's favourite auntie'. After all, it doesn't matter so much if your favourite auntie goes a little batty.

In 1973, Juliana again provided Nel with huge international press coverage with the celebrations for the quarter-century of her reign. Many German newspapers picked up Nel's story. Among these, the *Schwarzwaelder Bote*, Oberndorf, had a touchingly bland headline: '*Juliana is a nice woman*'.

An intriguing but frustratingly incomplete feature by Nel on Juliana, her husband, Prince Bernhard, and Princess Beatrix was written around the end of the 1970s. This was actually after the 1976 Lockheed scandal involving Juliana's husband, which provided Nel with a very big story towards the end of her long career with the AP (Chapter 18).

In the fragment, Bernhard remarked of his strong-minded queen: '*If my wife says no, there is nothing doing*.' Nel went on to say Juliana had an iron constitution and outdid her retinue when on state visits. This reminded her of an incident during the disastrous floods back in 1953. Juliana had been much photographed all day long, wading through the water in big boots. When photographers asked for one more, as she stood alone against a background of waves, she said no, that is enough. "Her aide said, you are right. She replied, the Queen is always right."

'*Queen Juliana, who had a lonely youth as an only child, is now the happy grandmother of ten boys and two girls between the ages of one to twelve*,' Nel reported in the fragment. '*They all gather at her 70th birthday at the rambling white mansion of Soesdijk where the queen lives. She is very popular and lives down to the people. Beatrix is a different generation – more a realist. As in the average modern family, there is a notable generation gap between the two*.'

Eventually, Juliana fell prey to Alzheimer's disease, probably also the undiagnosed disease that robbed Nel of her excellent memory. She died in 2004, just short of her ninety-fifth birthday.

In 1959, long before Juliana's abdication but after the Hofmans furore had died down, when her daughter Princess Beatrix was due to make her first visit to America, Nel set about moving heaven and earth to get an interview with the princess. "When the Hofmans period was on the wane, Princess Beatrix was sent to America. I also worked for *Newsweek* then, and made every effort to get an interview." First, there was no answer to a letter from Kersting. Then Nel had a tip-off about an American lady staying at the Soestdijk royal palace who belonged to 'a sort of sect à la Hofmans', and had allegedly been chosen to write a story about Beatrix for an American publication.

This was intolerable. Our irate reporter swung into action with a lunch with Beatrix's best friend Renée Roell, complete with early asparagus and strawberries. "I moved the chair in front of her and said down my nose, 'Of course I respect the fact that the princess is not giving any interviews yet. But,' I added threateningly, 'when she does do that, it should be with the person who first requested it in this country.'"

Not convinced that Mrs Roell would accomplish anything, Nel then charged off to see Joseph Luns, then foreign minister. She put it to him bluntly that "after an episode in which we had reported the Hofmans affair to the people in the most humane way, the minimal reward was an interview with Beatrix."

Three days later, the message came that Beatrix wanted to give an interview. "But UPI and the *New York Times* have to be there too. Disappointing, but better than nothing."

Beatrix had recently been on a trip with most of the European royalty of the day. This was a cruise organised by Queen Frederika of Greece on the *Agamemnon*. In the course of the interview, over tea in Soestdijk Palace, Nel asked interestedly how Beatrix found the trip. "*Wonderful*," said the princess, "*because I was among my own people.*"

Actually a very natural remark, Nel confided. After all, journalists would also rather sail with other journalists than, for example, construction workers. But it sounded bad and must have been a lesson for life for Beatrix. Nel made world news with Beatrix's remark, and in the Netherlands, there was no newspaper that didn't pick it up.

Dutch journalist Ageeth Scherphuis had a version of Nel's story with the *New York Times* popping the fatal question: This is how it went.

"Quite casually," says Nel, "we came to the cruise with European royalty that Beatrix had then recently been on at the invitation of Queen Frederika of Greece. 'Did you enjoy that?' asked Gilroy of the *New York Times*, 'with just royalty?' 'Well, of course,' she said, 'I enjoyed it.' And then, completely innocently, without her meaning any harm by it, she said, 'I liked it, because I was among my own people.'

"Sitting next to Nel in the car on the way back, Gilroy says, 'That was interesting, the remark she made about her own people, very interesting.' Ahhh, Nel thinks, he is going to make that his lead. If I don't, I will get trouble.

"And that Beatrix has never forgiven me. I am sure," Nel says ruefully. "Much later, I explained it to her, but that didn't make it any better." Nel tells Scherphuis she would not have used it if the *New York Times* had not been there. "I can imagine it was actually a very natural remark. I think I would not have wanted to do that to her."

This is an important incident. Nel was ambivalent about using this lead but felt forced into it by the competition. Possibly she was also anxious not to kowtow to royalty, as in another interview, she was more critical, saying, "She stood there with *beaucoup de presence*, very self-possessed... I thought: what a nasty remark!" She said the interview appeared in *De Volkskrant* newspaper with the same headline and Beatrix never forgave her.

"A little present in the form of a sixteenth-century print of Drakesteyn Castle didn't manage to make things up. As president of the Foreign Press Association, I asked if Her Majesty would take part in a *table ronde* one time, but she never responded to that."

But she went on to praise her: "She is enormously self-assured. She also did a good job in Japan. That was lapped up by all those Indonesian fellows. She also works day and night, that one." Sounds like Nel herself, I thought.

"That is a tremendously ambitious woman with an enormously inquisitive spirit. If she wants to know something, she calls up six professors from Leiden. She is a good queen. She also does not want to be unpopular, so she wanted to soothe that group of former Indonesian prisoners of war during her state visit to Japan, but still it was not overdone."

Nel was less impressed by Beatrix's relationship with the press. She said disapprovingly, "The only audience that she holds with the press is the meeting with a bunch of chief editors who are not allowed to publish anything about it."

Beatrix may not have completely forgiven Nel for that headline, but she did appreciate the print of Drakesteyn Castle, the little castle in Lage Vuursche where Princess Beatrix lived before becoming queen, and to which she returned following her abdication. Nel had found the print on a visit to Brussels. Among Nel's papers was a short letter on light-blue paper with a crowned B in the upper left-hand corner. In almost untranslatable courtly Dutch, it is undoubtedly a friendly note:

Drakesteyn, 21 May 1963

Dear Miss Slis,
Hereby I extend to you heartfelt thanks for the most charming, attractive old print of 'Drakesteyn' that you recently found in Brussels. I greatly appreciate your friendly gesture of buying it for me.
With best wishes, Beatrix

As queen, Beatrix was reasonably popular most of the time, but sometimes attracted criticism for being somewhat high-handed and interfering in affairs of state. It is true she has not warmed the hearts of the Dutch in the same way as her mother, Juliana. But I found her trademark beehive-like hairstyle and rather ugly big hats endearing. I also liked a story about her at the time of the EU summit in Maastricht in 1991, as relayed to a Foreign Press Association group.

Maastricht is known for its excellent food. In the Calvinistic north of the country, all comers, including top-ranking politicians or corporate leaders, are customarily given 'broodjes' (rolls) for lunch. But in southern Maastricht with its proximity to Belgium, even companies located there provide slap-up meals for all comers. One expects to eat well in Maastricht.

A restaurant owner was laying on a classy luncheon for the European Union leaders attending the summit, in his vast restaurant in a beautiful old castle. Proud of his cuisine, he wanted all the EU leaders to sign their names on a newly plastered wall in the restaurant, but the bureaucrats involved insisted this would not be appropriate. However, Beatrix spotted the wall and cried: "Come on, Europe," I imagine in her jolly-hockey-sticks kind of way, and they all signed his wall.

Beatrix's spouse, Prince Claus, will feature again in the chapter below on the Foreign Press Association, of which he was patron and loyal supporter. In the early years of his marriage, Nel was quick to dismiss rumours of Claus having an affair with a politician's wife. She also criticised some snide remarks made by Foreign Minister Josef Luns about Claus in a Belgian paper. Nel said of the prince, who became subject to serious depression and a series of illnesses in the 1980s:

"He was still his normal self then, that poor devil. But it is a good marriage all the same. *Enfin*. Some dirty paper also wrote that she [Beatrix] had an affair with that awful Laurens Jan Brinkhorst. I don't believe a damn thing about it. But Jan, of all people." *Another typical Nel roar of laughter.* What does she think of this muckraking by Luns in the Flemish paper *De Morgen?* "Completely indecent. Because I know for sure that [his depression] is genetic. Pa appears to have shot himself in the head in Kenya. If Claus suffers from the same thing, that is sad. Luns, I believe, has slightly lost his head."

Luns presumably suggested in *De Morgen* that Claus was a suicidal depressive. Paradoxically, just before he died in 2002 after a lengthy illness,

Nel as a little girl

Kennermer Lyceum secondary school: Nel gazes boldly out between two timid friends

Nel's father with his third wife, the dreaded widow (1948)

Middelharnis 75-year school reunion 1937-92

Dutch nurses on their return from nursing war-wounded
in Finland, September 1940

At St Moritz – Winter Olympics 1948

Indonesian Round Table Conference 1949

ECA press conference 1949. With U.S. businessman Kaufmann,
possibly related to Marshall Plan. Note Nel's splendid hat

With American actor Douglas Fairbank Jr 1949

International Court of Justice, The Hague c1950. Nel interviews members of Iranian delegation on oil consortium

Young Nel, glamorous at a dinner party

Nel at work

Nel Slis and Dan Schorr

Nel and Dan

Elysee Reception, Queen Juliana's State Visit to France, 1950

Nel in Paris

Nel with cats

Nieuwspoort reception for Nel's departure to Brussels, October 1963.
With Foreign Minister Joseph Luns, AP Bureau Chief Henk Kersting

U.K. Prime Minister Ted Heath, Brussels, c1964

With EEC Commission Vice-Chairman Sicco Mansholt. Brussels, early 1970s

Nel in conversation with Igor Stravinsky, US Ambassador
Celdon Chapen, Brussels cocktail party mid-1960s

U.S. Defense Secretary Clark Clifford at Brussels military
airport for NATO defence ministers meeting late1960s

'Behind the broad shoulders' of French Foreign Minister Maurice Couve de Murville at the beginning of the 1970s, when the UK's entry to the EEC was on the agenda

Tête a tête with a fellow-reporter from Le Figaro

Portrait of Nel

Nel in Brussels office

FPA 30th anniversary1955. Nel with FPA founder Paul Derjeu,
Foreign Minister Johan Willem Beyen (newspaper cutting)

FPA 55th anniversary, after speech by Prince Claus

FPA 55th anniversary, Nel and Claus dancing

A French decoration for Nel

FP 60th anniversary, Erestein Castle, Kerkrade November 1985. Nel introduces Prince Claus to FPA members Vera Vaughan Bowden, Caroline Studdert, Laura Raun

FPA 60th anniversary. A new award for Nel. With Claus

'Like a hair in the soup' Haagse Courant interview on Nel's 75th birthday, 1988

Robert Schouten interview on retirement from AP, 1979

Ivor Cornelissen interview, Nel's 80th birthday 1993

Prime Minister Ruud Lubbers at Nel's 75th birthday

Nel and NATO Secretary-General Joseph Luns. Photo used for Netherlands Press Museum 1995 exhibition, Vóór alles journaliste (above all a journalist)

Nel at home with a cigar

Claus won a libel case against a Dutch magazine for suggesting his father committed suicide, even though it seemed to be widely accepted that this was true – I'd even heard it myself. Whatever about that, the death of Claus in 2002 did reveal that from a difficult beginning, the prince had quietly achieved widespread popularity, both with the Dutch and internationally.

Nel criticised the RVD government information service for releasing practically no news about those illnesses of Claus when they become persistent, as she felt this led to too many rumours. Otherwise, she had no complaints at the time about the RVD or its chief.

"I have an excellent relationship with [RVD chief] Bax. He is very open with me. He feels very sorry for Willem-Alexander. Apparently he has the greatest difficulty in getting to grips with history and political science, while his two brothers take to this like a duck to water. That Friso [middle son] appears to be really brilliant."

Elaborating, Nel said, "The RVD has nothing to fear from me. I do not poach on their territory. *Je suis discrète*. They have told me a lot. I have used it, but *between the lines*. I do not publish everything. I have the reputation of total trustworthiness. I am somehow a bit straightforward. The Protestant is still in me, though, after all, they [Protestants] could go to hell. I have a certain propriety. I do not bring out the most sensational things, but I can write it in such a way that you still smell it a bit."

These comments, I think, give a good idea of Nel's considerable art of being a persistent and penetrating investigative journalist while also managing to remain a trustworthy contact.

Beatrix announced her abdication in favour of Willem-Alexander on 28 January 2013, three days before her seventy-fifth birthday, making her the country's oldest reigning monarch. She stood down formally on 30 April, which thus became the last traditional 'Queen's Birthday' festival. It was actually Beatrix who had instituted her mother Juliana's birthday as the official Queen's Birthday holiday, because her own birthday was on 31 January, rather a chilly time of year for these festivities. After Willem-Alexander took over, this became the 'King's Birthday' holiday.

Beatrix reigned for thirty-three years, just beating her mother Juliana's thirty-two years, before completing the hat trick of queenly abdications. Wilhelmina had the longest reign of the three, an imposing fifty-eight years. A sad note at the time of the royal 'changing of the guard' from Beatrix to her son was that Willem-Alexander's younger brother Friso was still in a coma after a skiing accident the previous February. Friso, who had given up his right to the throne to marry the woman he loved, died on 12 August 2013.

Nel herself was complementary about the young Willem-Alexander's other qualities, aside from those early academic struggles mentioned above. She saw a lot of his grandfather Bernhard in him. "*Il a du charme,* he has an easy manner, likes good food and pretty girls. *Il aime la vie.* I believe that he is good at dealing with people, but he is no big thinker."

In a final glance back at the older generation in her article on the monarchy, Nel sounded a poignant note: '*My last royal tour de force [for Wilheminia] was the White Funeral of Queen, or rather Princess Wilhelmina, which I found in a way pathetic. Wilhelmina towards the end of her reign had already frequently been 'out of the picture', while Juliana temporarily took over. The most pathetic thing in this bitter winter was the atmosphere in the little palace on the Lange Voorhout, where Wilhelmina lay in state. It had something strangely lonely that made you ponder about her perhaps interesting but rather arid life.*'

The funeral, in 1962, was known as the White Funeral not because of the weather, but because white was used instead of black, as Wilhelmina requested. An old newsreel film of it can be found on YouTube: Juliana and the other women mourners are dressed in white, and there is a white coffin. The hearse carriage is draped in white, and the horses drawing the carriage are wearing long white covers, making them look like a cross between heraldic jousting steeds and ghosts. The funeral must have brought back memories for Nel of Wilhelmina in exile in the UK at the very beginning of her journalistic career.

'LA SLIS' IN BRUSSELS
(1963-73)

CHAPTER TWELVE
EMERGING EUROPE
Prising open the door to Brussels

By the end of the 1950s, Nel found herself becoming increasingly bored with the Dutch, memorably calling them 'a nation of ten million nitpickers'. But as covering her country began to pall, a new age and a new reporting opportunity was dawning with the emerging European movement.

Nel had always had a very strong interest in the idea of a united Europe. Back in 1948, at The Hague Congress in the Ridderzaal (Knight's Hall), she was thrilled to hear Churchill, Schuman and Adenauer call for a united Europe. "And I still know exactly how I began my piece: *In green and leafy The Hague…* Europe has always impassioned me. I really wanted to get my nose into it."

Also known as the Congress of Europe, this event foreshadowing the European community was held on 7–11 May 1948, with 750 delegates from around Europe and observers from the US and Canada. Winston Churchill was honorary chairman. Churchill's speech calling for a united Europe, in a 'movement of people', can be found on YouTube.

Nel wrote about a united Europe literally from the beginning, even when the AP did not believe that it would ever happen. And she went on writing about it, even if they didn't use it. "I have always thought that a united Europe would come, and that it couldn't be otherwise…"

The European Economic Community was eventually set up in 1958, ten years after that congress in The Hague and a year after the foundation Treaty of Rome was signed. The founding six were France, Italy, West Germany, the Netherlands, Belgium and Luxembourg.

I like to remind myself sometimes of the litany of later joiners. The UK, Ireland and Denmark joined in 1973, Greece in 1981, Spain and Portugal in 1986, Austria, Finland and Sweden in 1995. Ten joined in 2004: the Central Europe quartet of the Czech Republic, Poland, Slovakia and Hungary; the Baltic states of Estonia, Latvia and Lithuania; tiny Malta, the Greek half of Cyprus, and Slovenia, first member from former Yugoslavia. Bulgaria and Romania joined in 2007, followed at a distance by another ex-Yugoslavia country, Croatia, in July 2013, the year the first edition of this book was published. Nel would have been delighted by the enlargement but distressed by the later spectacle of the UK's Brexit departure.

As the European movement gathered momentum through the 1950s, its importance finally dawned on the AP and the American business community it served. Their interest was further encouraged when the British began accession negotiations with the EEC in July 1961. As Brussels bureau chief Fred Cheval remarked to Nel, "The AP suddenly realised that it was serious. They ought to have someone in Brussels."

A short secondment to Brussels for a European Defence Community conference gave Nel the chance of a toehold, and she made the most of it. "Nel's work on the EDC conference deserves the highest praise," Cheval told Kersting. "She contributed greatly to the stories through her excellent contacts with the Dutch delegation and her constant spirit of enterprise and initiative. She was of tremendous assistance in the successful carrying-out of a tough coverage."

There was still some way to go, but things did begin to move after Nel returned from a holiday in Italy in August 1962. Her holiday, incidentally, caused a friend in the American Embassy to complain that The Hague seemed even duller with Nel away. "Even the Dutch don't seem to hate us with any interesting intensity."

Henk Kersting sent Nel a confidential letter, dated 19 September 1962, giving her strict instructions to throw it away after reading it. Kersting was passing on his reply from Lloyd Stratton on having a full-time AP staffer in Brussels to cover the Common Market (EEC). This was positive, despite an ominous and prophetic note about Germany:

I would not object to assigning Nel to the job. She is an excellent reporter and possibly under the tutelage of the London desk her writing would improve to suit. I believe Cheval would not complain, although possibly Germany might not be too happy. However, no other solution to the Market staffing problem has been found and Nel has worked hard and well.

Scenting victory, Nel mustered her ammunition to press her suit further. In a letter asking the advice of New York colleague Relman Morin about how to go about this, Nel wrote: '*I frankly feel that the AP can use me to greater advantage in Brussels than in The Hague. My assets – speaking French, Dutch, German, Italian and English – would benefit the AP... I – virtually single-handed – disposed of New Guinea and old Wilhelmina. Successive weekends went into Wilhelmina's obit, her death and finally her white funeral. The EEC, however, needs someone who likes the work, which includes also careful filing, updating and lots of meticulous doings which I happen to like and am used to, having pottered on my own for almost twenty years.*'

The fact that Nel spoke all the languages of the EEC's founding six as well as English did win the AP over. "*We'll send Slis*, because she speaks five languages," the AP eventually decided after much humming and hawing.

So the door to Brussels at last creaked open. As Nel put it, she was sent to Brussels 'to see how postwar Europe was doing'. After some months of toing and froing between Brussels and The Hague, 'disposing of Wilhelmina', whose funeral was held on 4 December 1962, a letter from New York dated June 25, 1963 confirmed Nel's appointment as full-time Common Market Correspondent.

Nel's departure received remarkable media coverage, highlighting the impact she had made as The Hague Correspondent over nearly two decades. Following her official appointment, she was given not one but two well-attended farewell receptions. The first was hosted by the Foreign Press Association on Thursday 22 August, while on Monday 2 September, politicians in The Hague could say their goodbyes at a reception given by Henk Kersting and his wife.

Among the guests at Kersting's reception was Foreign Minister Joseph Luns, reputedly the only minister who sometimes called her 'Nel' instead of 'Miss Slis' during press conferences. "At any rate, if he was really excited," Nel said blandly.

The last official event Nel attended as a reporter was that reception described earlier given by the Indonesian chargé d'affaires on 23 August, the day after her own Nieuwspoort press reception. Remarkably, this produced one newspaper report headlined '*Hearty leave-taking of Nel Slis*' rather than anything about the Indonesians. The reporter was effusive about Nel:

With her, we are losing a unique figure of whom people can say at her leave-taking that she is already legendary now. Tough and thoroughly indefatigable and at the same time loudly grousing that she is knackered, never dull, knowing everyone, appearing at all receptions and sometimes saying things to Dutch heavyweight men which make her fellow journalists exchange shocked looks with each other. Later saying: "But Nel, you really can't do that!" And she: "Why not? Surely he can have manners."

He recalled the last press conference given by Frits Philips, founder of the eponymous flagship Dutch multinational. "'Gentlemen,' said Philips. And Slis, over everyone: 'Gentlemen? Are ladies forgotten here?' She was the only woman."

The reporter concluded: "And now Nel Slis is leaving us. Too bad!"

Another article, by G. Toussaint in *De vrouw en haar huis* (*Woman and Home*), October 1963, had more warm words about Nel:

The Hague and actually the entire country is the poorer from the loss of an important woman. The journalist Nel Slis, loved and feared by many who have had dealings with her: press officers, ministers, ambassadors and press chiefs have taken leave of her in an exceptionally warm way. She was always and still is a cock-of-the-run, somebody that never minces her words and also does not need to do so, because she turns out to be well informed about all topics which she has come across in her profession. A cheeky hussy maybe, but a sympathetic hussy...

In 1944 joining the AP and in 1945 in The Hague. For all these years she has put everyone through hell whom she suspected could have news. But she got it out of them. Modesty becomes a person, they say, but 'pressing on' and getting on top of the news is also a characteristic that apparently attracts people. Because there will seldom have been a reception as well attended, as animated and as varied as that which was offered to Nel Slis on her departure from the Netherlands. It is too bad that she is going away, but it is a delight to have known her.

Other newspaper clippings revealed that as well as Luns, the ambassadors of Belgium, the US, Britain and Poland were among those that turned up in Nieuwspoort to say farewell to Nel. One of these items, headlined '*Missed*', complained that while warm words were spoken, Nel was not given a decoration by the government, '*because Miss Slis has disseminated much good about the Netherlands around the world via this American press agency. In commentary and news. And there are those who are honoured for very much less.*'

This unnamed reporter also raised an interesting point about American journalism being 'different', with which I would agree. Describing Nel as '*a woman who held her own ground*', the writer added, '*No small performance, as it is not so easy to work for an Associated Press. American journalism is different to ours. This is sometimes too easily forgotten in judging her performance – or simply not even understood. And how often did she not set the ball rolling at international press conferences for Dutch colleagues who could not get their questions out so quickly. People will miss that too, as well as the warm personality that she has.*'

CHAPTER THIRTEEN

BRUSSELS!

La mer à boire

Nel moved with characteristic speed to change her address to Avenue Molière 168 in Brussels after her appointment. Tyna Wynaendts, then aged about fourteen, helped her to move her belongings to Avenue Molière and stayed on for a few days to paint a wardrobe. First, though, Nel had a surprise for her Dutch removal men. Tyna told me the story:

"They were very simple, and in the beginning, they showed a sort of mistrust, that she was this eccentric woman – because she bossed them around and they were a little bit grumpy. Then, when it was all done, they said, can we go now, but Nel said, oh, no, it's much too late, we are now going to the best place in Brussels to eat mussels, near the Grande Place.

"No, madam, they said, no, no, no. But Nel wouldn't listen to them. She said no, we should go. So very reluctantly they just followed, and it turned out to be an evening of delight, because with the beer helping, they had such a good time and afterwards they just slept in their truck, because they couldn't drive after all that beer. I'm sure they're still talking about it."

Once in residence, Nel found she had to begin all over again in her new working sphere. Right at the start, there was a hassle about her accreditation: Was she a Dutch journalist, or an American one because of her press agency? Dutch Foreign Minister Joseph Luns, a recurring presence in Nel's journalistic life, helped her out. I didn't discover the outcome, but my guess is that she remained Dutch.

Once again, Nel was working from early morning to late at night, reading up on new subjects, going to cocktail parties and meeting as many people as possible. And once again, she had to fight her way in as a solitary woman among hundreds of men. Furthermore, she was now in more direct competition with the correspondents of Dutch newspapers, as the AP news from Brussels was regularly picked up by the Dutch papers.

These Dutch correspondents closed ranks against her. "I could not get in because I did not work for a Dutch newspaper," she recalled angrily. "The Dutch boys took care of that. This man from *Het Vrije Volk*, that was a very bad one. Luckily, I don't remember his name any more. That is an advantage of getting old. I still have a nasty taste in my mouth from that." I would love to know what he did. For Nel to pick him out from the rest, it must have been pretty dire.

Some 200 journalists were accredited in Brussels in 1963. Three of those were women, and Nel was the only press agency woman. "In Brussels, I dared not ever turn up unprepared, did my homework down to the last iota, more than the men," Nel declared. "Most of all so that they did not find you *less*. And along with that, you had to look smart and be well dressed. That was watched out for there."

In an early EEC briefing, Nel was completely swamped by trigger prices, threshold prices and other peculiarities relating to Common Market agricultural policies. Her Dutch colleagues were 'like a wet blanket'. Louis Metzemaekers, future editor of *Het Financieele Dagblad* and at the time working for *Het Parool* newspaper, was the only one that was friendly. He came to her rescue.

"'Metz, I'm dying, I don't understand a bloody thing.' 'Well then, we'll have lunch,' said he, and then he wised me up," said Nel.

"But mark my words," she recalled with a grimace. "In those first couple of years, I didn't go to the theatre or a concert on a single evening. For two years, I read up about European politics every evening. Yes, sure, Slis always did her homework. I went nowhere, only to receptions where I could 'pick the worms out of their noses'.

"But Metzemaekers was always a very decent colleague, *pas un petit bonhomme*. Whenever he saw that I understood nothing, he said that he would take me with him and explain it to me later."

On top of grasping these esoteric Common Market goings-on was the difficulty of reporting on them in a palatable form for AP's customers. Even in the 1990s at my more specialised financial news service, it was difficult to arouse interest in EEC affairs still bristling with technical jargon. I always felt the EEC specialist in my own news service (AFX News) was very much undervalued as a result.

And then there was the sheer exhaustion of all these lengthy EEC meetings. "Brussels was *la mer à boire*: I was in the thick of potatoes, gas, ecus," Nel recalled. "I did learn a lot there, but writing short pieces which could be understood by people was very difficult sometimes… It was a killing job." Still, she added with satisfaction, "I was often the only one that wasn't completely wiped out by all these meetings. If I had not had this Zeeland iron constitution, I wouldn't have made it."

I had to look up '*la mer à boire*'. It means an insurmountable task, but maybe it's even better literally – an ocean to drink.

By way of compensation, there was the excitement and camaraderie of those early days in the emerging EEC. "Very many journalists were still really inspired by Europe then. Sometimes we clapped if something was achieved after long negotiations… At the start, it was a sort of starry-eyed business. I thoroughly enjoyed it, nothing was too much. I worked day and night and did plenty of homework at weekends on agricultural and monetary affairs, and I didn't mind, it was like a popular university, you learned a lot with a wonderful crowd."

Taking the longer view, Nel enthused, "Professionally, it was a most interesting time with a wonderful press fraternity; excellent, keen, interested, hard-working." Rather unexpectedly, she added, "With 200 journalists from all over the world, there was no such thing as jealousy and pettiness." Well, apart from some of her Dutch colleagues, I thought.

Still, it was exhausting, and after two years Nel found herself craving a holiday. She asked her half-sister Jaan and the faithful housekeeper Aagje to come and look after the cat. "Because I so madly want to get out at last for a month's holiday, as I am dead tired after two years' hard work and scarcely a decent weekend." Apparently they couldn't come, but a solution was found for the cat and Nel enjoyed a summer break in Turkey.

Nel's own admissions about how she leaned on Metzemaekers made me curious about his perspective on Brussels. I already knew of him, because from 1967–77 he became the highly respected chief editor of Dutch financial newspaper *Het Financieele Dagblad*, where I worked in the 1980s. Fellow journalist Friso Endt also often impressed on me how much Metzemaekers helped Nel in Brussels. So in spring 2000, I asked Metzemaekers for a meeting. Friso told me he was completely blind, but that he was still writing by dictating to his wife. He died in 2003 aged ninety, so I was lucky to meet him.

On the telephone, Metzemaekers sounded clear as a bell, and said he would be glad to meet and tell me about Nel and those Brussels years. I arrived at the address to find the house was a building site, with new owners doing it up. Fortunately, he had only moved to the next village. Metzemaekers had moved into a plush crimson-carpeted old people's residence, his wife having meanwhile died. A big man with a deep voice, he was sitting in his rather dark room smoking and listening to a tiny radio.

Metzemaekers said Nel's biggest problem was that she was parachuted into Brussels by the AP with no preparation whatever. "She didn't know anything about the whole business when she arrived, especially all these specialist matters – I was the one that had to guide her, so to speak. She didn't have so much self-confidence."

Metzemaekers had already been in Brussels for five years, and she leaned heavily on him. "Loutje, give me a lead," she would wail.

Metzemaekers gave me a rundown on the general background in Brussels and the most important Common Market topics Nel faced on her arrival, namely the customs union and the Common Agricultural Policy (CAP). Under the Treaty of Rome, the customs union was supposed to be achieved in twelve years. A certain percentage of internal and external tariffs were to be harmonised annually. In the event, the customs union was actually achieved two years early, in 1968 – amazingly fast, Metzemaekers remarked.

In wading into these completely new subjects, Metzemaekers said Nel's best qualities were that she was extremely active and diligent. "She had no family; she had the whole day and night to be active. I always had problems with that because she always came to me. Was she driven? Yes, she was."

The European Commission held a press conference every week with a spokesman briefing journalists on whatever had already been decided. But the most important source of information was the meetings of European ministers, which had to approve all proposals from the Commission. Conversely, the ministers were largely making decisions based on proposals by the Commission, which Metzemaekers said had much more influence than in the new millennium.

In a major EEC rift in July 1965 that Nel would have covered, French President Charles de Gaulle broke off French negotiations on the Common Agricultural Policy and inaugurated the 'empty chair' policy. This meant France was still a member but was not present at meetings. Seven months later, in January 1966, France 'rejoined' under the Luxembourg Compromise, in return for retaining unanimous voting when major interests were at stake.

Many of France's early disputes with the EEC were about agricultural policy and financing of agriculture, Metzemaekers explained. Among the founding six, agriculture was most important for France. The aim was to achieve free trade between the six member states plus a common external tariff.

Another burning question of the day was Britain's accession to the EU. Metzemaekers noted that the 'pig-headed' French president had already caused a furore in 1963 by using France's veto to block Britain's application to the EEC, against the wishes of the other five members. He did the same again in 1967. There were fears that the whole community would break up because of de Gaulle, who 'threatened everything', he said. This would have been a hot topic for Nel and for the AP.

In 1969, Georges Pompidou succeeded de Gaulle as French president. This was an improvement, said Metzemaekers, though he still groused about Pompidou's Foreign Minister Couve de Merville. "Pompidou put in place a different policy for France; it was easier with Pompidou. But these men never gave press conferences. It was the foreign ministers that gave them. French Foreign Minister Couve de Merville was very difficult. He only gave press conferences for the French journalists."

According to Metzemaekers, relations between Dutch Foreign Minister Joseph Luns and the French were also acidic. He considered Luns had an anti-French attitude. Nel, who as we know got on well with Luns but was herself a confirmed Francophile, disagreed, telling me that despite his squabbles with the French, Luns insisted he liked France and the French 'personality'.

In all events, as Metzemaekers conceded, "France was an important EEC partner, and for that reason, the news from the French side was naturally important for us all." This would have played to Nel's advantage, as a fluent French speaker and a Francophile.

Luns and especially Sicco Mansholt, architect of the EEC's agricultural policy, were the towering Dutch figures on the European stage in this period. Nel painted a vivid picture of the two apparently very different men. Both were relatively big men physically, and they loomed large in political significance, far beyond their native Holland. I was impressed by the sheer volume of interviews, features and reports that the AP took from Nel on the two men. Her lively reporting must have helped make them interesting for the AP's American clients. Nel has also created enduring twin portraits for us of these two Dutchmen who played such a key role in emerging Europe, so I have awarded them a chapter to themselves.

CHAPTER FOURTEEN

PORTRAIT OF TWO DUTCHMEN: MANSHOLT AND LUNS

If the CAP fits...

The EEC's common agricultural policy (CAP) was essentially created by Sicco Leendert Mansholt, the Dutch member of the Common Market Executive Commission, later renamed the European Commission. Mansholt was put in charge of agriculture when the Common Market was set up in 1958, and was the only person to remain on the Commission throughout almost all of Nel's Brussels period.

Largely thanks to Mansholt, agriculture was actually the most integrated sector by the time Nel arrived, far more so than industry. Mansholt got a good press, Metzemaekers told me. "He was actually the most important player at that moment, as agricultural policy was made by him."

I found numerous photos of Nel and Mansholt in the EEC period. She already knew him well from her AP years in The Hague, as he had been the driving force in rebuilding Dutch agriculture after the war. In his thirteen years as the Netherlands' first postwar Agriculture Minister, his international career also began to take shape. He played a major part in the Food and Agriculture Organisation, which invited him to visit 'underdeveloped' countries such as Pakistan on several occasions.

Nel's stories on Mansholt show that he, like Luns, had quite a few spats with the French. In February 1964, she reported that 'the dynamic, six-foot vice president of the EEC Commission' had lost no time in denouncing France's refusal of Britain as a member. He called this a threat to the EEC's continued existence.

Mansholt, Nel reported, wanted a truly economically and politically integrated Europe based on the Treaty of Rome, working in close partnership with the United States. "I want a Europe open to all democratic European countries that can accept the Rome Treaty. A test for such a Europe is the preparedness to accept Britain as a member," he declared.

Nel wrote that Mansholt was the most outspoken member of the Common Market's executive, and the firmest in defending its principles, including Atlantic unity in the form of NATO: *'The fifty-five year old blunt and burly European statesman will defend the principles of Atlantic Unity with the same toughness as that with which he defended Dutch farmers' interests over his thirteen-year period of office as agriculture minister in Holland.'*

Mansholt was patient in pursuing his aims, but not always calm, Nel noted with a hint of amusement. *'He is an extrovert, and apt to lose his temper. People who have known him for a long time, however, say that he has calmed down considerably, although it does happen that he bangs his fist at commission meetings. Through the years, they say, he has developed into a true diplomat. He speaks in plain language, to the relief of many for whom the complex agricultural jargon of the Common Market (sluice-gate prices, target prices, threshold prices) is meaningless.'* Nel, like myself, was one of those who had been bewildered by all that jargon on first encountering it.

Among Mansholt's strengths was his solid expertise in agriculture, along with his determination that the EEC should succeed, helping to push it forward through many a crisis. In one such crisis on CAP regulations for cereals, eggs and poultry, in two months of uninterrupted conferences with little sleep and constant haggling, Nel reported that Mansholt *'patiently chalked up his facts and figures on a blackboard, to remind the six agricultural ministers of what was good for the community.'*

Nel also discovered that Mansholt was greatly influenced by his remarkable socialist mother Wabien Andreae, who ran away from home at the end of the nineteenth century to propagate socialism among the poor peat farmers in her area. That was how she met Sicco's father, Leendert Mansholt, a wealthy farmer's son who was inspired by her evening lectures on socialism.

'Coming by his socialism through both sides of his family, Mansholt remembers how he and his brothers used to sing the Internationale *in bed at night while his parents indoctrinated poor farmers and their wives,'* Nel wrote. In her nineties, Wabien sailed to Sydney, Australia to visit her married

daughter Aleid, teaching English to Dutch emigrants on the long voyage. She certainly sounds quite a woman. I did wonder what Nel's American readers made of all this socialism, back in the 1960s.

Manshold later settled on a farm of his own and married a former schoolteacher, 'gentle Henny Postel'. Nel reported that to Henny, *'he is a man with few close personal friends, fiercely absent-minded, not an intellectual. She tells of the time she came home to find he had eaten the dog's food out of the ice box...'*

Mansholt's organisational skills had first emerged in the war during the German occupation. He played a leading part in the resistance, supplying food, shelter and forged ration cards for Jews and the politically persecuted. When liberation came, he managed the lowering of the water level in Dutch canals so that barges heavily loaded with food and weapons could pass under the bridges.

After the war, Mansholt, aged thirty-seven, was picked by socialist Premier Willem Schermerhorn as Holland's first agriculture minister, with the job of reorganising Holland's agriculture and managing food distribution for a starving population. He spent the next twelve years making Dutch farming competitive again on the world market, raising farm incomes and improving the structure of farming.

Although Mansholt did speak fluent English and French, Nel said this was 'with verve rather than perfect grammar', and he had difficulty with '*le*' and '*la*'. The suave Dutch ambassador to Paris, Johan Willem Beyen, observed of one of Mansholt's visits to the French capital: "Sicco made a fine speech on agricultural integration in Europe. But not since Sodom and Gomorrah has there been so much sinning against the sexes."

In 1968, Mansholt clashed fiercely with French Foreign Minister Michel Debré as well as his own Commission president, also at the time French, souring relations within the common market. Nel gave her readers a blow-by-blow account of this clash, which gives a fair indication of the stresses within the EEC between France and the other five – and not solely due to de Gaulle.

Debré had complained to Commission Chief Jean Rey that Manshold was 'biased' against de Gaulle's government because he had described Gaullism as an obstacle to the community's political progress. To Mansholt's fury, Rey apologised, blaming Mansholt's 'politically dynamic personality' and 'fighting spirit' though conceding the community had benefitted from these qualities.

Obviously stung, Manshold told Rey he was disappointed by his reply to Debré, adding pointedly that it was regrettable that it had not been submitted beforehand for the approval of the entire commission. He said Rey should not have agreed with Debré about 'so-called interference in internal policy', fuming that "by doing so, you are reducing the executive commission members to a level to which the French government would like to reduce them… You had evidently the right to have a different opinion on the political task of the commission members, but this does not authorise you to condemn one of your colleagues."

About Debré's complaint about calling Gaullism an obstacle to EEC progress, Mansholt riposted that at his news conference, he reviewed the many differences between France and its five partners: over Britain's membership; council decisions by majority vote; the democratic future of Europe, and the role of a European parliament therein. As long as these and other important political differences were not cleared up, European political unity would remain an illusion, he warned.

Conceding that he did tell journalists de Gaulle's triumph in the elections would not help this situation, Mansholt said blandly he had too much respect for the President of the French Republic to suppose he would review his policy after his overwhelming victory in the elections. "What I have said is that differences among the member states will make a European policy impossible." And he wanted the people of Europe to be 'well informed and have no false hopes'. Finally, Mansholt concluded that the commission's task was to carry out European policy, and "being perfectly independent, the executive commission would judge for itself how to interpret 'a political opinion.'" Shucks to you, Debré and Rey, seemed to be his message.

Personally, of course, Nel deeply desired the success of the European venture and saw how obstructive the French could be, but she was a reporter first and foremost. So she could make a good story of this clash while at the same time conveying its political significance.

On a quite different topic, it emerges that there was already concern about pollution on Mansholds's watch. Nel reported that Manshold planned to sponsor a programme 'to give the community the necessary political strength to lead the world to overcome pollution, overpopulation and the exhaustion of raw materials'. He called for a planned economy, non-polluting production and increased recycling of waste.

Nel discovered that Manshold was also against excessive preoccupation with gross national product, instead urging concentration on a goal of 'gross national happiness'. In his view, the Community ought to set an example in seeking to make the world liveable for his grandchildren's generation. When asked whether he would steer the community in a socialist direction, though, Mansholt said his aim was democracy and that Christian Democrats were often more progressive than some socialists. Nel concluded that Mansholt was really a leftist liberal, despite his family background.

Finally, Mansholt also believed the US, with its huge social problems and international burdens, was no longer capable of carrying the burden of leadership alone. Many of the same issues, especially pollution but also perhaps relations with the US, have remained hot topics or become even hotter in the twenty-first century.

Mansholt served only briefly as commission president, stepping down in January 1972 to be succeeded by the Frenchman Francois Xavier Ortoli. Nel's final portrait of him as commission president, in April 1971, highlighted Mansholt's openness to new ideas, no matter how shocking, on the ever-vexed question of agriculture. Despite creating the EEC farm support edifice, Mansholt saw the dangers of overproduction and dared to suggest reducing farming numbers and taking farmland out of production. Nel painted an engaging picture of how Manshold was able to charm and disarm the farmers outraged by his proposals:

Another bombshell thrown into the European Economic Community (EEC) is not excluded as Sicco Laendert Mansholt takes over the top leadership. As vice president of the six-member European edifice, the blue-eyed, tall and balding Dutchman, whose strong physical condition belies his sixty-one years of age, shook the community to its core in 1968. He proposed that before 1980, some 5 million farmers should have left the land and 5 million hectares of marginal farming land be taken out of production.

Bavarian farmers shouted 'farmer killer', when the revolutionary Mansholt Plan for agriculture was published, and the West German parliament said instead of 5 million farmers off the land, out with Mansholt. Only last month a third, watered-down version of his plan was approved by the EEC Council of Ministers, who haggled over it for four years. A year ago, bloody and violent demonstrations in the

Brussels streets led the council to accept a resolution laying down the principles for spending more on farm modernisation than on support prices for inefficient farming.

But his great charm and personal warmth disarm most. Walking into meeting halls with hostile farmers, he usually walks out amid thundering applause, and has earned the sympathy of all young farmers' organisations in Europe...

Mansholt must have been a marvellous source for journalists, and Nel made the most of this. She also explained his reasons for talking so openly to the press. "Mansholt can be extremely blunt, when angered by the six ministers at a council meeting over pig-meat prices or other details, while more important issues are at stake. Getting impatient at council meetings, he is known to have put up a warning finger, telling them, 'I will inform the press of your behaviour.' Apparently he felt that since there was no close parliamentary supervision of the Common Market, there should be vigorous criticism in the press.

*

The other leading Dutch player on the European stage was Joseph Luns, Dutch foreign minister from 1956 to 1971 when he became NATO Secretary General. Politically, the socialist (or leftist liberal) Mansholt and conservative Catholic Luns were poles apart, but both were also pragmatists in the pursuit of their goals.

Flora Lewis had a somewhat more negative opinion of Luns than Nel. She also rejected Friso Endt's suggestion that Nel may have gone to bed with Luns to get stories. This was based rather tenuously on Friso's perception of Nel as doing anything to get a story and on the fact that Nel was the only journalist Luns ever addressed by her Christian name.

"Luns was very important," Lewis conceded. "He was a very stubborn and rather pompous man. I would be disinclined to believe Friso's suggestion. If she did, I'm absolutely certain it would not have been for the story. She might have because he was attractive. He was a tough, tough man, and an interesting man. He was foreign minister at a time of great importance when there was a big fight with France about what was going to happen with the Common Market, and later, he became Secretary General of NATO. So he was very much part of this postwar construction of Europe. He had strong opinions and he wasn't wishy-washy, so Nel might have thought he was attractive. But I'm sure she didn't go to bed with him to get a story. That is simply not Nel's style. I don't know whether she did, she would not have told me. I just know that she was such an independent-minded, strong-minded person, that she would disdain anything like that." Case closed, I felt.

Nel herself also covered a number of NATO meetings. One held before Luns took over, at the Juliana Barracks in The Hague, produced an entertaining 'FAST-MOVING NEL' snippet in the *AP World* magazine of summer 1964.

Part of the AP team, *AP World* reports, was '*Nel Slis, the AP news gal who covers the Common Market at Brussels. Fastest route from some news conferences to the tent bureau was through the men's room of the barracks. In moments of great stress, Nel Slis took this short cut. "She went through there so fast," says (staffer) Tom Ochiltree, "that maybe none of the men noticed her."'* Maybe.

In a profile for Luns' appointment as NATO chief on 4 June 1971, Nel gave a more extensive physical description of him than any I found of Mansholt. Perhaps he *was* more interesting to her in this way. She certainly considered he had charm, not a typically Dutch quality. Nel led with the contrast between Luns and his predecessor Brosio:

Lanky, long-legged Joseph Luns (60), of the Netherlands, will bring a new touch to the North Atlantic alliance, when taking over from Italy's aging and reserved Manilo Brosio (73) who retires next fall. Luns jumps on the Nato bandwagon after Brosio has oiled its wheels for changes in the seventies, that makes the emphasis shift towards greater European participation in the Nato defense effort and a detente in East-West relations. Contrary to serious and discreet Brosio, Luns is talkative and loves to quip jokes. At times he gets deliberately clownesque for the purpose of humouring his colleagues, to thaw a frozen meeting or to cajole his partners so as to get his way...

Six and a half feet tall, balding Luns is a great and versatile diplomat. Not an addict to sports, his long egg-shaped face, sallowed by tireless diplomatic activity, is mobile and occasionally turns into that of a sad clown.

Luns is extremely courteous. He turns on his charm whenever he feels like it. "A diplomat," he said, "must be nice." Chuckling, he admits that he loves to put his foot in it, when circumstances call for it.

On his new NATO post, Nel remarked, *'It will be a change, and not always easy for Dutch foreign minister Luns to serve fifteen foreign ministers in NATO... For fifteen years, Joseph Marie Antoine Hubert Luns has served the Netherlands as foreign minister in eight successive cabinets, with a growing authority at home and prestige abroad.'*

Luns gleefully informed Nel that his long term in office had made him familiar with the problems of some one hundred countries, from which he had collected some hundred or more medals. *'With disarming vanity he loves to wear as many as his chest will allow. Luns' globetrotting has endowed him with invaluable political and diplomatic experience, complementing his envied intuition for politics... He has made his foreign ministry officials breathless, when appearing seemingly unprepared at conferences, but unfailingly knowing the right answers, they say.'*

He was reticent about his designs for NATO – and here the stroppy French rear their heads again. *'Asked whether he sought to bring back France into Nato's military organisation, Luns carefully said that he could give neither a positive nor negative reply. Well aware of difficulties in President Georges Pompidou's political backyard, Luns said that one should not give the impression of wanting to force France.'*

But earlier, said Nel, he was less diplomatic. *'Angry over the Franco-German bilateral treaty, concluded outside the Common Market in 1963, he used to translate French foreign minister, Maurice Couve de Murville's name into German, calling him Couve de Murstadt. Despite Flemish-Belgian sensitivity over a Dutchman talking French... when disagreeing with Couve over Britain's entry, he used to stare Couve in the face, telling him: "When I want to be understood, I talk in French."'* Nevertheless, Nel believed Luns got on with the Frenchman in his own way, with his light touch untypical of his compatriots. She noticed he was the only minister who called Couve 'Maurice'.

This light touch was not always appreciated by Dutch MPs. *'Staid members of the Dutch parliament have blamed him for being light-hearted and flippant. "You can never do right in parliament," Luns said. "Parliamentarians are getting too critical."'* The Dutch parliament also often complained about his constant travelling. Foreign ministry officials used to say that Luns was visiting 127 countries each year, and Holland twice.

On home and family, Luns quipped: "When I am at home on Sunday, the children ask 'who is that pale man cutting the meat today?'"

Nel was complementary about his wife: '*Pretty baroness Lia van Heemstra, a quiet, distinguished-looking lady, who is a cousin of former film star Audrey Hepburn.*'

Born in Rotterdam on August 28, 1911, Luns graduated in law at Leiden University and entered the Dutch diplomatic service in 1938. He held posts at the Dutch embassies in Berne, Lisbon, London and New York before becoming foreign minister in September 1952.

Nel also reported that Luns was a vote-catcher. '*Luns has been the magnet in drawing votes for his Catholic People's Party, Holland's largest. The Dutch people have loved Luns' pre-election television shows. His tongue-in-cheek performance in reply to sharp questioning by reporters used to make people rock with laughter.*'

Politically, Nel described Luns as a pragmatist. '*For many years, Luns strongly opposed closer contacts with Eastern Europe. To the great surprise of Dutch socialists, when visiting these countries, they found Luns had become a popular man with both Yugoslav and Rumanian statesmen.*'

By contrast to Mansholt's socialist background, Luns, a convinced Catholic, was '*very conservative in religion and generally old-fashioned... He feels strongly about extreme forms of modern literature, the arts and contesting students. He condemns radicalisation of Dutch public opinion. "It points to a lack of tolerance, once the greatest virtue of the Dutch."*' Those attitudes did not always endear him to Dutch youth, Nel observed.

However, Nel found that like Mansholt – and despite certain Dutch-American tiffs, notably with Robert Kennedy over New Guinea – Luns had an unshakeable belief in Atlantic partnership. '*He has always stressed the need for good relations between Europe and the United States.*'

Overtly, Luns had qualified praise for the US, telling Nel, "One cannot deny that some American politicians show a lack of tact. But fundamentally the United States is a superpower, which in my experience, less than others abuses its power. More than any other big power, the United States will be reluctant to use its might as a steamroller."

From the American side, well-informed sources told Nel the Americans had reservations over Luns as Nato Secretary General, fearing that he might not be a 'model of discretion'. One American diplomat said worriedly, "He will need a very good second man."

Also like Mansholt, Luns was a true European, and was equally keen on UK entry into the EEC. '*In Luns' political thinking, Europe has priority.*

The recent French change of heart on Britain's entry into the Common Market has been a great satisfaction for Luns. He worked tirelessly to achieve this and felt satisfied that the European Economic Community was now a running concern. "It has promoted European economic integration and enabled the Six to avoid a dangerous economic slump," he said.'

More surprisingly, Luns also looked forward to a European parliament with real power. *'Luns is convinced that ultimately a United Europe needs a supranational authority responsible to a democratically elected European Parliament... He believes that imperceptibly Europe will advance in this direction to the point of no return.'*

He had therefore naturally clashed with de Gaulle back in 1961 on the Gaullist proposition of a European political union made up of sovereign nations, *'l'Europe des patries'.* Luns blocked the plan by using his veto, causing German Chancellor Konrad Adenauer to accuse him of 'impudence not befitting a junior minister'. Luns told Nel that Adenauer always disliked him, and that this was entirely mutual.

But Luns' respect for de Gaulle was also mutual, Nel concluded, quoting de Gaulle as saying, "Luns, you can trust. He is a man who loves his country."

On his background, Nel reported, *'Luns holds a Latin touch from his Belgian-born mother, Henriette Louvrier from Liege. From his father, Hubert Luns, a professor in art history at Delft University, he inherited his flair and culture. He is a good historian and a Napoleon buff, who rattles off by heart all of the French Emperor's marshals. Despite his squabbles with the French, Luns insists: "I like France and the French personality." Not to speak of the kitchen, because Luns is fond of French cuisine...'*

A small, undated item by Nel recorded the furore Luns caused in the Dutch parliament in one of his *enfant terrible* moods while head of NATO, when he compared the Dutch language to animal noises: *'Three Dutch Socialist members of parliament have asked Dutch Foreign Minister, Max van der Stoel, whether he had seen reports in the French daily* Le Monde *that Luns told Nixon during the Brussels Nato summit, "Of all animal noises, Dutch is most like a language, but even so, I don't think this is being nice to animals."'*

Nel's profiles of these two big men also show how thorough she was, leaving no stone unturned and no staff member, however lowly, uninterviewed, with plenty of feature-friendly colour touches to boot.

CHAPTER FIFTEEN
THE BRUSSELS SCENE: A PAINFUL FAREWELL
Parting is such sweet sorrow: Nel's Hartman nemesis

Nel wrote a long article on the EEC for Dutch publication, '*Women and their Interests*', published just after her return to Holland. This gives a detailed picture of the day-to-day life of an EEC reporter in Brussels during Nel's deeply involving stint there.

Describing how the press 'rummaged around' in the European Community in Brussels, she said: '*The word is well-chosen inasmuch that the headquarters of the EEC – called "Berlaymont" after the exclusive convent that stood there earlier – is a modern madhouse. Only after many months does a newly arrived journalist find her way or what she wants.*'

As Nel was leaving Brussels, King Boudewijn had just opened a brand-new streamlined, six-floor International Press Centre opposite the Berlaymont building. This was to become a very comfortable haven for the ever-growing EEC press corps – though Nel would have had problems with the lifts if she had stayed on.

During Nel's stint, EEC press service chief Beniamino Olivi gave a daily briefing at noon on the first floor of Berlaymont on new developments, as well as naming and shaming member states who had again infringed the regulations. '*A big attraction – a means used by Olivi to keep his horde together – is that immediately after this briefing, the bar in the corner of the press room opens and the journalists can fall on the tax-free drinks. Italian Anna, who every journalist knows, then displays a rare dexterity in distributing whiskies, beer, camparis and espressos in a few seconds...*'

These 'twelve o'clocks' were also a good chance to invite experts from the EEC commission for a drink. '*The press benefits from having the commission's sometimes very complicated proposals explained*,' Nel observed. She went on to explain the special role of a press agency for her Dutch readers:

> *Among the 270 journalists, there are only about half a dozen women who hold a full-time job reporting on the EEC. As correspondent for The Associated Press, I belonged to the press agency group. These are the 'busy bees' of the press world... As well as the national press agencies, like Agence France Press, Reuters, etc., new agencies have been born which are exclusively occupied with news about the EEC. Of these, Agence Europe is the best known and the oldest. It has the authority of a law gazette and lies on every diplomat's desk.*
>
> *Press agencies work 24 hours around the clock for their clients, who are spread throughout the whole world. This... means journalists keeping their ears pricked about, for example, the Mediterranean area, South and North America, whenever trade and prices of tropical and subtropical products come into play. They have to know the difference between soft and hard (durum) wheat, etc.*
>
> *Journalists... are normally no specialists. Those who venture to the EEC have to do their homework, have a memory like an elephant, an iron constitution and strong nerves. It is rushed work and there is much competition to be the first and the best.*

On the archetypal long nights of EEC negotiations, Nel explained: '*The famous "nights" of the EEC belong especially to agency journalists. Newspapers "go to bed"... But agencies have a paper or radio station somewhere that wants news at all hours... Many radio stations are on the air for 24 hours. That means that an agency journalist sometimes begins work at 10 o'clock on Monday morning and is not finished until 2 o'clock Tuesday afternoon, when the council of ministers can find no way to reach agreement, for example, on agricultural prices or energy policy.*'

She also highlighted the rewards, especially the camaraderie and sometimes sheer excitement of reporting on EEC developments. The most exciting nights for Nel were during the talks on British membership: '*In 1962, in 1967 and finally the last, successful talks in the 1970s. All the more so as the Six always first had to agree on what they wanted to offer the British, Danes and Irish...*'

Geographically, the council of ministers' meetings relocated from Brussels to Luxembourg for the months of April through to October. Not in winter, Nel observed, because that would cause too many accidents during the exodus from Brussels via the 'misty and often icy roads' through the Ardennes Forest. *'This is tiring, because it is after all still a two to three hour drive and not always good weather. But it also has its charm. The European journalists know all the beautiful spots in the Grand Duchy and all the good game restaurants that lie hidden away in the Ardennes.'*

The work was inspiring, Nel insisted. *'It was initially a group of fifty journalists, which has now grown to 270. It is a colourful mix of nationalities, with Russians, Chinese, Japanese, Egyptians, Israelis and Nigerians who have added themselves to the ranks of the Europeans, Americans and Canadians…*

The press corps in Brussels is exceptionally fraternal – nobody sees any possibility of gathering the opinions of nine delegations on their own – you help each other out.' When a journalist took a break to eat in one of the all-night restaurants, they would leave their phone number. Their fellow journalists would alert them if anything happened, she explained, observing that *'there only has to be a rumour running like wildfire through the press room and the journalists' work rooms and everyone flies to a corner where an expert is making some statement.'*

The ministers met on the fourteenth floor of the Charlemagne building, next to Berlaymont. *'Often experts are so worn out there that they set forth downstairs to chat with the press. Often there's nothing in it, but sometimes it means "news" and an interim report. Assiduous colleagues that don't want you to miss it alert you.'*

Often there were long nights with little action, sustained by lots of sandwiches, beer, coffee and whisky. *'German colleagues swear by beer and white wine, the French drink red wine and the Scandinavians and Anglo-Saxons throw in their lot with the whisky. There is also a lot of gambling. The Italians play poker; the Dutch play dice; the Germans play chess. Others read, sleep or work on something else. Heated political discussions are also held.'*

In view of the endless controversies among the Nine, *'one must above all not build anything on the remarks of a single delegation. Every country at some stage has its weaknesses. I remember the creation of the community sugar policy based on the production quota, which cannot be exceeded. The Belgian sugar lobby, a powerful group, just wanted to produce at [will]. In that case, you must not believe everything that a Belgian tells you. And whatever they may say, all Nine are afraid of losing some of their sovereignty – and it is often easy to hide behind France.'*

That last sentence has especial poignancy for me in post-Brexit Britain, with Brexiteers behaving both before and after Brexit as if the whole of the EU is against Britain and no other EU country shares their concerns about sovereignty. As well, so much of Nel's Brussels writing conveys how hard the Dutch in particular fought in favour of UK accession against French obstruction.

Finally, Nel reported that there was no discrimination against women journalists, but warned: '*One thing is sure: a woman journalist must come very well prepared, because an expert begins by thinking that a woman after all does not know much about it. If he sees in an interview that you are well informed, then you have no problems... But woe betide a woman journalist if she makes a mistake! This is much worse than if her male colleague makes the same mistake. Sometimes it is a thankless job... For many, it is difficult to get the fruits of their hard work into the papers. What seems very important in Brussels is often overshadowed in their own country by national events...'*

There was perhaps no discrimination against women in Brussels, but the case is murkier regarding the AP's attitude. It is a tribute to Nel's deep commitment to Europe that no trace of bitterness crept into that report, undated but most likely written after she was forced to leave Brussels due to an escalating conflict with her nemesis, Carl Hartman. I doubt it's a coincidence that the AP ultimately backed Carl, both a male and much younger than Nel.

In November 1969, Nel had a serious car accident on her way to the first key press conference for a Common Market summit in The Hague – not surprising considering her appalling driving. Yolanda Frenkel Frank remembered it; she saw Nel from time to time in Brussels. "Yes, she had a terrible car accident and had to stay in hospital with whiplash, cursing like mad – the whole time cursing bloody Dutch drivers, but *she* was a completely awful driver."

Near her old apartment in Javastraat, the one-way system around the corner in Frederikstraat had changed since she left, and Nel followed her old route and drove down it the wrong way. She crashed into a taxi and was badly injured and forced to spend time in hospital. Gradually, she recovered. While recuperating, she stayed with a friend who lived near Brussels, Viscountess Laure de Jonghe d'Ardois.

In January, she wrote to the AP's Wes Gallagher in New York to thank him for his friendly note urging her to take time to get well, and for a gold AP decoration she received the previous October. Nel was probably less impressed by the medal than she would have been by a bigger pay rise. But in any case, she assured Gallagher she would soon be back on the beat.

"Presently I am training to walk properly – a little better and longer every day. My doctor assures me that by the end of January, I will be able to resume sprints for the telephone."

The AP's November 23–29 World Service reported Nel's absence from the November Common Market summit. It featured the landmark introduction of the English language at the summit, in anticipation of UK accession.

"There were 450 journalists at the Common Market's summit conference, and they found the Dutch admirable hosts. Foreign Minister Joseph Luns personally escorted an overflow of more than one hundred journalists to the floor of the meeting hall with one mild request: 'Just don't sit on the tables.'

"But there was one absentee – the AP's Nel Slis, who knows the way through the mysteries of this organisation like few others. Nel was injured in an automobile accident on the way to the first important news conference and probably will be out of action for the rest of the month.

"The Dutch, with a bow to the great British interest in the meeting, opened up the Common Market's press relations to a new language – English. It had never been considered necessary before. The AP staff – Carl Hartman, Eric Esih of the Bonn office and Bernard Veillet-Lavellee and Stephens Droening of the Paris bureau – welcomed the innovation, although between them the AP correspondents could handle half a dozen languages.

"Hartman got the first tip on how it would all come out. He saw a Luxembourg official standing alone in the Senate lobby. Hartman asked him how the negotiations with Britain had been worked out, and the man told him. Six hours later, the final result was announced just as he said."

No wonder Nel was chafing to get back, livid about missing the summit. She must have been infuriated by the reference to Hartman's 'tip', as there was fierce rivalry between them and they did not get along well.

This became a growing problem. The AP appreciated Nel's qualities as a reporter but was inclined to carp at her sometimes strange English. It's also likely that AP reservations about a woman reporter were still at play, especially such an allegedly – and sometimes really – 'difficult' one. Also, news agencies generally had a weakness for 'hot young reporters' – traditionally male – as against age and experience. Nel was well into her fifties.

Her efforts had, however, received some recognition. In October 1966, she had received a pay rise to 1,950 *guilders* (885 euros) 'upon merit considerations'. Brussels bureau chief Fred Cheval, ever impressed by her energy and persistence, said in his letter to her at the time: '*No doubt, you have fully deserved it, if one considers your tireless, day and night aggressive gathering of European Affairs information. I do not believe anyone could have maintained your pace in that facet of your duties and remained alive. You have survived and deserved the increase granted. You are an almost unequalled master in collecting information.*'

Nonetheless, the AP still felt her style and use of language left some room for improvement. To Nel's fury, she discovered less than a year later that her *bête noire*, Hartman, was to be sent from Bonn to Brussels because of the increasing importance of the EEC and the UK's impending accession. Kersting had to work hard to prevent her from writing an angry letter to AP General Manager Wes Gallagher in New York.

Hartman himself was evidently aware of how sensitive Nel was about his imminent arrival, writing a conciliatory letter to her from Bonn: '*If this seems hard on you, perhaps you can believe that I would like to do everything I can – in my own interests – to make it easier… What can we do to make it as painless as possible for one another? It would be nice to have a word from you.*'

It would be nice to know whether Nel ever replied to him and if so, how. Nel also continued to fret about her salary, as it did not leave much room for salting anything away for retirement. She always told younger journalists she would have to work until she dropped after retirement because she had such a meagre AP pension.

At the end of 1967, she wrote about these money matters to Stan Swinton, whom she knew best among the AP chiefs in New York. But she got nowhere, and even her sympathetic local boss Henk Kersting eventually got fed up with her harping on the subject, writing an unusually acerbic note to her: '*I ask you emphatically not to phone me anymore about this personal salary question, and not to phone the bureau either. First you phoned up Anneke and me (both working people), in the depths of the night, and then you phoned again to Mr Van Mierlo at the bureau. Everything would have been easier with a little letter. We are not a grocery store.*' Nonetheless, on Kersting and Cheval's recommendation, Nel's persistence was eventually rewarded by another salary rise of 50 dollars a month from March 1969.

The Slis/Hartman rivalry, however, went on getting worse rather than better, and the AP was increasingly unhappy about their disparate and uncoordinated Common Market coverage. Critical letters from London Bureau Chief Dick O'Regan in 1970 described Hartman's stories as too superficial and written too much from an American perspective, while Nel's were too detailed and too regionally oriented – giving some inkling of their essential incompatibility.

"There is a job for both of you to do in improving our Common Market coverage," O'Regan insisted. But a year later, O'Regan said in a letter to Cheval, Hartman and Nel, dated 26 May 1971, that there were still complaints from some AP bureaus that *'Hartman's copy can be too elementary, and Nel's copy is too confused'*.

Because of the non-communication between Nel and Hartman, the AP was also becoming irritated by double coverage, and ordered them to confer every morning on what they planned to write that day and what press conferences they were attending. They were also told to read each other's stories and keep each other informed about long-term projects they were working on.

Despite the AP's pleas that "there should not be any competition, but organized teamwork to produce the reports wanted," these directives only added fuel to the fire. When the same message was repeated from New York, it added insult to injury from Nel's point of view by stating that whereas 'Miss Slis' came administratively under Cheval, the AP production relating to the EEC was 'the responsibility of Mr. Hartman'. All Nel's copy should be read by him for 'editorial control'.

That must have been the final indignity for Nel, with her vast experience, to have to submit to this younger, probably better paid and even in the AP's own view, 'superficial' reporter. No doubt her copy did need editing, but this was no way to resolve what was clearly by then a very serious personality conflict between the two.

Notes from Hartman demonstrate this, and must have rubbed salt into Nel's wounds. *'Please check with me BEFORE requesting interviews with members of the EEC Commission'*... *'When you give me information on the telephone, please do NOT send the story to London yourself unless I ask you to do so.'* This would have been impossible for Nel to swallow, and no doubt she gave Hartman hell in return. It must have been an intolerable situation for both of them.

In due course, a diplomatically couched letter dated 6 April 1973 came from New York, '*neither punitive nor in any way connected to your relationships in Belgium*,' informing her that she was being transferred back to The Hague with effect from 1 June.

CHAPTER SIXTEEN

LEAVING BELGIUM: VALEDICTIONS

Friendships, Belgians, Europe, Dale on Slis

Nel left Brussels with mixed feelings. The Hartman affair had soured her last years there, but it had still been a wonderful period for her and she had many good new and old friends there. Among the Dutch were Han Boon, who had become Dutch ambassador to NATO, and Rudolf 'Peek' Pekelharing, formerly foreign ministry spokesman in The Hague, who became head of the NATO press service. Old friends from America Isaac Stern and his wife also visited Nel in Brussels when he was on a European tour. And Nel's close friend Laura de Jonge d'Ardois lived at Ukkel, near Brussels, and she spent many happy weekends there.

Tyna Wynaendts often came to stay for long weekends and holidays, and was grateful to Nel for nagging her to study languages. "Her own career was built on languages, and she always told me to be careful of your languages – it's so important, in the modern world you have to be international. She also influenced my parents to send me to France. Maybe they would have done this anyway, but she was very insistent. And it is true that I got my job at the OECD library because of languages. I wasn't really qualified to be a librarian, but they needed somebody who was at least bilingual or trilingual. So it helped me – as she told me, when you have your languages, you can always find a job."

However, Nel observed that in Belgium, a country with two official languages for everything, "It isn't always easy for the Dutch here, partly because of the linguistic problem. People don't realise that we don't take sides on the matter." In an interview with Brussels English-language magazine *The Bulletin* before leaving Belgium, Nel also spoke of a perennial misunderstanding between the Dutch and the Belgians on more fundamental grounds.

"They are so different. I think it's partly because the Dutch, whether they're Catholic, Protestant or Jewish, think like Calvinists, while the Belgians have a more flexible Catholic way of life. It's also a question of history. Belgium has been the victim of war and the balance of power; the country has always been a battlefield. It's very different from Holland, which has never had any wars except the Spanish and the German occupations." I'm not sure why she skipped the Napoleonic occupation of Holland here, but Belgium, sometimes dubbed the 'battlefield of Europe', has certainly suffered more from wars.

At the height of Holland's socialist era in the 1960s and early 1970s, Nel noted that there was a strong element of protest among the young, with movements like the Kabouters (hobgoblins) and Dolle Mina. But there was nothing comparable in Belgium.

"I think partly because of history: under stress, the Dutch protest, the Belgians are saboteurs. Also partly because of the preoccupation with the linguistic problem. Partly because the social structure here is more rigid than in Holland."

Nel had praise for Belgian women: "In Holland, women put great emphasis on getting university degrees, then they get married and give up work and just settle down to giving coffee parties. In Belgium, the number of women who work is much higher. And whereas the Dutch woman spends very little time on her looks, her Belgian sister takes great pains and looks much prettier."

Enlarging on this theme, she went on: "There are certainly just as many capable women in the Netherlands as in other countries, but I find they are way behind the women in other countries... [Holland] is the only country where emancipation is subsidised. In Belgium, where they still have Napoleonic laws, where women... until recently still needed written agreement from their husbands if they wanted to take a trip to England, [women] are much more independent. They work harder and take care that they still look good."

What Nel most admired about the Belgians was their ability to cope. "I admire the way they've absorbed the big international organisations like the Common Market and NATO."

Asked by *The Bulletin* whether journalism was a suitable profession for a woman, Nel was predictably emphatic. "Certainly. Women are discriminating and perspicacious, which makes them good journalists. But it's not true, as some people claim, that their sex gives them an advantage over men: or it may give them a short-term advantage, but this is offset by the fact that men find it hard to take a woman seriously on a serious subject."

In many ways, the Brussels period was the high point of Nel's career, especially in view of her huge interest in the European project. And after the initial struggle to master the EEC's complexities, she surely hit her mature journalistic prime, becoming a dominant figure on the Brussels scene.

Mulling European developments in 1981, seven years after leaving Brussels for The Hague and not long after she retired from the AP, Nel told me, "I still believe in Europe, very much. We mean nothing any more as individual countries, in world politics, and I think Europe is still the best place to live, personally – I love other parts of the world, but I wouldn't live anywhere other than Europe.

"Economically, we would benefit enormously by a united Europe. Also culturally. That [culture] is not even in the Treaty of Rome, though it's done a little bit, but not enough, by the Council of Europe. I very firmly believe in the great advantages of a united Europe politically, economically and culturally, while maintaining our differences…"

Nel's views on the potential size of 'Europe' and on de Gaulle's idea of Europe from the Atlantic to the Urals seem quite prophetic in the new millennium: "Well, I think personally we should start with what we have – and, of course, we now have Spain, Greece, Portugal coming in…Mmm, why not the whole Slav world? I often wonder if the Russians would ever go in for that, but the satellites, yes."

How did Nel see Holland's contribution? I wondered. "Well, it's a belief in Europe. Mostly selfish – its bread is buttered by Europe, certainly in the agricultural field but also in many other respects. Also Belgium and Holland are so central, we *are* Europe in a way. The achievements of Europe are, I think, enormous – very fast. In the beginning, it was a starry-eyed period. It has slowed down enormously, but imperceptibly it makes constant strides. A great breakthrough was Britain joining."

Summing up progress at that point in 1981, she said, "The first thing is getting people across borders. The agricultural market, however you want to say it, it's still a major feat, because had it not been achieved, south Italy and Germany would be empty with all the poor farming people going to the cities, and there boosting communism. It prevented extreme leftism.

"Secondly, the free market – you can move goods across very easily – Camembert and French wine here; that was impossible before the war – now you can get anything anywhere. Perfume costs the same here as in Paris. Thirdly, the exchange of capital. The European Monetary System has greatly helped the movement of capital and money matters. It helped to stabilise the system."

On Europe and the US, Nel said, "We'll always be interdependent, more and more so. We in Europe have become, not so much tired, but wise. It no longer makes for great civilisation – it's an old civilisation." So for Nel, 'Old Europe' would not be a dishonourable badge.

I have saved for last a crucial reminder, as we move further into the twenty-first century and World War II seems more distant:

"People always forget what has been done since we emerged from war, when people were at each other's throats. Now, in less than thirty years, it's made a lot of progress. Europe can play a very important role in the future, if it plays things well…"

For a personal sketch of Nel in Brussels at the height of her powers from one of her fellow journalists, my Paris-based journalist friend Alan Tillier came up with the name of Reginald Dale.

Dale arrived in Brussels in 1968 to report on the EEC for the *Financial Times*, when Nel had already been there for six years. Alan himself also met Nel in Brussels around that time and later visited her in her apartment in The Hague with Reggie Dale. He was complimentary. "Nel always made the EU understandable to a visiting fireman like me, cutting through the gobbledegook."

Dale spoke enthusiastically on the phone from Washington about Nel in her Brussels heyday:

"I can still see her clearly, a wonderful person. She could be very aggressive – that's not the right word; feisty, that's the right word – when dealing with people who weren't very cooperative. She was incredibly friendly to new journalists arriving in Brussels and often took them under her wing.

"She knew a lot of people, all the main players. She was close to the Dutch, of course, and also to the French, as she spoke French. Also to the Luxemburgers, Boschette, the Luxembourg commissioner; Jen Dondlinger, his successor. She knew everyone, and everyone knew her.

"Another friend was a Dutchman in the Commission, Edmund Wellenstein, a very senior official with a very good brain… A great friend of Nel's in the Commission was Clara Meyers, spokesperson for agriculture; they'd go off to places together. Another good friend was Emanuel de la Taille, well known on television. Later, when he stopped doing television, he ran a club for journalists in Paris...

"I can see Nel now, driving her little car, peering ahead with a determined expression. She was an erratic driver... but when she got stuck into something, she stuck to it. She had huge concentration in everything, whether it was complicated European questions like agricultural prices, it was the same spirit. She would go on and keep pestering until she got enough to explain it, enough for a story.

"Everyone knew her, she was a charismatic figure. You always knew when she was around, she was a huge presence. You'd see her frown of concentration, then she'd suddenly burst into a radiant smile.

"The main subject while I was in Brussels was enlargement: Britain, Ireland, Denmark, Norway. And the whole question of how the EEC should adapt to take in more members. The Hague triptych [the three pillars of policy] for enlargement and deepening came from a summit in The Hague in 1969. We also covered NATO, and I went on covering it afterwards.

"But I remember Nel much more in the EU context. We would wait for hours and hours outside, often all through the night; the press corps all knew each other well. Commission meetings were then in the Berlaymont building. You walked across the road to the Charlemagne building, where the Council of Ministers met. The press were on the ground floor and the ministers met on the fourteenth floor, so they had to get by us.

"Because Britain was not a member but the Dutch thought they should have been, they would brief journalists as an unofficial favour, first their own in Dutch and then the others in English, though in England there wasn't much interest in the EEC. There were only three British staff reporters at first: Charles Stevens at Reuters, P. Taft of *The Times* and me. Then de Gaulle died in 1969, and the negotiations started in 1970. It was the beginning of a huge influx of journalists.

"I didn't see Nel outside work because work took up so much time – occasionally, we would go riding, if there was a meeting in The Hague. When I moved to Paris later, Nel came for a short stay. I was in Nel's apartment in The Hague a couple of times. I was with her on the night they announced the new pope [Pope John Paul II]. Neither of us liked the cut of his jib.

"I loved seeing her there, but she was much more in her element in the huge press area in the EU, her laughter… So much of life there was in public. Nel liked a drink, but I never saw her the worse for wear for drink. At the time of the British entry negotiations, we'd be up three nights running to three or four in the morning.

"I can just picture her now very vividly, laughing. She had a great sense of humour, and a lot of funny stories, strange things in Dutch, which she'd translate. Quite obscene, some of them. Part of her good heart. A very generous person with a big heart.

"As you go through life, you meet a handful of people who are clearly larger than life. It's a privilege to have known them, and Nel is one of those."

HELLCAT OF THE HAGUE

(1973-2001)

CHAPTER SEVENTEEN
RETURN TO HOLLAND
Slis on the Dutch; a few more scoops

When she left Brussels, Nel still had yearnings for her first love, Paris. If offered it, she would have gone there like a shot. But the AP wasn't offering Paris but The Hague, where they had a staff shortage. Besides, the meagre AP pension she complained about so much made the generous Dutch state pension very attractive. She needed to be living there for five years to qualify for it, and coincidentally, she had just five years to go to the AP retirement age.

As she said, "It was time to think about the future. My pension from AP is *poor*. Americans do not understand what a pension is and Europeans are in their eyes *second hand*. They come completely at the bottom of the ladder."

As soon as she heard about her transfer to Holland, Nel wrote to her new bureau chief, John Gale, to thank him for letters he had written to her. They "contributed to soothing my traumas due to a lack of Brussels office courteousness," she told him. There was an understandable tinge of bitterness in this thinly veiled reference to that thorn in her flesh, Hartman.

On the money front, Nel had another financial ace up her sleeve in the form of that fertile piece of land in Goeree-Overflakkee. Almost the first thing she did back in Holland was to sell her land. She told me she was happy that she went there in person to sell it instead of leaving it to intermediaries, finding the islanders appreciated the personal contact. I feel this was mutual.

With the money from the sale of the land, she bought an apartment in The Hague found by her friend Johanna Beek, Yolanda's mother. Here she was to live for the rest of her life until she had to go into a home, and it was here that I used to visit her in the 1990s. A light and airy first-floor apartment in a modern apartment block by the sea, it was about twenty minutes by tram from the city centre.

The rooms were arranged off a small hallway. In Nel's study, the faithful filing cabinet, telex, telephone and fax were still there when I visited. And there were the piles of newspapers no journalists could do without before and, for many, even after everything went online.

A comfortable, relatively large sitting room was on the same side as the study. On the other side were Nel's bedroom and a guest bedroom, as well as the bathroom and small kitchen. Antique furniture inherited or acquired by Nel along the way, bookcases, paintings and photos of friends and places lined the walls. The surrounding balconies gave a glimpse of the nearby dunes.

Nel's finances were a bit of a mystery to me. She was always complaining about her meagre AP salary and the extra expenses that a woman correspondent incurred in order to be well turned out. But she still managed to buy expensive clothes and she always looked extremely smart. She also travelled extensively, well into her last years. How, I sometimes wondered, did she manage all of these expenses?

Part of the answer is that, like other journalists, she supplemented her AP income by those *schnabbeltjes*, writing for magazines and other publications. She also inherited the Biarritz house from her friend Jacqueline, and presumably salted something away when she sold it. But probably the biggest help in the last stretch of her life did come from those 'fat hectares' of Goeree, enabling her to buy the apartment in The Hague outright and live rent and mortgage-free. So for the first time in her life, Nel had a home of her own.

She remained in Holland thereafter, much as she sometimes kicked against the pricks. "Yes, I found it very difficult to get back," she admitted. "I feel, frankly, at home in most countries in Europe – I'm even getting used to postwar Germany, a beautiful place. Personally, I find other countries more attractive and if I had money and time, I would have a second house in France or Italy – still the cradle of European civilisation."

Indeed, Nel always considered herself more European than Dutch. But while I was looking into what John Gale called her 'last fling at covering the Dutch', I came across some of her pieces showing what she thought about her own country, its culture and its people. One that appealed to me was a thoughtful article actually written about a decade earlier, just before the Brussels phase. This seems to me to encapsulate many enduring characteristics of the country and its people. Some warmth about the Dutch nation and its peculiar history percolates through, along with evocative images of the countryside.

The Dutch are, Nel wrote, *'conditioned by three C's – the climate, Calvinism and curiosity about people and things abroad'.* First, the climate:

The Dutch are apt to apologise for their climate, as though they themselves had invented it. Most Dutchmen take a wry pride in the fact that the climate of the Netherlands is damp, that the skies are always a luminous grey, and that the sun only makes its appearances on the birthdays of the members of the House of Orange. Making depreciatory remarks about the climate is one criticism that the Dutch themselves still enthusiastically agree with.

And yet the Dutch evidently thrive in this climate, for they are an active, bustling lot, almost bursting out of the dikes which protect them from the ever-covetous waves.

Then it's on to Nel's perpetual gripe about heavy taxes on single employees, and her preoccupation with Holland's high birth and low mortality rates and ever-growing population. Paradoxically, population density seemed to be a bigger concern back when it was at 10 million than in the twenty-first century at 17 million and rising – though as in other European countries, there have been intermittent immigration stresses and strains.

Presciently describing efforts to reduce the population as Quixotic tilting at windmills, Nel then homed in on the iconic Dutch windmill, much reduced from 7,000 in the seventeenth century – and peaking at over 9,000 – to about 1,200 at the time she was writing. In those past centuries, before becoming pretty tourist attractions, she reminds her readers that windmills were literally the engines of the Dutch economy. They drained land for agriculture, powered production and were an essential force in shipbuilding, driving the Netherlands' seafaring Golden Age.

By the 1960s, the population of 10 million was living in an area of 12,530 square miles, over half of which were below sea level, including Amsterdam,

Rotterdam, The Hague and Haarlem – and with Schiphol Airport some fourteen feet below sea level.

As well as those windmills of old pumping out water to make land, Nel remarked that "ever since the thirteenth century, the Dutch have been building dikes to keep their feet dry." Hence a country of dikes and bikes – the title of that little book Nel wrote about Holland – as well as windmills.

Noting that windmills left over from the pre-technological era were 'reverently' guarded by the Dutch monuments organisation, Nel confidently predicted they would remain a feature of the flat Dutch landscape. She was right about that too, as they are still there, guarded like an endangered species. Kinderdijk, with the world's biggest collection of windmills, is on the UNESCO world heritage list. Nowadays, the windmill's successor, the lanky 'sustainable energy' wind turbine, is more prevalent, dotting the land and seascape around the Netherlands as in other countries. Despite such changes, I found Nel's description of the Dutch landscape still resonated with me:

> This landscape, dead and dreary in winter and blossoming in the summer with green foliage and the white sails of boats floating along the canals, is always dominated by the huge expanse of luminous and ever-changing sky. This wonderful light helped to create the golden age of painting in 17th-century Holland, when wealthy Dutch merchants were immortalised in canvas by such masters as Rembrandt and Frans Hals.

Controlling nature has been an integral part of Dutch history, she reminded her readers. 'In the last 2,000 years the Dutch have gained 1,453,000 acres from the sea and lost 1,400,000.' Even as Nel was writing, a twelfth province was being created, 'turning the eel-rich Zuyderzee into the province of Flevoland, wresting 550,000 acres from the sea.'

Nel rated the southwest province of Zeeland a major bulwark of Calvinism, the rather harsh strain of Protestantism that took root in various degrees of dourness in the Netherlands. She recorded that when the Zeeland farmers' wives were saved from the disastrous 1953 flood, one of their main concerns was to have their sea-soaked white lace caps stiffened in time to go to church the following Sunday.

Another side effect of the various branches of Calvinism that flourished in the country was that even up to the late 1960s, everything in Holland was still run along denominational lines, including education, radio and television, trade unions and even political parties.

'*There are some fifty different shades of protestant Christians, and arguments about such things as the role of the snake in the Garden of Eden take place even among Dutch right-wing political parties.*' Only three of the eight parliamentary parties were non-denominational. This denominationalism gradually dissipated over the following decades, but I believe some element of Calvinism will endure as an ingredient baked into the Dutch psyche.

Nel also claimed that denominational thinking influenced Dutch literature, little known in the outside world because of the language barrier. Three of the great figures of Dutch literature were internationally known, but that was because they wrote in Latin. They were fifteenth-century humanist and theologian Erasmus, seventeenth-century jurist and theologian Grotius, and his contemporary Spinoza, the theologian and philosopher.

'*Spinoza's Jewish-Portuguese parentage is also evidence of the open-armed welcome that Holland has given to refugees. This attitude, a blend of charity and of stern justice, is a natural result of the country's strong religious tradition,*' Nel wrote. Here again, although churchgoing may have gone out of fashion, I believe this charity-and-justice blend is another ingredient written into the DNA of the Dutch.

Nel's piece ended up with the adventurous, exploratory side of the Dutch. I felt this was what Nel liked best about her compatriots, as it chimed with her own nature. As she put it, '*the average Dutch citizen is far less reserved, serious, non-effusive and plodding than he looks. Climate and Calvinism may stiffen his spine, but his curiosity, imagination, individualism and sense of humour make him far from stodgy.*'

She claimed the discovery of Australia and New Zealand for the Dutch and listed their former colonies in the two Americas, in Asia and in South Africa. The Dutch sailed up the Hudson and they founded New Amsterdam, now New York. '*In the Dutchman, brought to a halt by the sea, there is that deep-lying urge to pioneer and explore, to innovate and invent in all spheres of human activity... Throughout the centuries, the Dutch have sailed the seven seas...*' And Nel's observation that '*world travellers will run into Dutchmen all over the globe, from the Far East to Africa*' remains every bit as true today.

They are, she declared, a nation of traders, transporters and brokers. As well as the sea, the great rivers have played a key role in trade, with two of Europe's main arteries, the rivers Rhine and Meuse, reaching the North

Sea through Rotterdam. Europe's largest harbour, Rotterdam sprawls across the Rhine estuary, forming a major gateway to the European continent. Remarking that Rotterdam breathed activity, Nel also singled it out as the only Dutch city endowed by wealthy citizens with works of art.

Her piece finished with a nod to the capital, Amsterdam: '*Holland's pride, because it is Holland's most beautiful city.*' After her return, Nel frequently drove to Amsterdam for press conferences, Foreign Press Association meetings and parties – including mine. This went on until well into her seventies, with her driving becoming increasingly terrifying for any unwitting passengers.

While she was discussing the Dutch with me, Nel also remarked on another element: their lack of moderation. "They either go overboard one way or the other. In the 1960s with sex on the radio, they had it up to the point of impudence, on TV and radio. I mean, I'm all for freedom of sex and such things, but there were such unsavoury programmes on these things, it was totally unnecessary. The same is true when they go the other way, being too priggish. There is a lack of moderation sometimes."

When I asked her what she considered the country's strengths, she said, "A country of tremendous freedom and charity. I think it comes from Calvinism – there's a good and a bad side, the Dutch get nice when you're really in the soup. Of course, I feel why not profit from it earlier, but here, you have to be really *dans la merde...* But they stand by you then; it's a good quality. They immediately collect for the Chinese or whatever – partly Calvinism, you know, the Bible, guilt feelings. They're helpful, they don't like to see people in trouble."

Nel had a couple of other approving comments, though she couldn't resist a sting in the tail: "And I do think, on the whole, culturally, they make a great effort. We have wonderful music, better than Belgium, and there's still a lot of art, painting. The bookshops are thriving, much better than we had in Belgium. I mean, there are advantages to Holland – art, culture. Even though the Dutch always know everything better, they sit there judging, they're very, very smug."

On her return in the 1970s, Nel found herself writing about the relatively novel topics of prosperity and revolt. The Netherlands was changing from a 'staid and stable country' into an 'avant-garde land with a radical youth and aggressive media' and action groups on everything under the sun. A new openness on television was demonstrated by the filming of an abortion and by TV discussions of death and other taboos. And she was pleased to find the formerly meek press corps at last getting tough with taboos and authorities.

From her regular coverage of religious affairs, Nel had an acute grasp of the role these played in Dutch society. Despite the shift to free thinking, the 45% of Roman Catholics versus 25% Protestants and 30% humanists in the population in the 1970s still seemed surprisingly high. But as Nel pointed out, even the Catholics and no doubt also the humanists in Holland were in a certain way Calvinistic. Meanwhile, the Roman Catholic Church itself had come a long way from 1955, when the Dutch bishops prohibited 'their' politicians from joining the socialist party. By the 1970s, almost half the 150-seat parliament was leftist, and this included many Roman Catholics.

Older people were most aware of the increased prosperity, Nel discovered. Her own faithful Aagje was roped in here as a seventy-eight-year-old charwoman who said she had 'never had it so good'. Among the young, Nel found a growing tendency to revolt. A wave of rebellion that started in the early 1960s against the establishment and obsolete traditions came from groups calling themselves the 'provos' and '*kabouters*' (gnomes). These groups also took up the fight against pollution, which they considered the most acute symptom of a sick society.

Nel was often quite scathing about her compatriots and their culture, but never more so than about women and emancipation. In her 1981 interview, this produced quite a rant: "I think Dutch women are a case apart – they're so smug and self-satisfied on the whole. One, they're the most backward, even compared with Ireland, Italy, Austria. The younger women are a little different, but I find even among Dutch women journalists very little solidarity, very little interest one for the other." The best crowd, she reckoned, were the countrywomen, who ran courses on politics.

"But in all the places where I've worked, London, Belgium, France and all over, I've found there's greater friendliness and solidarity among women journalists than in Holland. Here, they're still, as they say, catching flies off each other."

Warming to her theme, she burst out: "I think it is GROTESQUE the way they go about subsidising so-called emancipation. The Rode Vrouwen and the countrywomen are the only two organisations that have some goodness in them. WHY subsidise emancipation? Why not have it come from the various organisations to help each other push for women's rights?

They should subsidise creches – what women need – so that women who want to work have the facilities. If they don't know what they need, then they should not be subsidised. Now they use the subsidies for sitting and meeting and commissions, and all sorts of useless things. It is a scandal.

"Here, women are all divided – the academics pooh-pooh the businesswomen; they pooh-pooh the soroptomists, the soroptomists pooh-pooh someone else. They're all divided in little clubs, and they're an unbearable lot anyway."

Many foreign career women settling in the Netherlands in the 1980s and 1990s would have been inclined to agree. When I came to live in Holland in 1979, I was shocked to discover the meagre extent of women's participation in the working life of the nation compared with other European countries. And single men as well as working women suffered from the fact that society was arranged on the assumption that anybody going out to work would have a wife at home to take care of things and do the shopping, let the plumber in, and so on. Virtually all the shops closed at 5 pm. After debating later shop opening hours for more than two decades, these eventually arrived at the end of the twentieth century. Unfortunately, progress in women's participation continued rather slowly, though it has speeded up in the new millennium.

In her day, Nel herself was an almost unique career woman role model for other Dutch women. If Nel had married Dan Schorr and had children, though, I'm afraid that she would have found it virtually impossible at that time to combine this with a career in journalism. The ambitious Schorr was hardly house-husband material. Also, even into the 1970s, combining motherhood and work was still extremely difficult for journalists in most parts of the world. As Irish journalist Isabel Conway said:

"You see all those photographs of Nel in the old days. Oh, she was so stylish, she was the real thing. She was tough because you had to be as a woman journalist then, and there was no compromise, you just had to, you were married to your job, that's how it was then. To be honest, when I started in the 1970s, it was very similar in Ireland. You couldn't combine it with other things. You were either in for it, the whole thing, or you didn't do it. You retired, got married."

It was Tyna Wynaendts who conveyed to me the depth of Nel's belief in the importance for women of independence and access to wider horizons. This was the core of her own emancipation credo, and was also what she encouraged in other women. Growing up in Goeree-Overflakkee, she must have seen how the wives lived, "a slave to their husbands," said Tyna.

Nel also detested the small-mindedness and cramped, watchful attitudes, "where everybody knows everybody else and comments on them." This was certainly not confined to her island. One can think, for example, of the small mirrors still to be seen outside the windows of Dutch houses for spying on everything going on outside.

Therefore, said Tyna, "knowing how difficult it was for women to get on professionally, Nel would privilege women and help them a lot." Occasionally, Nel's determined support for women could have bizarre results. When Tyna became engaged to Jean Jacques, the ambassador in Brussels remarked that she was very lucky. "Nel said no, HE was very lucky, and that became a real fight. They were both competing on who in this new couple, Jean Jacques or myself, was the luckiest one to have found the other one. And it was a real fight; they never spoke to one another again."

Nel very consciously sought to help women in their professional lives. When she was younger, she left her money in her will to an association in Holland that promoted birth control, because she felt that was what women needed to obtain their freedom and to be able to build up their careers. "She thought women should be able to choose whether to have children or not, and she wanted to help this," said Tyna. Later, with contraceptives widely available, this became unnecessary, and Tyna became Nel's heir.

Though doubtless delighted with the arrival of contraceptives, Nel was out of tune with the provocative sexual liberation movement and somewhat aggressive feminism she encountered on her return to Holland. "They had a very revolutionary way of looking at it. These people often are provocative, and she would have nothing to do with that. She was very much a lady," Tyna recalled.

This seemed paradoxical to me, considering Nel's own often unladylike behaviour. Tyna thought this over and said, "She was too neutral to be engaged politically, but she had very strong opinions – without being like others who had similar opinions. She would never mix with the Dolle Mina ('Mad Mina' feminist group)."

"Perhaps she felt they put more emphasis on shouting about their rights than actually going out and doing something," I suggested.

"But sometimes you need those kinds of people too," Tyna said. "But I think Nel was very much a *lady*, with all that that means. She had a very high sense of quality for all things – in her personal life, but also in literature, in the friends that she chose. She was not influenced by the idea of being a part of a social section of society. She made up her own mind on everything."

Tyna learned from Nel to perceive the world from a broader perspective than the confines of Dutch opinion. "She always said, don't just stay here in Holland, there's much more. And when we were travelling, she always gave me another perspective on things – really, that it's not just the opinion of high society in The Hague that's important. The world is a lot larger and there are other opinions. And that was very valuable."

Independence was also the pleasure of simply being able to buy things. "She liked buying a lot, and that's one of the things she said, it's wonderful being independent, you don't have to ask anybody whether you can or not, and if you spend it foolishly, it's your own responsibility and nobody can tell you maybe you're spending too much on shoes or whatever. She said make sure you're in that position, so that you can do exactly what you like."

When Tyna was growing up, Nel's influence complemented that of her mother, Nel's best friend from the island. "I'm grateful that the adult woman I could identify with was my mother, for many, many very good things, but Nel was sort of additional, a role model of a woman who could look after herself and earn her own living, and who was intellectually creative, and I'm very grateful for that."

Nel's often derogatory views on Dutch women and their movements did not prevent her from taking a professional interest in matters relating to women and feminism in the 1970s, and she was always willing to write for women's publications. She wrote about feminist magazine *Opzij* when it was launched in the early 1970s, and later she herself wrote for *Opzij*. Privately, Nel must have had a pretty low opinion of its early efforts, though it later became far more professional and successful.

Another of Nel's reports I found was on a woman who made it to an important political post in the Labour (PvdA) Party. In an odd slip-up in the lead, Nel likened her to Peggy, presumably meaning Maggie, Thatcher. There are no obvious clues in this piece to Nel's private reactions, but she probably approved of this Labour leader's undogmatic, democratic views and of her contacts with other women socialists around Europe.

With her indefatigable nose for news, Nel continued to have her share of 'primeurs' or scoops through the 1970s. She made a big impact with her coverage of a French embassy hostage-taking by Japanese Red Army terrorists in 1974. Then there was the armed hijacking of a train by South Moluccan independence fighters in 1977, the assassination of a British ambassador and KLM hijackings.

The Japanese Red Army hijacking of the French Embassy in The Hague in 1974 provided a particularly dramatic scoop. In the AP obituary for Nel, journalist Anthony Deutsch recorded that '*Slis actually witnessed the takeover by Japanese Red Army terrorists of the embassy. After scrambling to the rooftop of a nearby bookstore, she lay crouched in the shadows as they emerged with heavy weapons. She later told the story in an eyewitness report.*' Nel's reporting received wide international coverage.

In the 1976 hijacking of a KLM plane by three Palestinians who boarded it in Spain, the Palestinians threatened to blow up the plane in mid-air unless Israel released eight jailed guerrillas. The Tel Aviv government refused, but passengers and crew were eventually released unharmed in Abu Dhabi. Nel got hold of the story of the plane's cliffhanger in Tunis, where it landed with enough fuel for only another fourteen minutes flying:

"The airport horrified the pilot by refusing landing permission, turning off its approach lights and placing obstacles along the runway to prevent the aircraft landing. Captain Janssen was furious. 'I think it's a disgusting scandal that the authorities there bluntly refused to allow us to land. We were an aircraft in an emergency situation. We didn't have enough fuel to go anywhere else.' Fortunately, they were able to touch down safely because the airport had forgotten to switch its automatic landing system off. The landing gear was slightly damaged when it hit some oil drums on the runway."

On Dutch politics and premiers, always among a foreign correspondent's special interests, she wrote solid pieces on the socialist government that took office in May 1973 and on its premier, Joop den Uyl. An important event under den Uyl's premiership was the granting of independence to Surinam, marking the end of the Dutch colonial period.

Nel's first piece on den Uyl homed in on the new government's income-levelling plans for taxation and what people thought of these. For this, she roped in her friend and advisor Piet Wackie Eysten, who provided a coolly negative assessment, arguing that low wage earners already had numerous advantages over higher earners.

Nel also interviewed den Uyl on Europe and on his wider foreign policy stance. Den Uyl, I felt, enjoyed being interviewed by Nel, and the pieces were historically significant. Den Uyl was a backer of European integration but wanted democratisation via a strong European parliamentary system. He also wanted to bring the Scandinavian countries into the EU.

In Nel's 1975 interview, den Uyl, then about to be the first West European leader to visit US President Gerald Ford after the fall of Saigon and the ending of the Vietnam War, took a fairly hard line on the US, expressing his preference for a strong Europe, independent of the US. Privately, Nel probably found some if not all of his views quite attractive.

On decolonisation, den Uyl put his money where his mouth was, with Surinam becoming independent at end-1975. The last piece I found while den Uyl was premier was written about Surinam just ahead of its independence. Considering that most of its miniscule population wound up in the Netherlands, it was startling to read that Surinam is four times the size of Holland and that 80 % of it was then unexplored jungle.

While he was prime minister, den Uyl personally recommended Nel for the Orange Order, symbol of knighthood. His recommendation was an honour in itself, as most journalist candidates were nominated by the culture ministry. As a result, Nel's name appeared at the top of the list of decorations in the official Gazette.

Piet Wackie Eysten remembered Nel receiving letters, telegrams and telexes of congratulations literally from all over the world on her knighthood. From Brussels, the AP's Fred Cheval lauded the honour as coming from 'those you have been after, all these years', while a former Dutch ambassador from the Indonesian decolonisation days recorded that he never had to hesitate in trusting Nel.

Den Uyl also presented the decoration to Nel personally. One of the many interviews with Nel around her eightieth birthday recorded that den Uyl stuck at least three safety pins in her chest trying to put it on. Former government information service chief Gijs van der Wiel said she was the only journalist in his entire career to be awarded the decoration personally by a prime minister. That AP obituary of Nel quoted den Uyl as remarking, "She is certainly difficult, but I still love her a little."

Just a few years after her return, and also during den Uyl's premiership, Nel was to find herself once again embroiled in covering a scandal involving the monarchy, as the Lockheed bribery affair involving Queen Juliana's husband, Prince Bernhard, broke. We take a closer look at this next.

CHAPTER EIGHTEEN
THE LOCKHEED AFFAIR

The Prince and the Aircraft-maker – The Big Fudge

It was during Nel's last stint with the AP that she found herself covering the biggest scandal of the century involving the Dutch royal family. In 1976, Queen Juliana's husband, Prince Bernhard, was implicated in a US bribery inquiry into US aircraft-maker Lockheed.

The scandal broke during Joop den Uyl's premiership. In February 1976, a US Senate subcommittee on multinational corporations revealed that bribes to promote Lockheed aircraft sales in the Netherlands were paid to an unidentified high-ranking Dutch official. The official was subsequently inferred to be Prince Bernhard. A commission of three distinguished Dutchmen was set up to investigate the allegations, specifically that one million dollars was paid to the 'official' in 1960–62 and a further 100,000 dollars in 1972.

Voluminous quantities of AP copy in Nel's archives took up the story from the completion of the commission's report in August. Although the huge output was a team effort, I find it easy to imagine Nel herself engaged with the story virtually round the clock for weeks on end. She was by then approaching her sixty-third birthday, but with no sign of flagging energy.

Besides, it was an exciting news story: the queen's consort apparently caught with his hand in the Lockheed till. Would the queen survive, let alone Bernhard? A constitutional crisis seemed quite probable.

Nel's bulky Lockheed archive started on Monday 17 August, when the independent commission had delivered its report and the government was studying it. Den Uyl planned to report to parliament a week or so later. Ahead of den Uyl's statement, the Dutch press were claiming that Bernard had not been cleared, or alternatively that there was no evidence that he took the money but he must have known that some of his associates accepted Lockheed payoffs.

A Slis report six days later said Queen Juliana had returned home from Italy to take a hand in the political situation, along with Bernhard himself. Nel's 'highly placed source' informed her that it seemed clear that there would be no proof that Bernhard accepted Lockheed funds, but that 'there are indications his business dealings have created a delicate political situation for the monarchy'. The source did not, however, believe an enforced abdication likely, as no cabinet minister would support so drastic a step.

Another government source added that nothing in the Dutch constitution said the monarch would have to go, even if the commission's seventy-page report failed to absolve the prince. Bernhard, Nel noted, was inspector general of the Dutch armed forces and a member of two government advisory bodies – the defence council and a cabinet committee that helped prepare the Dutch budget. This was among an enormous number of other posts he held.

The queen retreated to Italy the next day, after talks with den Uyl. As head of state, it turned out that she had an important voice in the final formulation of the government's conclusions about the report's findings. On Wednesday 25 August, the government announced it would report to parliament the next day. The royal couple flew home yet again. They did quite a bit of commuting between Italy and Holland just then.

The next morning, an unattributed report in *De Telegraaf* newspaper said Prince Bernhard would resign as inspector general of the Dutch armed forces. When den Uyl reported to parliament later in the day, this turned out to be true. From seven that evening to five-thirty the following morning, a vast flood of AP news reports and text excerpts from the inquiry report flowed out, scarcely pausing for breath in the morning before launching into commentary. The AP continued to pour out reports well into September.

The first Slis report on Thursday 26 August trumpeted: '*Prince Bernhard was accused Thursday of damaging the Dutch national interest in the Lockheed affair and was swept out of his various defence posts, including his job as Inspector General of the Dutch armed forces.*' Among wide coverage of the story in international newspapers the next day, it made it to the front-page lead in the *Salt Lake Tribune*. This is relatively succinct, so I can't resist putting most of it in here.

Dutch Prince Resigns Posts Over Lockheed Affair
By Nel Slis
Associated Press Writer

THE HAGUE, Netherlands – An inquiry commission accused Prince Bernhard on Thursday of damaging Dutch national interest by improper dealings with the Lockheed Aircraft Corp., and he resigned his public functions.

Premier Joop den Uyl told a tense and sombre parliament the government has asked Queen Juliana's 65-year-old husband to resign all posts where a conflict of interest might arise, including his duties as inspector general of the Dutch armed forces.

The Socialist premier said a three-member independent commission reported there was no conclusive evidence to prove the allegation that the prince received $1.1 million from Lockheed to promote the sales of its aircraft in the Netherlands, and there was no evidence the prince had influenced official procurement policy.

But the inquiry had concluded he "entered much too frivolously into transactions which were bound to create the impression he was susceptible to favours," den Uyl said.

"Later, he showed himself open to dishonourable requests and offers. Finally, he allowed himself to be tempted to take initiatives which were completely unacceptable and which were bound to place himself and the Netherlands procurement policy in the eyes of Lockheed – and it must now be added also in the eyes of others – in a dubious light."

Den Uyl's statement, broadcast to a nation that held the royal family in high esteem, said the prince would also get out of business life.

Official spokesmen said there was no constitutional crisis affecting the queen's position. They said none of the five parties in den Uyl's left-center government want the queen to step down as a result of the Commission's finding and the government's decision to force Bernhard to resign his public posts.

There had been speculation in the Dutch press that the 67-year-old queen, an immensely wealthy woman who has an unpretentious style, might abdicate...

Considerable background on the prince was given in the AP wire reports. The prince had been a key figure in the Dutch armed services since the end of World War II. On his return to the Netherlands with the liberating allied forces from exile in London, he held advisory posts with the navy and air force before becoming inspector general for the combined services in 1970. This entailed informing and advising the defence minister.

Den Uyl read out in parliament the prince's somewhat mealy-mouthed letter of resignation from his defence posts. Bernhard said contacts of many years' standing with old Lockheed friends had developed along 'the wrong lines', and he had not observed the caution required due to his 'vulnerable position as consort of the queen and as prince of the Netherlands'.

The commission report failed to provide conclusive evidence that the prince ever took possession of the 1.1 million dollars in Lockheed funds, but said it could not be ruled out that money reached the prince or his nominees without being recorded in the royal bookkeeping. It noted there had been increasingly friendly contacts between the prince and Lockheed's former head Robert Gross in the 1950s.

In 1959–60, Lockheed officials had apparently considered making a gift of a Jetstar business jet to the prince for his personal use. However, because of difficulties in registering the title, Fred Meuser, the company's Dutch-born former Swiss representative, suggested a one-million-dollar gift instead. Meuser turned out to be an old friend of the prince.

There was also testimony given by former Lockheed vice chairman A.F.C. Kotchian to the US Securities and Exchange Commission and the US Senate subcommittee on multilateral corporations, saying that payments were made abroad using Swiss lawyer Hubert Weisbrod as an intermediary: 300,000 dollars in 1960, 300,000 dollars in 1961 and 400,000 dollars in 1962, authorised successively by Robert Gross in 1960 and other officials in the later years. Weisbrod had been appointed by Meuser.

In a letter to the Dutch commission, Prince Bernhard told the investigators he neither received the money nor had it directly or indirectly at his disposal. But he said about 100,000 dollars went to 'a few mutual acquaintances' who needed financial support for social reasons.

In tracing the transfer procedure from Lockheed to bank accounts in Europe, the commission came across the name of a former Polish army officer, Col. Pantchoulidzew, who was a personal friend of Bernhard's late mother, Princess Armgard. The commission concluded that Pantchoulidzew's role was to tell Weisbrod to which accounts the money should be transferred. Under the circumstances, the report said, Lockheed had a valid reason to assume the money intended for the prince had in fact reached him.

After den Uyl's speech, the AP proclaimed: "In twenty crowded minutes, den Uyl signalled the end of Bernhard's long career as one of Holland's leading men of affairs," leaving the Dutch to take stock of the shattered image of their merchant prince. The speech was broadcast live on television and radio. MPs listened 'somberly' and then went off to read the 240-page commission report. The many business activities from which the prince was also to withdraw included seats on the boards of the national airline KLM, Dutch-German VFW-Fokker Aircraft and Hoogovens steel group. He was also patron of over 300 other organisations.

The commission said in its report that it could not state with certainty the destination of nine-tenths of the famous one million dollars. It did, however, succeed in establishing that in 1967 to 1968, Lockheed management approached the prince on several occasions for information and intervention in the possible procurement by the Dutch of the P-3 Orion naval aircraft. The prince was offered 500,000 dollars if he used his influence on their behalf. Although he refused, this was only based on the impracticality of the request and not on principle. His friendly relationship with Lockheed continued.

In another piece of financial skulduggery, it emerged that in around 1968, Lockheed established an off-the-books account of 400,000 dollars, administered by the Paris law firm Coudert Frères. From this, a 100,000 dollar payment was made to a Swiss bank in the name of Victor Baarn. Baarn is the name of a Dutch village close to the royal palace at Soest, which seemed decidedly fishy. The commission said Bernhard explicitly denied receiving the money, and it had found no evidence to the contrary. Nor had it been able to identify the person using the 'apparently fictional name' of Victor Baarn.

A more damning revelation was a handwritten letter in September 1974, in which Bernhard returned to the subject of the P-3 Orion and asked for a commission on the sale if the Dutch decided to buy the aircraft. This would have been worth about one million dollars. The prince told the commission he wanted the money for the World Wildlife Fund, of which he was the long-time head. Commenting sourly that 'the end did not justify the means', the commission report continued with a further genteel rapping of Bernhard's knuckles:

'*The concealed threat contained in the second letter written by H.R.H. and the reference to the many efforts he had made to get the right decisions based on political considerations, form a whole which must be described as extremely questionable.*'

The commission also pointed out that with a company like Lockheed that was permanently in the market for the sale of its aircraft, it was absolutely essential to avoid even the appearance of being open to influence. '*Through his conduct, the prince achieved exactly the opposite and this must be regarded as extremely imprudent and unwise,*' it remarked, rather mildly in the circumstances.

Although the commission found no evidence that the offer of gifts influenced the prince's judgement, it did stress the fact that Lockheed felt able to make such 'improper requests' and offers – which were furthermore not unequivocally refused. Besides, the prince himself approached Lockheed with equally improper requests for commissions.

In the event, the Orion project fell through. The proposal to purchase new naval aircraft was scrapped from the Dutch defence budget on economic grounds.

Perhaps most mind-boggling was the commission's statement that although it found no conclusive evidence that the prince ever took possession of the 1.1 million dollars, it could not exclude the possibility that the money reached Bernhard or his nominees without being recorded in the prince's books. In effect, it appeared to be saying that we can't prove you have the money but we can't prove you don't. Overall, the whole thing looked like an almighty fudge.

When the Donner report went on sale to the public the next day at 15 *guilders* (5.60 dollars), the first two impressions of 5,000 and 10,000 copies sold out within hours, and the state publishing house had to hastily print a third impression.

Dutch newspapers were quick to condemn Prince Bernhard. The leftist *Volkskrant*, for example, found the Donner Commission's report extremely painful reading, and Prince Bernhard's statement no less so. '*The display and admission of actions which are contrary to the views and values of the Netherlands is in itself depressing. And when it concerns the husband of the head of state, it is a traumatic experience for a large part of the population.*' Further, '*the prince has moved in a corrupt atmosphere that is to be abominated and which has injured the feelings of very many people towards the royal family.*'

Den Uyl commented that the government had allowed the prince a great deal of freedom of movement in the exercise of his functions, based on the confidence that members of the royal house were aware how interwoven their private lives were with the national interest. If the national interest could be damaged by contacts or activities, there was a duty to consult with responsible ministers. It was unacceptable that the prince should have failed to report on his relations with Lockheed.

Den Uyl endorsed the inquiry's view that Bernhard's performance had been 'fruitful and admirable' in many fields on behalf of his country, but added that the government 'deplores all the more that Prince Bernhard has become involved in relationships and situations which are unacceptable'.

An opinion poll the following Monday showed an astonishing 71 % said their feelings about Prince Bernhard were unchanged, with only 28 % saying their feelings had changed. While 61 % agreed that the prince should no longer carry out official functions, no less than 90 % said the monarchy should stay.

That Monday was another hectic reporting day as the parliamentary debate took place. Nel's wrap was running on the wire in the small hours of the next morning. She reported that the Dutch government was committed to a 'searching' review of its future relationship with royal figures and their freedom in fulfilling their public roles. A new bill would be submitted to parliament defining which royals would be subject to ministerial responsibility and thus supervision.

As Nel pointed out in her wrap, Bernhard had operated throughout his long career with very little reference to the government. This had been possible because the constitution failed to spell out ministerial responsibility in precise terms for any royals except Queen Juliana.

Parliament also endorsed the government's decision not to proceed with any criminal investigation into Bernhard's activities, as that would have 'serious consequences' for the position of the head of state.

Dutch parliamentarians appeared most concerned with keeping the monarchy intact while seeking future safeguards for the government. "The prince has brought the royal house into a delicate position," Frans Andriessen, spokesman of the influential Catholic People's Party, told parliament. "A repetition might be fatal. The knowledge of this must weigh very heavily on the prince."

In further fallout, a furore arose over two Dutch MPs being approached by Lockheed in 1974 to win support for the Orion. This rumbled on for a while but eventually fizzled out, as there was no sign of improper activity. The two, Joop van Elsen of the Catholic People's Party and Adrianus Ploeg of the conservative VVD party, visited the Lockheed and Fairchild plants in 1974 when they were in the US for a NATO meeting. Ploeg told *De Telegraaf* rather plaintively, "We just had a cup of coffee or orange juice with them."

Yet another revelation followed in September, when letters surfaced showing that Prince Bernhard had discussed the purchase of planes produced by Northrop Aircraft Corp, as a replacement for Lockheed F-1046 Starfighters, with West German Chancellor and former Defence Minister Helmut Schmidt.

The *New York Times* said it was widely assumed in The Hague that Prince Bernhard's links to Northrop, Lockheed's rival in Europe, would be investigated. Major Dutch newspapers were said to have teams working on the prince's ties to Northrop, whose former chairman was yet another of his closest friends. However, apparently nothing came of this. It would certainly have added an extra frisson if Bernhard had turned out to have been conducting a sort of private 'Dutch auction' between the two US aircraft-makers for his commissions.

A report by Nel on 8 September ahead of Bernhard's official resignation from his various posts gave more background on the prince, especially his pet Bilderberg conferences. Predating the Davos World Economic Forum (of which Bernhard became a patron), these were a kind of private version of Davos started by Bernhard in 1954. His idea was that personally invited top government and business officials from North America and Western Europe should have a chance to talk freely behind closed doors.

The meetings were named after the hotel in the east of the Netherlands where the first conference was held. Bilderberg's initial aims were to 'foster dialogue between Europe and North America', later redefined as to 'bolster a consensus around free market Western capitalism and its interests around the globe'.

The Bilderberg meetings actually survived into the 2020s under other chairmen, including three Brits: Sir Alec Douglas-Home, Eric Roll and Lord Carrington. But in later decades, they attracted negative comment, including a rash of conspiracy theories.

Nel's piece on Bernhard noted he was stepping down from his leadership of the annual Bilderberg conference and was also expected to give up his presidency of the World Wildlife Fund. *'The 65-year old prince cancelled this year's Bilderberg conference scheduled for April at Hot Springs, Va.,'* she wrote.

Although Bilderberg was literally Bernhard's baby, giving up the WWF presidency probably stung too, as he had held the top post at the fund aimed at saving animals threatened by extinction since 1962. Nel noted that Bernhard had travelled around the world for the WWF to support fundraising dinners and auctions, 'meeting the prominent and wealthy'. He also set up its 'Panda Club', an elite of 1,001 top people who each paid 10,000 dollars into the fund for their membership.

Bilderberg and the WWF were always regarded as the major private interests of the prince, who had already announced his resignation from all his official defence and business functions, she wrote. Nel hinted that losing control of the Bilderberg movement was more painful, as one channel through which Bernhard might have hoped to exercise some lingering influence. As she remarked:

"The prince has known or been on terms of warm friendship with every American president since Franklin D. Roosevelt. He had a distinguished World War II record and later bustled around the world in search of big industrial orders to help Holland's postwar reconstruction.

"Strictly at Bernhard's invitation, the statesmen and big industrialists came flocking to the annual Bilderberg meetings… including a host of other political and business luminaries including such figures as Giovanni Agnelli of Fiat and David Rockefeller of the Chase Manhattan Bank." No wonder giving up his pet Bilderberg project stung.

In mid-September, a poll conducted for Elsevier's magazine showed that after the dust had settled a little, 62 % of Dutch citizens believed the official inquiry had failed to reveal the full facts on Prince Bernhard's involvement in the Lockheed bribes scandal. Only 27 % thought all had been revealed.

Fifty-one percent found it right that Bernhard should quit public office. But there was still an astonishing 41 % who thought he should have stayed on. Despite his disgrace, the poll showed the Dutch firmly backing the monarchy, with 87 % in favour of keeping it, only 6 % wanting a republic and 7 % uncommitted. It also showed 76 % wanted Queen Juliana to stay on the throne, though a significant 19 % thought she should abdicate shortly in favour of Crown Princess Beatrix.

Reporting on the poll, the AP added some rather more negative 'vox pop' quotes:

"Since the report was published, I've been looking twice at pictures hanging in public buildings of Bernhard and the queen," declared Jos

Lenteren, a twenty-eight-year-old bank clerk from Amsterdam. "If he's been in this deep with Lockheed, it makes you wonder what else he's been up to…"

Willem Burg, a twenty-two-year-old student from Alkmaar, said, "It's the worst example since Watergate of what so-called top people can get away with. He should have been prosecuted."

"It brought me to tears," said Wilhelmina Smits, eighty-two, a widow from Arnhem. "I've been through two world wars with this royal family but I've never experienced anything like this. It's terrible, just terrible."

"What bugs me," said Johan van de Heuvel, a forty-seven-year-old engineer from The Hague, "is that Lockheed should even think of the idea of bribing a member of our royal family."

The comparison with Watergate is noteworthy, as the US scandal was relatively recent, in 1972–74, and was evidently still on people's minds.

One other AP piece, on the government's legislative moves following the scandal, gives some insight into the workings of the Dutch royal family at the time. The legislation, aimed at more control and supervision of the Dutch royal household, was hampered by differences of opinion between Queen Juliana and the government on the definition of a member of the royal household. Here are a few excerpts:

The queen, they said, is loath to have differences established between any of her offspring, children and grandchildren alike. The government for both reasons of cash and responsibility wished to limit the number of members of the royal household to the Queen and Prince Bernhard and Princess Beatrix and Prince Claus…

Even though Princess Irene resigned all royal prerogatives after marrying Roman Catholic Prince Hugo Carlos of Bourbon, and Princess Christina did likewise after marrying Cuban-born Jorge Guillermo, the royal household has grown since former Queen Wilhelmina with just one daughter, Juliana…

Juliana's other daughter, Princess Margriet, married Pieter van Vollenhoven and they have four children, and Princess Beatrix has three boys. The question is that the government feels reluctant to undertake responsibility for all of these, but the Queen so far has insisted on this…

Authoritative sources said that often Dutch royalty is too much surrounded by yes-men. People with their own opinion usually do not stay long. These same sources feel that the example of the British royalty should be followed by appointing independent, worldly-wise advisors with a solid legal background.

Still, those worldly-wise British advisors didn't seem to be much help when it came to Queen Elizabeth's offspring, especially in the case of Prince Charles' very public break-up with Princess Diana, not to speak of all the other divorces littering the family, from the queen's own sister, Margaret, onward. Princess Anne, Andrew and Fergie… it was hard to keep track of all those royal divorces. It's true there were no political scandals like Lockheed, but there have certainly been plenty of personal ones to keep the gutter press and gossip magazines busy.

The above excerpts were not under a specific byline, but it seems certain Nel contributed to them, with her vast experience of the Dutch royals.

For another angle on the Lockheed/Bernhard scandal, Nel's fellow journalist Friso Endt was more than happy to tell me the story of how he got his scoop literally 'from the horse's mouth', though he unsurprisingly lost Prince Bernhard as a contact thereafter. Endt, who was writing regularly for US magazines, said he had a good relationship with Bernard dating from the Hofmans affair, when a story Friso wrote for *Fortune* helped get Hofmans' role curtailed. Bernhard was grateful and told Friso, "Call me any time."

"When the story about his involvement with Lockheed was in the *Wall Street Journal*, his secretary told me, 'I know it's not true.' But I wanted to hear it from Bernhard. The Government Information Service was not talking either. Bernhard was a patron of Davos so I went there to Bernhard's hotel, where he was having dinner with Wagner, the head of Shell. He came out and I said, 'We were called by the palace, saying they know it's not true, but I have to hear it from the prince himself. Your Royal Highness, can you say it's not true?'

"'Friso,' he said, 'I cannot say that it is not true.' I immediately phoned *NRC Handelsblad*, but they did not dare to publish it. *Newsweek* did dare. I never spoke again with the prince after that. Bernhard was as poor as hell, he didn't have a penny…"

This last remark of Friso's seems an important clue as to why Bernhard might have got involved in the bribery business. After all, he was married to one of the world's richest women, so it must have been a little galling for him to be strapped for cash on his own account.

The Lockheed affair also had serious consequences for Beatrix's depressive husband, Prince Claus. Because Bernhard had to resign all his public functions, Claus was never able to take up any significant job. A serious and intelligent career diplomat, many people believe this contributed to his deepening depression. In fact, one of the few functions he was permitted was to be honorary patron of the Foreign Press Association, in which he took a genuinely warm interest.

In Beatrix's reign, as in those of her predecessors, the protocol of not quoting the queen and other royals was strictly enforced, though there was the odd slip-up. One was during a visit to the Netherlands in the early 1980s by the black rising star of the day in US politics, presidential hopeful Reverend Jesse Jackson.

After Jackson met with the Queen, Abner Katzman, who succeeded John Gale as AP Bureau Chief, managed to get into a car with him, and Katzman then reported his remarks about the interview with the monarch while I was working in the AP office. This created quite a diplomatic furore, but Katzman was naturally happy enough, as his story was already widely reported around the US. Sitting on my desk in the AP-Dow Jones corner, he made a charming and clever apology over the phone to Jackson, ending: "Just remember, when you visit the Netherlands as President of the United States, I'll probably still be an unknown journalist in Amsterdam."

In 1999, a visit by Queen Beatrix to the society of chief editors produced another fracas: "Over-hasty talent reported that the sovereign had said of the press that 'lying reigns'. The context in which she had said that was not made clear," the Dutch ANP news service sniffed later. A television programme was then actually launched under the title *Lies Reign*, in which journalists' behaviour was examined.

Claus, as far as I know, never made any *faux pas*, probably helped by his diplomatic background and considerable personal charm. However, he did have to overcome the initial problem of being German – and of learning Dutch. Claus features in the next chapter, on Nel's long association with the Foreign Press Association in the Netherlands.

CHAPTER NINETEEN
THE FOREIGN PRESS ASSOCIATION
Nel and the FPA, Prince Claus, Lubbers and many others

Nel's fruitful if sometimes stormy involvement with the Foreign Press Association spanned nearly all her life as a journalist. She joined it in 1945, when she moved back to the Netherlands after the war. She became the first woman both to chair the association (1978–86) and to be elected an honorary member.

The Foreign Press Association in the Netherlands (FPA) or Buitenlandse Persvereniging in Nederland (BPV), as it is formally known, was founded in 1925 by fifteen foreign correspondents to promote the interests of foreign journalists working in the country. It all began appropriately enough with a bunch of these journalists meeting in a pub, 'De Twee Steden' in The Hague. All fifteen founding members were male, but a month later, the association acquired a solitary woman member: French-born Mrs Livia Jars de Gubernatis.

Initiator and founder Paul Derjeu found that an association was urgently needed to improve the position of the foreign press. "On several occasions, even of important and international interest, the foreign press simply didn't exist in the opinion of the organisers," Derjeu lamented.

The dramatic event through which the Dutch establishment finally came to realise the value of the foreign press didn't arrive until nearly three decades later, in the form of the catastrophic flood of 1953. In the FPA's anniversary publication in 2000, Friso Endt recalled how the world rushed to Holland's aid, '*in response to harrowing reports of the tragedy filed by our members*'.

During the post-flood clean-up, Prime Minister Willem Drees told the FPA he had never realised how vital and valuable a Dutch-based foreign press could be. In recognition, trees were planted (by Friso Endt among others) in Ouwerkerk on Schouwen-Duiveland, where a street was also named 'Weg van de Buitenlandse Pers' (Foreign Press Street). A nice gesture, but Schouwen-Duiveland is the island neighbouring Nel's Goeree-Overflakkee. So I can't help thinking what a shame they didn't pick a street in Goeree-Overflakkee's little town of Middelharnis.

Two years after the flood, Drees wrote an appreciative foreword for FPA chairman Henk Kersting's thirtieth anniversary magazine:

'*The work of the representatives of the foreign press is important, for our country and people as well... especially in the flood disaster, when it was precisely the modern communication methods that carried the news of the calamity across the world in the twinkling of an eye, as a result of which sympathy and help was awoken and offered from all quarters.*'

Telex would have been the main 'modern' communication method in the 1950s, apart from the telephone and possibly still the odd telegram. Morse was also still occasionally mentioned. Telex remained pretty dominant until fax took over in the 1980s.

In his 1955 foreword, Drees also lauded the value of the foreign press in 'everyday living': Through their correspondents, he wrote, '*they project the picture of our country abroad, so that understanding is created for our ups and downs.*' The foreign press were very much valued by the government, he said, and suggested they could even contribute to '*peoples having more understanding of one another throughout the world.*' I find it hard to imagine any present-day prime minister being so complimentary about the press.

In an extremely polite foreword by Queen Juliana's husband, Prince Bernhard, he observed that readers back home saw the country through the correspondent's eyes, reading 'his *(sic) praise but also* his *criticism*,' and said he was grateful to FPA members for handling this responsibly. '*They have become good friends of the Netherlands. Perhaps sometimes the friend that "points out shortcomings", but still a friend.*'

The FPA were certainly going to do a lot of pointing-out of Bernhard's own shortcomings a couple of decades later over the Lockheed scandal. Another comment still seems true today, if no easier to achieve: '*People have more need than ever of a better understanding of what goes on outside their own borders.*'

The same 1955 magazine featured Nel's decorous article quoted in Chapter 4, '*We – Women Correspondents – Want to be Taken Seriously*'. There were still just a tiny handful of women in the FPA then, but by 2000, women would make up one-third of the total.

As chairman, Nel's bureau chief Henk Kersting wrote a lengthy and thoughtful but rather turgid piece on the 'Task and Role of the BPV'. David Post, later Nel's vice chairman, told me Kersting was an effective FPA chairman. "A very nice guy, very proper, almost German in a way, he was so correct, and always beautifully dressed." Perhaps this super-correctness weighed on his prose.

Kersting did seem to labour the point on membership criteria, but there was a good reason for this. Membership regulations had to be tightened up during the Cold War period, after the FPA uncovered a spy who had passed himself off as a foreign correspondent. The fake journalist then tried to get access to strategic information via his FPA membership.

Kersting also revealed a surprising British honorary member of the FPA: "Sir WINSTON SPENCER CHURCHILL, spontaneously appointed after the war to honour him, the former foreign correspondent, as liberator." When Friso Endt died in 2016, I discovered from his obituaries that he once interviewed Churchill. But his obituary writers gave no details, being more interested in recording the riveting fact, also previously unknown to me, that Friso actually saw nightclub owner Jack Ruby shoot Lee Harvey Oswald when he was in police custody after being charged with the assassination of US President John F. Kennedy.

Although the 1953 floods did give the FPA a big boost, an exodus to Brussels was also beginning, with many foreign correspondents of global papers such as The *New York Times*, *Neue Zürche Zeitung* and *Time/Life* opting to locate in Brussels rather than The Hague.

"With the result that The Hague as a centre for international reporting slipped sharply behind Brussels. A feeling of uneasiness and even disquiet arose," complained Herman Bleich, Kersting's predecessor as chairman. One contributing factor was the Netherlands' very poor press facilities, so Bleich set off on a long and ultimately successful drive to set up the modern Nieuwspoort press centre. The centre opened in March 1962.

Bleich was apparently well enough respected too. But there could, of course, be tensions within the FPA board. David Post, Nel's vice chairman at the time, described clashes between Bleich and Nel when she was chairing the FPA: "Nel could handle anyone. But she was more or less a dictator. Things were done her way, or they weren't done at all. When I joined, I was the youngest person by far, it really was an old person's club, and also because I was an American, I was very welcome there. Particularly by Friso and Nel, because the Krauts were trying to take it over... Herman Bleich was one of the Germans. He wanted to run it, and there were awful fights."

Where Endt, Bleich and Slis all agreed was in worrying about the decline in the FPA's influence as the EEC became more important and siphoned off international journalists. By 2000, the Brussels press corps of around 1,000 would actually surpass that of Washington. In the event, though, other journalists replaced those that left Holland, partly thanks to the growing international importance of financial news.

For a tiny country, Holland has a disproportionate number of big global companies. As well, several international bodies are based in the Netherlands and need to be reported on. Many of these are legal bodies, probably the best known abroad being a relative newcomer, the International Criminal Court in The Hague. Helped by these two factors, the FPA would continue to flourish into the new millennium, which would have delighted Nel.

The later FPA anniversary magazines made sure to include a few jokes. For the 1985 magazine, Kersting dug into the war years in his archives. War or no war, occupation or no occupation, he remarked, AP New York was always asking its correspondents for 'smiling briefs' on dull days, and he offered a few that appeared in American newspapers in 1940. The one about the unknown cow appealed to me:

"*War and occupation have not squelched Dutch humour. We Netherlanders are going to erect a statue to the unknown cow at the end of the war," a Dutch farmer solemnly remarked. When asked to explain, he said: "Well, the daily official reports of Britisch (sic) bombings on Dutch soil always state that only cows were hit.*"'

I particularly liked Nel's wry contribution: '*Shortly after Margaret Thatcher first became Prime Minister of Britain, a journalist was seated next to the British ambassador at a European Covenant luncheon. The journalist allowed as how she admired Mrs Thatcher for her courage, intelligence and articulateness, but wondered aloud about her experience abroad. With dry British wit, the ambassador replied: "She once danced with Mugabe."*'

And Friso Endt had a good one about Wim Dik, then State Secretary for Foreign Trade and Exports. In a speech at the World Trade Center in New

York, he must have mystified his audience with his closing remark: "*And that ladies and gentlemen is other cook,*" *a* mis-transposition of the Dutch expression '*andere koek*' meaning 'another story'.

Nel had got to know Prince Claus long before she chaired the association, thanks to his association with the FPA as its honorary patron. He was its guest of honour several times, and back in the 1960s, he and Princess Beatrix had attended an eventful press ball at the Amsterdam Hilton hotel. Friso Endt recalled the event. A performance by the Edwin Hawkins Singers blew the electricity circuits, after which, "we sat with all our guests, including the royal couple, in the dark. Princess Beatrix and Prince Claus were clearly amused and enjoyed the rest of the evening with us by candlelight."

David Post told me about what was probably the rowdiest Foreign Press dinner in Hotel des Indes in The Hague in the 1970s, when the Labour Party's Joop den Uyl was prime minister: "It was during the oil crisis, and only Holland and America were being boycotted because of their support for Israel, and there was this popular song in the country at the time, *Den Uyl is in den olie* (Den Uyl is in the oil, i.e. 'in the shit'), and the prime minister actually got up and sang it. It was the rowdiest one I was ever at – it was out of control."

When Nel was chairing the FPA at the fifty-fifth anniversary celebrations in 1980 in the Kurhaus Hotel in The Hague's seaside suburb of Scheveningen, Claus himself made a speech, which was a hit. He cleverly interviewed himself, dredging up all the stereotypical questions he had faced. Friso Endt reminded Claus of his speech when he was FPA chairman at the 1990 celebrations. "Claus said to me: 'Did I really say that then?' I told him I still had the original text. 'It still sounds completely topical,' he replied." I don't actually know which bit of the speech they were referring to, but I've picked out his thoughtful and nuanced reply to the last question he asked himself, namely, whether he was happy.

Noting that conditions in the affluent West had never been more favourable, Claus wondered whether people were happier than a century ago, or happier than those in poor countries down south. "A very difficult and also intriguing question. Especially for those of us who... are trying hard to help the poor countries in their development. It is too much to be treated in a short interview. The fact, though, is that we in the materialistically rich countries have come to question the rightness of the equation: material welfare and affluence equals personal happiness..."

"All I can say is, sometimes I am happy, sometimes I'm not. But then there is nothing in a normal person's life like a permanent state of happiness. At least when one is aware of what is going on around you in the world at large. Hunger, deprivation and the ultimate threat of global annihilation… You have children and you worry about their future. And there are many other worries, small and big, which concern our country and people and the world as a whole…"

A report of the event in the *Haagsche Courant* was headlined: '*Great hilarity in Kurhaus – Prince Claus interviews himself at press ball*'. It quoted much of the prince's speech, and commented on his good English. Photos showed Claus buying a lottery ticket for the tombola, and Claus and Nel dancing and laughing. Another showed Foreign Minister Chris van der Klaauw rather dashingly sweeping the American ambassadress around the floor.

Nel chaired the FPA for eight years with characteristic style, vigour and vigilance – though as David Post said, she was also quite autocratic. No doubt like most FPA chairpersons, she had her trials and tribulations, the biggest one in her case being the scandal of one Erich Hoos, who ran off with a chunk of the FPA's cash. Friso told me the story:

"Hoos, who had been a very good secretary, was temporary treasurer, and one day Nel came on the phone yelling and crying, in tears really, in a panic, and said Hoos took 9,000 *guilders* from the FPA's cash, which is a lot of money… He falsified the signature on the cheque and he disappeared."

It turned out that Hoos had fled that night to a hotel in Maastricht. Friso went there and found out he had crossed the border into Belgium the next day. Friso went to the bank and berated it for accepting a cheque with a false signature, and the bank agreed to pay back the money.

Months later, Erich Hoos was sighted staying by himself in a little pension (B&B), 'on top of the Brenner Pass', claiming to be working for his old press agency, Agence France Presse. Friso said he thought he must be crazy. "A couple of months later, his wife called me and said, he's back, so I went there, and there was Erich, now under treatment by a psychiatrist. He was fired by AFP, of course, so they were in great trouble. I think she later divorced him."

Friso took over as chairman shortly after this incident. He gave Nel much credit for remaining a vigilant watchdog of press interests. "Nel, when I was chairman, often called and said we should not take this, we should protest, and I did."

While chairing the FPA, Nel presided over two memorable celebrations, the first being that fifty-fifth anniversary, actually held on Valentine's Day 1981, when Prince Claus gave his much-applauded speech. Nel's own speech came after the main course, followed by Prince Claus' speech, followed by a decoration for retiring FA secretary Pal Balázs, so guests had to wait a while for their dessert.

In Nel's speech, she bade farewell to the US ambassador of the day, among other notable departures, with a special word for Balázs. Then she reminded her audience of the physical dangers faced by reporters elsewhere in the world, along with pressure from governments seeking to manipulate or distort the news. "We are grateful for our freedom in this country," she declared.

She also expressed satisfaction with the growing number of women journalists. "I think it is not as difficult for my younger female colleagues as it was for me in 1945 to get a start in this game. They had never heard of a woman reporter... This organisation seems to be coming of age – it has elected a woman president for the first time in fifty-five years..."

Technological innovation, she remarked, continued to change the working life of journalists. Compared with the Morse key used of old to move the news from one country to another, "now the news is sped to the papers at speeds of 1,200 words per minute, using satellite circuits and computer systems. John Gale of the Associated Press can tell you there will be an ultra high speed news transmission system operating in Holland by the end of 1981.

"Presently a one-hundred-word-a-minute bulletin filed in Istanbul can be read simultaneously in Paris, London and New York within minutes of clearing a central computer. In future, it will be even faster, and huge amounts of information will be transmitted just by pressing a button."

Boy, was she ever right, though it took a little longer than perhaps she thought. And she was speaking before mobiles, iPhones and pads, Facebook and other social media and all the other paraphernalia yet to come.

The following year, 1982, Nel was elected an honorary FPA member, joining a short list of people 'who have made themselves of exceptional service on behalf of the association or the foreign press in general'.

One of the BPV's most splendid celebrations was its sixtieth anniversary in 1985, also under Nel's chairmanship. It was held in Erestein Castle, Kerkrade, near Heerlen in the southern province of Limburg. Prince Claus was again guest of honour, with Prime Minister Ruud Lubbers giving the keynote speech.

Nel's speech was in three languages this time, not that she couldn't still have made it in five. Recalling Prince Bernhard as guest of honour in 1961 and Queen (then Princess) Beatrix attending with Prince Claus later in the sixties, Nel declared, "Continuity is the life blood of any organisation. For that reason we are particularly pleased to have with us Your Royal Highness, who has always taken an interest in the media."

Nel also expressed her worries about the fading international profile of the Netherlands, as well as her fear that Europe itself might be in decline: "Geopolitical realignments over our six-decade history have… in many ways reduced the Netherlands' significance. Reporters go where the stories are, as they should. But because of that, the spotlight is not on our beat the way it used to be. Is it because Europe is in decline? Afflicted with Eurosclerosis as some journalists would have us believe? True there is plenty of action and plenty of journalists in Brussels, but many of them specialise in and are limited to specific economic areas.

"Are fewer foreign correspondents covering the big picture because there no longer is a big picture in Europe? Perhaps with another visionary like Robert Schumann, De Gaspery, Churchill or Paul Henri Spaak, the EEC would again be a heavyweight. Fortunately, the Netherlands still remains a financial and economic centre, and a seat of international law…"

At this anniversary, Nel received yet another honour, being promoted by Lubbers from Knight to Officer in the Order of Oranje-Nassau. This took her by surprise, and she was visibly moved. Prince Claus presented the decoration to Nel, and in one photo taken just afterwards, she looks quite overwhelmed. Other photos show her in sparkling form presiding over the celebrations and dancing with Claus. Afterwards, I heard that Claus enjoyed it all so much that when he wanted to go home, Beek Airport was closed. The BPV board had to call in the governor of Limburg, who had the airport opened up again so that Claus could fly back to The Hague.

I can vouch for it being a good party, as I was there too. In fact, I made a terrible *faux pas*, which revealed Lubbers as a particularly kindly PM. I was staying with a friend of my sister's. Carla was so shocked when I unwisely let slip that I'd found a much-loved velvet skirt that I was thinking of wearing to 'meet the prince' in a Dublin dustbin that she made me wear one of her dresses. I didn't much like it, but I guess it looked respectable.

When we arrived at the castle, the journalists were herded into a grand panelled chamber to meet the prince. We stood around in a circle, and Nel introduced us to Claus one by one, starting with my *Financial Times* friend and ex-boss, Laura Raun, and myself. When she got to my friend Naomi Wimborne, she got her right as Reuter's bureau chief but momentarily looked nonplussed by her Moroccan boyfriend next to her. Undismayed, she promoted him to Moroccan television.

At the end of the circle, she and Claus wound up back with Laura and myself. Claus chatted amiably to us for what felt like hours but was no doubt just a couple of minutes. We were not expecting this and had no idea of the correct protocol. He made interesting comments about the role of journalism, and sometimes we both felt like saying I do agree, but didn't want to sound sycophantic, surrounded as we were by our fellow hacks with ears on stalks. Conversely, we might have wanted to say "yes, but…" but were not sure if this was permissible. So we just stood there nodding and smiling like a couple of proverbial Chinese mandarins.

Afterwards, we all went downstairs to the marquee. I was exhausted, what with two young children, a recent divorce and struggling with learning the trade of journalism, so promptly relaxed into a pleasant coma. A familiar face swam up out of the crowds of Dutch business people and politicians and shook my hand in a friendly way.

"What did you say your name was?" I said cheerily.

"Ruud Lubbers."

Oh cripes.

"*Really*, AP-Dow Jones!" said someone, I think later FPA president Vera Vaugan Bowden. But Lubbers, seeing how embarrassed I was, tossed off this little story against himself. While he was studying French in Paris, he told me, he went into a museum.

"*You're* not French," said the concierge. "Where are you from?"

"Guess," said Lubbers.

"Spain," the concierge shot back at him.

"No, I'm from Holland," said Lubbers, who was very dark, and famous for his five o'clock shadow – long before the days of designer stubble.

"Oh well, there were a lot of Spanish soldiers stationed in Holland," riposted the concierge.

I'm still amazed to this day by his kindness. I can't imagine Maggie Thatcher or any other UK PM telling a story against themselves just to make some unknown hack feel better.

Sandwiched between the two awards from Dutch premiers, in 1982, Nel received 'La Croix d'Officier de l'Ordre National du Merit'. The French government was honouring her as a 'friend of France'. The insignia was presented by the French ambassador, Claude de Kemoularia, at his residence. She told a Dutch newspaper, which was impressed by her fluent French: '*I received the award for my journalistic efforts... I worked in Brussels from 1961 to 1973. At the EEC. The French gave the lead at that time.*'

In presenting the award, De Kemoularia made quite a flowery speech, saying, "In her character we recognise courage, loyalty and dedication, and above all also love for France, for the country, its culture and its civilisation." He also outlined her remarkable career, especially her resistance work in London while monitoring broadcasts for the BBC.

In 1990, when the FPA celebrated its sixty-fifth anniversary with Friso Endt as chairman, the world was undergoing huge changes: The fall of the Berlin Wall, German reunification, Soviet *glasnost* and *perestroika*, the emergence of Eastern Europe. Nel was in serious vein in this anniversary publication, now called *The Foreign Correspondent*, with an article on the EEC and Eastern Europe. Helmut Hetzel, who followed Endt as chairman, wrote on German reunification, and Herman Bleich also had a somewhat paranoid article on the same subject. But at that time, many people who remembered World War II were extremely anxious about the prospect of a resurgent Germany.

A Russian, Sergei Melnikof, TASS correspondent since 1985, contributed a short, optimistic piece about *perestroika* and the press, saying his work had become more difficult but also more interesting since TASS lost its monopoly. And board member Frank de Jong again reminded readers of how technology had changed:

Back in the '60s I worked as AFP (Agence France Presse) bureau chief in Jakarta and the only way to file copy was a Morse-cast transmission of up to two pages, twice a day, to Singapore. Even worse, during the four-week telecommunications blackout after the aborted coup attempt in 1965, I had to go to Jakarta's airport twice a day and ask passengers to take my copy to Singapore, where my AFP colleague would pick it up...

At the 1995 celebrations, it was Crown Prince Willem-Alexander's presence that made the biggest impression, as Endt and Conway reported:

The Foreign Press Association even made headlines itself in the Dutch media. We had succeeded where it had failed… in meeting Crown Prince Willem-Alexander, who spent a couple of hours chatting with our members… Naturally, he was queried about his love life, views on the disastrous goings-on at the time in the British monarchy, and his ambitions, at this extraordinarily frank and fun-filled get-together.

Willem-Alexander completely outshone the underwhelming keynote speaker, European Commission President Jacques Santer, who could chiefly be congratulated for saying absolutely nothing for twenty minutes.

This anniversary, under Helmut Hetzel's presidency, was the last one attended by Prince Claus. He missed the celebrations in 2000 due to ill health and died in 2002, preceded by Nel in 2001. Nel did join both the 1990 celebrations in Ootmarsum and also those in Scheveningen's Kurhaus in 1995. She, too, was unable to attend the seventy-fifth anniversary celebrations in 2000 in the Ridderzaal (Knight's Hall) in The Hague. But she was not forgotten in the anniversary magazine.

She would doubtless have been delighted to see a woman heading the FPA again, as Vera Vaughan Bowden had become president in 1998. Also that Queen Beatrix, who eluded Nel's own efforts to get her to meet the FPA, was guest of honour in 2000. Nel would have applauded Vaughan Bowden's short, dignified address in Dutch – and would definitely have laughed her head off at Haagse Courant columnist Floor Kist's brilliantly hilarious one.

Kist's best joke had Beatrix rolling around in her seat along with everyone else in the room. Talking about how Dutch tulip growers liked to name tulips after famous people as a good way of getting some publicity, he said Eleanor Roosevelt was one of these. The then first lady said she did feel quite honoured at first to have a tulip named after her, until she read the description of the tulip in the catalogue: '*No good in bed, but good up against a wall*'.

This was a grand millennium celebration for the FPA, which Nel would have enjoyed enormously.

CHAPTER TWENTY
AFTER THE AP
The light that failed

Q uite exceptionally, the AP kept Nel on after its very strict retirement age of sixty-five, as it was thought Queen Juliana was about to abdicate. But as Juliana was taking her time, she did actually retire the following year, in 1979.

Nel went on working as a freelance journalist through her late sixties and seventies and would probably have carried on right through her eighties had her memory not failed. By the start of the 1990s, she could still list *Europe Magazine*, Washington, McGraw-Hill Publications, New York, *European Chemical News*, and *Oilgram News*, New York among her publications, and she was also still working regularly for Agence Europe. Europe remained her special interest, rather more than Holland. And following the collapse of the Soviet Union, her old EEC beat was enlarged by the new world of emerging Eastern Europe.

In *The Foreign Correspondent* of March 1990, Nel reviewed the cataclysmic events taking place in Eastern Europe and their implications for the EEC. Her piece, 'Eastern Europe crowds EC agenda', also pinpointed feelings of nervousness about German reunification prevalent at the time: '*The West European countries have clearly not forgotten World War II. They fear super-patriotism. All hope that a European Germany will emerge, and not a German Europe.*'

While it remains a historically interesting report, the sparkle was beginning to fade from her writing. However, the following year, Nel was able to enjoy a burst of journalistic life covering the 1991 EU Maastricht summit for Agence Europe, rediscovering her old expertise and gusto from the Brussels years.

She and I both joined a pre-summit FPA visit to this gem of a Roman city on the Maas River in the summer, ahead of the summit. On a limb of the country stretching deep into the south and surrounded by Belgium and Germany, Maastricht has a completely different atmosphere from the Calvinistic north. The local dialect is soft and sometimes quite incomprehensible to those of us from the north. Women are smartly dressed, and the food is excellent; the historic streets are beautifully preserved.

The old town hall has glorious dark colonial-era wallpaper covered with fabulous birds and flowers, a big contrast to the modern MECC conference centre. Here, all the journalists were to be corralled, attend press briefings and meet the European Commission and EEC ministers. An ultra-modern complex, it looked quite confusing. Nel hissed, "Always make sure to see where the lavatories are."

Nel wrote a well-composed curtain-raiser for *Europe Magazine* on Prime Minister Ruud Lubbers, who held the EU presidency for the six months which was to produce the Treaty of Maastricht. Though it may have needed quite some editing at that stage for all I know, it encapsulated a lot of information about what was going on in the Netherlands and in Europe at the time. It struck me as an extremely solid piece of work at age seventy-eight, and also showcased Nel's favourite politician.

At the Maastricht summit, Nel was bustling around happily, working with her Agence Europe friends and tipping fellow journalists off on anything she thought might be useful to them. Like Nel back in the 1960s, I myself was just discovering how bewildering the EEC could be to a newcomer. The EEC nights were every bit as long in Maastricht as in Brussels. I slept for four hours the first night, two hours the second and not at all on the last night. It was like a fever, the obsessive attempt to figure out what was going on.

Nel's former FPA board colleague Laura Raun, my second boss at AP-Dow Jones, was there for CNN News wearing a dashing pink suit. BBC heavyweight John Simpson criss-crossed the floor looking grumpy; John Cole, known for his years of excellent Northern Ireland reporting for the BBC, snoozed cosily on a sofa through the first night.

This was the summit at which British premier John Major extracted the UK's opt-out clauses for the Economic and Monetary Union plan, so the

UK's formal press briefings were always packed out. They were run cabaret-style by a young successor to Margaret Thatcher's famous – or infamous, depending on one's point of view – press chief, Bernard Ingham.

Each and every official that appeared through the long nights acted like a magnet, instantly attracting a big clump of reporters. In their absence, reporters went on trawling around talking to anyone, including other journalists. On the first night, I was surprised to be interviewed by a TV station from somewhere remote, I think in Australia. In the middle of the second night, I found a small group of Eastern European journalists from Latvia and Estonia encamped in an otherwise empty room somewhere in the depths of the MECC rabbit warren. They explained to me how it was necessary before the collapse of the USSR to report to the KGB both before and after doing an interview. There was no alternative. Either one complied or one could not work. That was a glimpse of a very different world.

The summit produced the 1992 Treaty of Maastricht, setting the conditions for Economic and Monetary Union (EMU) and the single currency. To most people's surprise, the exchange rates of twelve EU countries were in the event fixed only seven years later. The introduction of the euro as legal tender followed in 2002, forming the biggest European currency union since the Roman Empire. In the new millennium, it has had its decidedly shaky moments, but so has the whole European enterprise at many stages. Personally, I remain a euro-optimist, even after the terrible blow of Brexit.

Back in Maastricht, the Economic and Monetary Union proceedings were settled fairly quickly. At an early-morning Dutch press briefing, Finance Minister Wim Kok had one bright red eye after his long smoke-filled night, but looked happy. For the rest of the summit, all kinds of other bizarre issues were on the agenda. As often happens in this evolving European institution, many ended up being swept under the carpet or glossed over in blurry compromises.

In a press conference concluding the summit, an extremely weary Prime Minister Ruud Lubbers confessed his disappointment that more had not been achieved. He was unhappy about the UK opt-outs but expressed satisfaction about the EMU agreement. He must have been pleased when the euro was launched a few years later.

Nel would have been happy about the eurozone too. She would certainly have appreciated not having to change money between countries so often on her tours around Europe to see her friends. But she would also have been delighted by this symbol of a somewhat more solid and maturing European union – despite remaining ever prone to the odd seismic upset.

Even apart from Maastricht, the last decade of the century began for Nel as a glorious celebration of her life, with a series of anniversary parties and interviews marking her achievements. We return to these in the final chapter. Later in the 1990s, though, dark clouds started to gather for Nel.

During the last phase of her life, three key people looked after Nel and her interests: Tyna's lawyer brother Piet Wackie Eysten, producer Yolanda Frenkel Frank and fellow journalist Friso Endt. Another Dutch journalist, Frank de Jong, also helped out before he himself became ill. Friso Endt said he bore much of the day-to-day brunt as Nel became more difficult as her memory failed.

I did find that whenever people recalled the encroaching difficulties with Nel, they were also inclined to remember Nel as she had been earlier. Many long-standing friendships survived through these troubled years, as long as her elderly friends were able to drive or were at any rate still alive. And she continued to travel.

David Post, Nel's former FPA vice chairman, noticed signs of eccentricity long before the memory loss really became apparent. "She had one horrible habit of asking questions at press conferences and then never listening to the answer because she was in a private conversation with her neighbour. I remember being at Fokker [the Dutch aircraft-maker which later went bankrupt], and she asked [chairman] Frans Swarttouw a very complicated question, and then she started talking to me, and Swarttouw was saying Mevrouw, Mevrouw…"

David also told me about a particularly hair-raising drive with Nel. They had been in the Hilton hotel in Rotterdam for an American Chamber of Commerce lunch, at which the then transport minister Neelie Smit-Kroes was the speaker.

"There was a Foreign Press meeting in the evening in The Hague, and I took the train knowing it would be quite a boozy day, and she said oh, I've got my car here and I'll drive you back to The Hague. It was parked right on the pavement in front of the Hilton Hotel, and she came out and the doorman started yelling at her, and she said there wasn't time to get a parking place." Nel still had her habit of just dumping her car right beside wherever she wanted to go.

"So I leapt into the back seat, knowing it would be awful. It's four o'clock in the afternoon in Rotterdam, and we're driving back to The Hague on that busy highway. She had some sort of DAF car that journalists could get ten percent off in those days, and she decided she wanted to talk to me. I was in the back seat, so she just turned around, looked me in the eye and kept talking, while big trucks were zooming all around us. We finally got to the Binnenhof [parliamentary building] and she parked the car right there, and a man came up. 'Oh, it's you, yes, all right,' he said."

Driving aside, David wanted to stress that Nel was a very generous person, particularly with young journalists. "In what sort of way?" I asked. "Introductions?"

"Yes, she introduced you to everyone, and if you ever needed to know something, you could call her up and she'd tell you who you could get hold of, and she usually would call them up first so they'd know who you were. She was extraordinarily kind to younger journalists, particularly Americans like me and Jim Smith."

Jim Smith was a young AP reporter in The Hague in the late 1970s, who was Nel's vice chairman at the Foreign Press Association before David Post. I met the slender, quiet-spoken Jim Smith myself once in the AP office on Amsterdam's Keizersgracht, just before he moved to South Africa in 1981.

Of course, David said, Dan Schorr was one person Nel would definitely have married, but added with a touch of humour, "This Jim Smith at the AP – despite being young enough to be her grandson, she would have married him too."

David also mentioned Nel's old friend Rudolf 'Peek' Pekelharing, the former diplomat who he said was once slapped by Nel but forgave her. He visited her regularly, as long as he could still drive a car. "They were really good friends. Rudolf would always talk about her in a very nice way."

Flora Lewis described Nel as an exceptionally loyal friend. Apparently when her old friend Jacqueline who lived near Biarritz became ill, she would go and stay with her and help her, for long periods of time.

"I guess that's why Jacqueline left her house to Nel?"

"Yes, but by that time, Nel wasn't able to keep it up, so she sold it. She had a lot of friends whom I didn't really know, going way way back to her childhood. She kept up her friendships, and some of these went back fifty or sixty years."

Tyna Wynaendts told me Nel didn't actually nurse Jacqueline when she got ill, as some people claimed – nor did she nurse her great friend, Tyna's mother.

"Why not? Might she not have been happy to use her old skills?"

"She didn't want anything to do with nursing. She went to Jacqueline in the last months, but more to hold her hand. Also when my mother was dying and she came often, my mother sometimes suggested it. We had nurses in and out all the time, and when one was going on holiday, she asked Nel would you maybe stay? No, no way."

"Why?"

"She was probably afraid that she no longer knew how to do it – yes, she wouldn't do it unless she could do it well."

Laura de Jonghe, who lived near Brussels, was one of Nel's greatest friends, and Tyna recalled that after Laura was widowed, they travelled together frequently. Nel had first met her when she was working for the BBC in London. After Laura died, Nel spent more time with her friend Jacqueline, a former Agence France Presse journalist, travelling and spending summers with her in her little house near Biarritz.

Tyna also described a slightly bizarre Geneva routine that Nel had evolved. Apparently, after visiting Tyna's family, she would often visit friends in the Dordogne, then Jacqueline, and then go to Switzerland, to 'see her bank account'.

"Then she went to see her counsellor, and that was always a big joke because she was called Madame Corrupt, a wonderful name for a financial advisor. She didn't stay with her, but she always took her out for lunch."

"Where did she stay, then?"

"In a Salvation Army place, because in Geneva, apparently, the army has a hostel for women only, nice and clean, and Madame Corrupt had given her the address. Going to the bank was just habit, that's what she had done in previous years, and I don't think it was really needed."

Nel's friend Laura also had a brother in Portugal. Tyna said Nel didn't like the climate in Holland. She was prone to rheumatism and wanted to move to a warmer climate. "She had gone to Portugal for a holiday and met Laura's brother, and there was an elder brother and a whole circle of friends. But they were all elderly. She was probably one of the youngest of the group. So when the time came, it was too late, because they had all died."

Tyna believes Nel would have settled happily in Portugal. "Sometimes I asked, wouldn't you be afraid to be on your own, not knowing anybody? And she said, well, I've settled in so many places, I would go to the yoga class and see if there's a nice woman and I could take her out for a coffee and then one thing would lead to another – it doesn't scare me at all."

In The Hague, Nel gave Dutch lessons to Portuguese workers after she retired. "Probably the lessons were not very good, she was already [losing it], but she could explain things to them in Portuguese, as she spoke that language a little bit too."

Once when Tyna was staying on Belle Ile, off the coast of Brittany, Nel came to visit with her friend Clara Meyer, who had been the agriculture spokesperson in the European Commission.

"We went for a walk with the two old ladies and I said now, Clara, you have the choice, you can go left back to the house, or right – this way is a bit more difficult but that is a bit longer. So Nel said right and Clara said no, no, that's too steep, left, and there was no way of making them give in – they were exactly the same kind of person. So we ended up taking a middle road that wasn't really a road. It was terrible – I didn't know which one to go with, because they were determined to go their own way, and I felt as I was the hostess that I couldn't leave one or other by themselves."

Tyna's children got on very well with Nel, who always took them out shopping when she came to stay. "Sometimes when I said no, you can't have that dress or that pullover because you don't need it and I don't like it, they'd say, we'll ask Nel, and Nel would buy it for them."

Nel did also acquire a few good friends in The Hague along the way, despite remaining somewhat underwhelmed by her own country. Two of these also went travelling with her late in her life.

I met Gonne Hollander in her elegant house in The Hague in 2002, soon after Nel died. She was the same age as Nel; a stout, smartly dressed woman with a neat halo of permed hair, only slightly lame. She told me she first met Nel in 1958 through her husband.

"I liked her from the first meeting. She was so keen, fierce – open."

Gonne travelled with Nel in the south of France and Spain. While her friend Jacqueline was in hospital, they stayed at her house. "It had all sorts of weird noises in the night – Nel got a bit afraid. Perhaps it was the heating, or the fridge, but it would burp in the middle of the night. In the daytime, we visited her friend in the hospital."

Gonne said Nel always drove on these trips. "I didn't dare. She always smoked at the crucial moment, and at one moment, she drove straight through a barrier. What an adventure!"

Later, they went by train to Berlin, as Nel would not fly. "It took an enormous time, and we had difficulty finding a hotel that wasn't a skyscraper, with no lifts… Then Nel had a brainwave – we'll go to the cabaret. It was just after the Berlin Wall had fallen – they had lots of East and West Berlin jokes."

"Did you enjoy those trips?"

"I didn't like her smoking the whole time, but she was fun to be with."

Gonne had started giving '*eettafels*' – informal dinners for the various single people in town – back in 1975. Nel still managed to make it to these social events even when she was beginning to lose it, but was sometimes quite obstreperous.

"She made rows, she could be so unreasonable. One time at an *eettafel*, a gentleman said something about the Red Cross. 'Red Cross,' said Nel, and launched into a whole tirade – nothing good about the Red Cross. And he was president of the Red Cross! I didn't like it, her fighting – I had to smooth it over. She could hurt people.

"After Piet Wackie Eysten sold Nel's car, she came by taxi or with Yolanda, but she was always looking for her car keys. Oh, the last years were tragic. She had a lot of dear friends. She was very friendly with the neighbours, two nice homos [gays], she loved them. There was also a woman who made clothes for artists… and Rudolf Pekelharing, they smoked and drank together the whole time. He was a bit short of breath as he smoked too much, but a very nice man."

Gonne said Nel loved telling a story about when she got the second, Officer of the Order of Oranje Nassau, decoration: "Someone wrote to her and said, '*I always associate you more with officers and their language than knights.*'"

Gonne was obviously much taken by Piet Wackie Eysten and seemed faintly annoyed that Nel made Tyna her heir. She said she nagged Nel to remember Piet too in her will, as he did so much for her. "I don't know whether she took any notice. She didn't like his wife very much."

Gonne also spoke highly of Nel's "dear Indonesian charwoman, Sandra, who did everything for her." Sandra was a quiet brown woman, I guess in her late thirties, and I felt she was a soothing presence in Nel's apartment.

At the end of our interview, Gonne said, "Nel had a heart of gold. Everyone who knew her well, knew that. Tyna said at the funeral – remember they lived in Goeree, provincial girls and boys – that Nel opened the world to her. 'Thanks to Nel, we had a wider view of the world.'"

Nel's last big trip, as far as I know, was with her and Gonne's mutual beautician, with the remarkable name of Elizabeth de Jong van Beek en

Donk. A tiny, rounded woman in a lilac tweed skirt and jersey, with neatly curled hair coloured dark honey blonde, she talked to me in her light and airy working room with beautician chair, steamer and other tools of her trade around. She produced excellent coffee and cakes.

Elizabeth met Nel at Gonne's *eettafels* and became her friend as well as beautician. Nel would come to her once a month for a facial and massage. Among other trips, Elizabeth travelled with Nel to Brussels for the funeral of one Sylvia Fentener van Vlissingen, a member of a wealthy Dutch family, who had died in a car accident.

In the second half of the 1990s, by which time Nel was suffering from serious memory loss, she suddenly wanted to go to St Petersburg. Fragile-looking little Elizabeth arranged for a three-day bus trip there and back, with three days in St Petersburg. Though it must have been very difficult to cope with Nel by that time, Elizabeth insisted it was great fun. She said the other passengers on the bus looked after Nel from time to time to give her a break.

Nel was not so keen on the drive right through Germany, threatening to start making unpleasant noises about the war. But by the evening, they were in Copenhagen and could stroll around its great park. They then drove across Sweden and took the ferry from Stockholm to Helsinki and the bus to St Petersburg. They had three days there, and then the whole long trip back again. This seems to me a remarkable achievement for Nel at that time, and I should think even more so for Elizabeth.

"What do you miss about Nel?" I wondered.

"The atmosphere, openness – everyone was welcome, the warmth. She was really trustworthy. And also her candour, honesty. Yes, she could be difficult, but that was also her power. Perhaps because of her lonely childhood, she became so strong – I was very protected as a child, but then you are not so combative as if you are alone, like Nel – it had its good side, in her independence. She was really a big figure in the world, as a woman – you could see that at her eightieth birthday celebrations."

Yolanda once remarked that Flora Lewis was "very much the same kind of... tough old lady journalist [as Nel], no way to fight them." Friso Endt claimed Nel imitated Flora. Perhaps there is something in that, but where Flora sometimes seemed to positively enjoy intimidating or upstaging more lowly journalists, many people, including myself, have attested to Nel's unfailing kindness to those starting off in the business.

British journalist June Dole was among these. Her first encounter with Nel made a big impression.

"I was a newcomer to The Hague when Nel Slis, the colourful grande dame of the FPA, introduced me to the then Dutch Prime Minister Ruud Lubbers with the maximum of impact and the minimum of protocol: 'Her boss can be pretty tough and if you don't answer her questions, she will be fired.'"

I thought, Nel knew Lubbers very well and I'm sure that amused him no end. June goes on:

"This first sip of vintage Slis was heady, leaving me somewhat stunned. But politicians of all labels knew her as one who shot remarks from the hip in a multitude of languages, so the Premier wasn't at all flustered. He reacted with humour, courtesy and candour in answering the questions we raised."

All the same, Nel certainly understood herself to be the Grande Dame of Dutch journalism and occasionally clashed with AP-Dow Jones' Victoria English, another strong woman of journalism. Short, somewhat stocky and intense, with abundant short dark hair, Victoria was not inclined to give any quarter to the older journalist.

Nel, always so immaculately turned out, was genuinely outraged by Victoria's American bobby sox and lack of stockings. Victoria was unfazed. She claimed that years of modern dancing enabled her to focus her energy, for which I can vouch. She was my first boss, an excellent and powerful journalist who taught me the trade. I was lucky to have such a good teacher.

She certainly rated herself a queen bee in financial journalism at the time, with good reason. Not for nothing, for example, did Dutch Central Bank President Wim Duisenberg, the future first President of the European Central Bank, come to her leaving party in the AP office in Amsterdam when she, like Nel years ago, was moving to Brussels.

This reminds me that Victoria was somewhat piqued to be given a lady's shaving kit by Philips as a leaving present: "All those interviews when I thought they were pondering my astute questions, they were just looking at my legs and thinking, why doesn't she shave?" She had an excellent sense of humour.

Meanwhile, in The Hague, it was becoming harder to cope with Nel's pestering habits. Friso Endt was often in the firing line. Eventually, he said, "I called Henk Kersting, her former boss, and I said what am I to do? Nel sometimes calls on Sunday morning at eight o'clock and starts yelling, and

[now] twenty times a day. Henk said, Jesus, Nel is so difficult. If she starts yelling, you yell back. It's the only thing she understands."

One of Friso's hardest jobs was getting Nel off the board of the FPA which she had chaired so successfully. By then, she was becoming a real problem. Vera Vaughan Bowden, who became FPA president in 1998, told me, "She would sit at the annual meeting, and she would say, where's that bloody Italian who walks his dog every day and lets it shit in my garden? And then another day, she would say, the bloody Brits, they think they're journalists, no way they're journalists, and she would go on about that, and then another day it would be the French. It depended on the mood."

Eventually, Friso persuaded her to resign by agreeing to do so at the same time, but the board persuaded him to stay on, as he was on the board of the Nieuwspoort press centre and dealing with its approaching move into new premises. Nel refused to talk to Friso for a year, and told everybody in Nieuwspoort he kicked her off the board and she hated him. Nevertheless, Friso was persuaded by the chairman, Helmut Hetzel, to give a farewell speech for Nel.

"So I said, Nel, you are already an honorary member, you are a member for life, but we have a medal – I think Ballasch invented it – for people who did a lot for the FPA. It's a nice silver thing, and it says, in gratitude for everything you did. You know what Nel said? I have that already – but it was a lie! So she got it anyway."

Hetzel believed Nel might have understood a tougher approach better, along the lines of Kersting's advice to shout back at her. Hetzel had first met Nel back in the early 1980s.

"What was your first impression?" I asked.

"I was very much shocked because of her impoliteness, straight words and strong voice – not fitting for a lady! But after getting to know her, I found she was an interesting person. But very impatient, of course, and very choleric. She could shout in all languages – French, English, German, Dutch."

Nel, who had certainly attacked Helmut on occasion, would nevertheless have been pleased with his final assessment:

"Most important was her attitude. She was completely independent, criticising the government. She was a critical journalist, as a journalist should be. She did not believe what politicians said, she was investigative and critical... Like a bee, buzzing around to get the honey out of the story... And she had tremendous power. She was like a volcano who could explode again and again.

"There's a good Dutch saying – she was a '*vreemde eend in de bijt*' (literally, a 'strange duck' in our midst). She was provocative – the opposite of the average silent, reluctant Dutch journalist…"

The last regular briefings Nel went on attending were the then Prime Minister Wim Kok's press conferences. In his obituary on Nel, Friso wrote: '*When Kok appeared at the annual pre-budget day press conference with the new secretary general of the prime minister's office, Ad Geelhoed, it was Nel who asked, "Mr Kok, who is the gentleman who is sitting next to you?" A young reporter said later, "We were all thinking that, but Nel asked it."*'

Eventually the day came in June 1999 to move Nel into a nursing home, the Gulden Huis on Steenhouwersgaarde in The Hague. The move was well managed but was quite nerve-racking, as her friend Yolanda Frenkel Frank recounted.

"Piet (Wackie Eysten) took Nel to the hairdresser, and Sandra and I packed stuff and put it in the moving van. She did care about clothes, she never threw them away. Ones she'd had twenty or thirty years ago were still there, hundreds of pairs of panties, cardigans, silk blouses – really a lot… Nel was quite a striking lady, very pretty when she was younger."

Tyna Wynaendts was likewise impressed by Nel's huge quantities of clothing, as well as how very well organised these were, possibly as a result of her early nursing training. Tyna said Nel also used to insist on 'hospital corners' when she was making beds with her, remarking, "You know, I'm a Swiss nurse and this is how it must be."

Over the years, Tyna said Nel squirrelled away and hoarded everything: "Thousands of doubles of everything. But it was very well organised, in neat piles, and every spring, everything came out of all the cupboards and was put back again. She was a bit of a hamster [hoarder] – Yolanda wasn't exaggerating. I've never seen anything like it. She had all her old lipsticks that were not quite finished, about twenty of them.

"We were trying to give things away and clear things out, and then we would open another cupboard, and there was more and more of it – it was incredible. Even in the cellar, there were suitcases full of clothes that were still taken out, cleaned and put back again. That was a bit of nursing mentality."

While Yolanda and Sonia were still struggling to deal with all the clothes, the hairdresser called to say Nel was finished and wanted to leave, way before they were ready.

"Piet rushed over and plonked her by the television at his house, after some yelling and screaming. She really loves him. Piet's brother and I put up her things, hung up curtains… We had come up with the idea of saying the house is being painted, you have to go out for a while.

"I had to go with her to her room. When she saw all her stuff, she sat down and stopped grumbling… A lady in the home came in – it was really very funny – with an enormous list of questions, what do you like for breakfast, porridge? Nel hooted, you must be absolutely crazy. A question about hobbies – her eyes were nearly closed, she was tired. 'HOBBIES? Hobby, I never had a hobby, don't be silly.' Working was her hobby.

"Piet and I were really sad – such an amazing woman, kicking and screaming. Why am I here with all these mad people? After the first day, she took over one of the chairs by the elevator, made it her chair for a couple of months. The nursing staff liked her very much, the only one that was more or less alive…

"Nel was quite nice to the other people too. There was one old lady, she would come by and offer her chocolates. Nel loved chocolates and cheese, she stuffed them in. They were playing bingo – can you imagine? She hadn't got a clue what everyone was doing."

This gusto for favourite foods proved an enduring characteristic. For Friso's seventieth birthday, he hired a boat and invited all his friends on a canal trip. Yolanda said he wanted Nel to be there, although she was already pretty far gone.

"'No problem,' Yolanda told him, 'I'll take her…' So she made for the herrings, she loved herrings, and Friso had only reckoned on one per person. She ate about three. Typically Nel. She sat down on the boat and it was lovely to see her with all her old mates, probably old enemies, the way they told stories – everybody in Nieuwspoort still watching her – how much admiration they had for her, it was really quite stunning."

The best part about the move, Friso said, was that once she was in her room, with some of her furniture around her and the pictures put up on the wall by Yolanda, she looked around and said it was quite nice. "Though half the time she thought she was in Brussels."

The move into the home, which took me by surprise and upset me a lot, became necessary because Nel had started to go walkabout from her flat. She wandered all over The Hague, completely lost, and was sometimes picked up by the police. There were other distressing stories about incontinence and tantrums at the Nieuwspoort press centre, but the staff there always remained completely understanding and kind to her. But getting lost was frightening; she would feel safe and be well cared for physically in the home, Friso pointed out.

A number of people continued to visit her in the home. Yolanda found she could make her laugh over a pile of old photos, but as her memory got shorter and shorter, it could be painful. Tyna said Flora Lewis didn't like visiting Nel.

"It drove her crazy, Nel asking the same question. But I gave her the same answer. Why vary it when she asks exactly the same question? And that kept her happy. And it doesn't really matter so long as you are communicating. People found it annoying when she couldn't remember them, but I would always get her to talk about the past and my mother when they were small, and then she remembered a lot better."

The end was particularly distressing, Yolanda said. Nel simply stopped eating, but still took some days to depart. Right up to the end, her will remained strong.

*

Nel Slis died on Monday 17 December 2001, aged eighty-eight. The funeral and cremation arranged by Tyna, Piet and Miek and Lars Wackie Eysten was held on 20 December at Crematorium Ockenburgh, The Hague.

CHAPTER TWENTY-ONE
CELEBRATIONS AND REFLECTIONS

A series of interviewers, myself included, made their way to Nel's apartment in The Hague in the years after her retirement from the AP to record and transmit her story to the public on some particular anniversary, or simply because they had got wind of it. As well as the gaps these helped fill in her earlier history, I found they provided a satisfying series of sketches to round off the picture of Nel and her career.

Dutch newspaperman Robert Schouten was one of her first visitors, remarking, "Journalists are not supposed to interview each other, is the normal opinion in journalism. But Nel Slis simply has to be an exception to this rule. After all, she also belongs to the category of women-who-have-made-a-career." And after all, she was breaking new ground in so doing.

The Schouten interview photo is one of my favourites, with Nel, cigarette in hand, gesturing towards her interlocutor with a thoughtful expression on her deeply lined, still handsome face, pearls over her chic Chanel-style cardigan.

Nel had finally retired on May Day, 1979. She was quick to remind Robert that she had wrung an extra eight months from the AP, which was completely exceptional. "It is an iron rule that you have to go when you're sixty-five."

So why did they keep her on? Schouten asked. "Among other reasons because they thought that the queen would abdicate on her seventieth birthday, and I am well informed about royalty… But that abdication is now no longer expected for the moment."

Schouten's interview was headlined *'Give me the nub of the business'*, which must have pleased Nel. He started with a riff on Nel's voice: "'Madam, you are blessed with a strong voice.' Nel Slis glances, not a bit surprised, at photographer Kurt Boekenkamp, who is setting up his camera. Behind her back, men are apt to compare her voice to a foghorn."

Nel's strong, smoky voice was the first thing that struck me as well. Robert spotted its usefulness as a journalistic tool: "The awe-inspiring noise that this astute woman can produce – if necessary also in English, French, German and Italian – is undoubtedly one of the qualities that has made her, as correspondent of the powerful American press bureau Associated Press since the war in The Hague and Brussels, into a professional difficult to circumvent."

Government officials might dislike and even deride her approach, he said, but they respected it: "No long stories, please. Give me the core of the business. What are you doing there the whole goddam day, if you can't do that."

Schouten noticed the telex still rattling away in her study. "I shall miss that thing, not the noise, but the information," Nel remarked. Then, "looking rather helplessly at enormous piles of newspapers and reports on the floor, looking for photos that refuse to appear, she says, 'I can't find anything anymore. One of these days, I must just chuck everything out…'" Fortunately, the typical journalist's reluctance to throw stuff away prevailed; otherwise, it would have been near impossible to write this book.

Igor Cornelissen's interview in *Vrij Nederland* in 1982 was headlined *'And on top of that I had the good fortune to have a nose for news'*. It was Igor who suggested Nel should have gone down in history as 'That woman who stopped Molotov', rather than 'that difficult broad'.

Incidentally, Keith Fuller, who succeeded Wes Gallagher as President and General Manager of the AP, also recalled some of Nel's other big stories in a letter of appreciation on her retirement: *'I know you will look back with pride on the big stories you helped cover, including the Moluccan siege, the Prince Bernhard story and the Common Market. It will seem strange to think of anyone else covering the tough political scene.'*

The photo for Igor Cornelissen's interview was taken head-on, with Nel sitting bolt upright and looking almost regal. He considered Nel what the English called a 'character'. Noting the AP house magazine once described her as vivacious and charming, he commented, "Charming we would not want to dispute, but vivacious is definitely too weak a word. Slis is the writing tornado of the Foreign Press Association."

In November 1988, when Nel was seventy-five, the Foreign Press Association celebrated her forty-five years as a journalist with a reception in Nieuwspoort. As I was standing at the reception with Nel's former FPA vice chairman David Post and a friend of his from England, the English friend was astounded to see Prime Minister Ruud Lubbers stroll in and amiably heckle Nel from the back of the room, without a bodyguard in sight.

Endt, who arranged the celebration, had assembled a book of multilingual tributes from dozens of friends. Among these, Herman Bleich called her 'the terror of press officers' and Manuel Santarelli, director of information at the European Commission, '*la personnalité la plus craquante, la plus attachante*'.

An article in the *Haagse Post* was headlined by her favourite tag on how she became a journalist: '*I fell into it like a hair in the soup*'. She told the paper her career had been '*a long and often also a hard time. But I would do it all over again with pleasure*'.

In 1991, Monique Smits' portrait of Nel Slis appeared in the *Mediakrant* under that modest remark of Nel's: '*If it's about news, I trample them all into the corner*'. Smits, too, was impressed by the dynamism of the seventy-eight-year-old, still in harness, though becoming a little chaotic.

"Who sent you?" she asked Monique, looking her up and down curiously in her hall full of bulging bookcases. Smits thought of other journalists' descriptions of Nel: "The terror of many an authority and spokesman, but with a soft heart. *Never a dull moment* with Nel." She, too, remarked on her voice; 'sonorous' and 'from the back of her throat, deepened a fair number of octaves by cigarettes'.

Nel then '*rushes irrepressibly hither and thither and in a bird's eye view unveils her wanderings around the world and landing up in journalism,*' Monique wrote. Later, she produced her framed photo of Han Boon, Foreign Affairs State Secretary under Joseph Luns as Foreign Minister, inscribed by Boon: '*To Nel Slis. Dynamic, intrepid, a true friend over the years*'. At the end of the interview, Nel was already getting back to work.

In 1993, Ageeth Scherphuis' extensive and sympathetic portrait, '*Nel Slis' 80-year War: The Lady of the Press*' in *Vrij Nederland* newspaper was one of several marking Nel Slis' eightieth birthday. Her introduction is a reminder of how unique Nel was and what a battle she faced.

The only women among a hundred wily correspondents. "That difficult woman", on facts and checking and bolting barefoot to that godforsaken telephone. The news must get onto the wire. On her male colleagues: nitpickers. And on women: milksops, they were, and still they don't do anything.

A nice girl from the South Holland islands at Associated Press, one of the biggest press agencies in the world. She had to hammer away harder than such a nice little man from NRC. It made her more aggressive than she was, she says, and it gave her a bigger gob. Definitely.

A big gob and a smart face were her best assets, Nel declared. "And then if you are also a bit intelligent."

Ageeth reckoned Nel was better known in the world than in Holland. "In Brussels, she is La Slis and in New York every journalist knows her. In The Hague, she's that difficult woman, who always wants to hear everything twice before she reports it."

However, she had mellowed somewhat. "She is a lamb now, compared with earlier," Gijs van der Wiel, former director of the government information service, told Ageeth. Van der Wiel described a typical dialogue he had had a hundred times with Nel:

"By night and at breakfast she called me with this heavy, smoky voice, put her questions and drew her conclusions. If I then said, 'Nel, that's not how it is,' she shouted back, 'How is it then, goddammit?' And I came back again: 'That I can't goddam tell you yet.' A manner of conversation that I did like, but the younger spokesmen were not all charmed by it."

Nel had 'an extraordinary journalist's intuition', Van der Wiel told Ageeth. "She is very persistent and she has unheard-of energy. Intuitively, she knows what's going on and then she sticks to it, stopping at nothing.

"But nobody will run aground with this woman – she is trustworthy. Never have I heard a minister or civil servant interviewed by her complain: *that I did not say.* They can be shocked by their own remarks, especially because it goes to the world abroad…

"'I will read [what they said] over to you,' she says then.

"And me: 'Yes, but can't there be a word in between? It is really so very strong.'

"'They goddam said it like that.'

"'But if you tone it down a bit.'

"'No, then it would be such goddam flabby trash.'"

Her knighthood from den Uyl did not make her any softer or easier, Van der Wiel told Ageeth: "Difficult she is, and impatient. Always with the hot breath of the competition on her neck. 'Don't you goddam have anything for me yet, UPI will soon be running away with it.'"

"So," Nel said to Ageeth at the end of the interview, "now you know my whole history. Why should people be afraid of me? As you see, I am a lamb."

Algemeen Dagblad reporter Sjef van Woensel was impressed by the eightieth birthday reception for a 'trustworthy big mouth' given for her by the European Commission, at which she was presented with an entire edition of *Europe Tomorrow* devoted to her:

To whom does it happen that the prime minister comes to address you because you are having your eightieth birthday? And who gives you a free reception with hundreds of people attending? This happened yesterday to Nel Slis, a very well-known journalist in The Hague who worked as correspondent for the Associated Press in the Netherlands from 1945.

Among the eminent people coming to shake her hand were Foreign Minister Pieter Kooijmans and – again – Prime Minister Ruud Lubbers, the latter praising Nel for her tenacity in questioning and the trustworthiness of her reports. '*The premier also put up happily with the big mouth that made Slis a colourful and resonant figure in The Hague,*' Sjef wrote.

"What do you think of the Dutch press after forty-eight years?" Sjef asked Nel.

With her 'harsh, penetrating voice', she said it should sometimes be a bit more critical. "They could hit home a bit more often. That does not have to be hard or improper."

What irritated her was that the Dutch news media had so few correspondents abroad. "You are a little country..." Nel often distanced herself from her own country... "but the papers should really invest more money in correspondents. Young dogs that build up experience abroad and can accomplish very good work in their own country after that. They would also be more critical then."

Sjef wanted to know if Nel saw changes. "Oh yes, certainly. The Dutch have evolved very much in their opinions. Earlier, when I began here, they were very reserved. Now they are much more free, for instance, in the political area and as far as sex is concerned."

And finally, he asked, "How long will you go on with your work?"

"As long as I can talk and walk. So I hope a long time yet."

The last interview I found was Ineke Geraerdts' piece in *Nieuwspoort Nieuws*, in October 1993. When Geraerdts complained to her editor that *Vrij Nederland* had covered everything conceivable in its spread of three full pages, she was advised to ask Nel what she missed in that interview. The piece she wrote, '*News has become second nature to me*', has considerable atmosphere and a revealing sad note:

She lights up another cigarette. A slim, well-dressed woman, with lively brown eyes that assess me curiously. "What I missed? Something about my work. There is a lot in it about my career, but my work never came up. It is still very important for me. I could not do without it. That would bore me to death."

Her home on The Hague's Ranonkelstraat breathes the atmosphere of a student flat. Furious clean-up attempts stranded on the impossibility of throwing away books, magazines and other valuable piles of paper. The walls are good for reminders of former times, well-loved people, foreign countries: a print of a San Francisco swimming bath, a photo of a good friend who is no longer around, a watercolour of a country lane on Goeree-Overflakkee…

She looks around. "Good, isn't it? But now and then I have to get away for a month or two, when I've had enough of this fiddling around here."

Would she move? Ineke asked.

"Moving again? I couldn't think of having to drag all this mess with me. No, just now and again going away for a couple of months is a fine solution for now. It is like the Rock of Gibraltar here in the winter. Then I go to the south of France… If I was not Dutch, I would only like to be French. I still have a few good friends, but they are becoming fewer. Sometimes I think: what have I done to deserve it that I'm still here? All these boys that I have known, apart from a couple, are already in their coffins…

"My big trump card was of course my knowledge of languages. I still remember that Gijs van der Wiel called me up one time with a cry for help: 'Can you come to the Portuguese prime minister's press conference? I'm stuck here with twelve young press guys who don't even understand a word of French.' Underestimating the importance of languages is a mistaken way of thinking."

Ineke also asked Nel about Joseph Luns, Dutch Foreign Minister and later NATO chief. *'You had the nickname in The Hague of "the terror of Luns". Were you so difficult for him?'* Nel responded to the question but moved on quickly to Lubbers.

"Of course not. I was maybe not the easiest, but Luns was such a conceited man that he was actually scared of everyone... Do you know who I really have admiration for? For Lubbers. After Drees, Lubbers comes top for me. If he goes, I go too. Lubbers is an extraordinary man. Exceptional. The fact that he is Catholic, I don't blame him for that. You might as well know, I'm not mad about these fine Holland Catholics, but I find Calvinists just as creepy.

"I have known Lubbers so long, first as MP, then as economic affairs minister. He has only had ten years as premier after all. He has flair, talent for ironing out messes. I do not believe that he has many enemies. An international career should suit him. Delors is stepping down next year."

Jacques Delors was the departing European Commission chief, and Nel, like many others at the time, was hoping that Lubbers would succeed him, but this didn't happen.

Ineke's interview was headlined: *'If Lubbers goes, I go too'.*

Geraerdts concluded: *'Nel Slis is now eighty and not yet "at peace". She still takes care of reports for 'Europe, agence internationale d'information pour la presse', writes features for Europa Magazine (an EEC publication in New York), writes articles for the chemical magazines of DSM, Akzo and Gist Brocades...*

In the winter months her car is parked in the Lange Lombardstraat every Thursday evening. Nel Slis polishes up her Italian. Soon she is going to start learning Russian as well: "I met such nice White Russians in those days in France at the Sorbonne."

Oh yes, some people are unstoppable...'

One of the interviews inspired a letter from an amazed seventy-seven-year-old woman from Gouda, saying what Nel had achieved '*borders on the unbelievable. Nurse, Sorbonne, Oxford, almost psychiatry, English, French, German, Italian, translating from New York for the Netherlands Purchasing Commission, AP correspondent in a man's world, and then still to look so nice!*'

In 1995, Nel featured as '*the grand old lady of the press*' in a centenary exhibition mounted by the Netherlands Press Museum, entitled '*Voor alles journaliste*' (Journalist above all). The exhibition leaflet says: '*She distinguished herself from her male colleagues by her direct approach, tenacious persistence in asking questions, and lack of respect for authority*'. Its centrefold is a photo of Nel with Luns when he was NATO Secretary General.

Shifting the emphasis from celebrations to reflections, when I visited Nel's old friend Flora Lewis in Paris in 2001 not long before Nel died, I asked her what she missed most about her.

"Oh, just an old friend. Comfort. We had little junkets, excursions, which I couldn't bear to do later, because she insisted on driving and she was a terrible, awful driver."

"Where did you go?"

"Oh, in France, places we wanted to go, or I had some reason to look at, or because we thought there might be a story. A place that I was eager to visit, that had some artistic or historical or picturesque interest or that was attractive. She was adventurous..."

"How would you describe her as a journalist?"

"I think she was a kind of role model, rule-breaker, that made it easier for women... I think her contribution was just steady, honest reporting. Sturdy, sober, getting the information, reliability, credibility. She was honest. She would ask tough questions because she wasn't about to play softball – to give someone an easy ride because she liked them.

"But on the other hand, even if she didn't like someone, she wouldn't ask mean questions, she wouldn't ask trick questions. It was all very straightforward. The sources who knew her, because it's a small country and they all know each other quite well, learned quickly that they could rely on her. She wouldn't distort, pretend, twist. She didn't try to trip people, but she didn't give them a puffball either. She was a very straightforward, hardworking, uncomplicated reporter. She was about exactly what she said she was about."

"She was very curious, wasn't she, right from her childhood?"

"That's what makes a reporter. She had some problem with her father...

She said that was one of the reasons she was eager to get off and be a newspaperwoman, because she wanted very much to reach this stage of independence.

"She would try very hard, she was very persistent, but she wouldn't pretend to be somebody she wasn't. Lots of people do that. Woodward and Bernstein tell in one of their books about Watergate that they broke into an apartment and stole documents: Nel would never do that.

"And you get – particularly with television people – this pretending to be somebody that they're not, pretending to want to ask about one thing, when they're really trying for something else. Nel was always honest.

"Practically everybody who knew Nel was fond of her. You saw that Lubbers was also. Well, because one admired her, it was exactly this independent-mindedness, this honesty, this certainty that you knew who and what she was, and that's extremely attractive. Particularly in a society where that kind of woman was unusual."

As I was typing up Flora's thoughts and adding a mental proviso that there were in fact a fair few people who actively disliked Nel, I had an email from Texas. It was from Laura Raun, a friend of Nel's and previous fellow FPA board member, with this charming image of Nel in the kitchen:

Oddly enough, my most vivid memories are of Nel in her personal life, not her professional one. For example, Nel was meticulous about cooking. When she made an oil and lemon dressing, she was very careful about measuring out the ingredients and mixing them thoroughly in a small, clear bowl. I can still see her in the kitchen, the sun silhouetting her, stirring that dressing.

I loved Nel's flat in The Hague because it had windows in every room. It was a virtual glasshouse, close to the water. We would go for walks on the beach, sometimes stopping for a coffee on the boardwalk.

I would stay overnight and she was a perfect hostess. Nel adored having a captive audience to hear her colourful tales of friends and colleagues across Europe. Her throaty voice painted the picture. Her cigarette-wielding hands accentuated it.

Yolanda, too, remembered Nel's salad dressing. "It always tasted better than anyone else's, even if we made it exactly the same way. She was a very good cook, liked to make salads, that type of thing."

Nel's favourite politician, Ruud Lubbers, who promoted her to Officer of Oranje-Nassau at the second of the FPA anniversary celebrations over which she presided, has the last word on her. Lubbers, the longest-serving Dutch prime minister (1982–1994), went on to chair the World Wildlife Fund and in 2001 became UN High Commissioner for Refugees. He died 14 February 2018, aged 78.

In autumn 1999, I wrote to Lubbers to ask for his help during my early struggles with Nel's biography. He phoned me back at once. He said he was coming to the Nieuwe Kerk in Amsterdam to meet the Dalai Lama and told me to come along there and 'say you have an appointment with me'.

A very young lad on the door looked totally disbelieving when I dismounted muddily from my bike in the pouring rain and told him this as instructed, but at that moment, Lubbers rushed out, grabbed my arm and whisked me inside, saying, "I need this woman," leaving the doorboy gaping.

Sitting on the steps of the crowded Nieuwe Kerk., Lubbers said, "I liked Nel. The strangest thing is that she was a Francophile and I also am – I was intrigued by the fact she was a Francophile. Though in the European context, she was more British – communitaire – a no-nonsense approach to Europe." Lubbers himself was famous for his 'no-nonsense' politics.

"A very straight lady, and open. And I found her typically Dutch – *Les Gueux*. At the beginning of the sixteenth century, the aristocrats joined with the ordinary people… they protested – if you go, we go too. It's the French for beggars. So Nel was one of *Les Gueux*, and I had something in common with her."

I was mystified by this *Les Gueux* business, but with the help of Wikipedia discovered that the sixteenth-century Dutch protesters against Spanish rule were called beggars by their Spanish regent's advisor and they then adopted this as the name of their revolutionary movement.

Lubbers went on: "She was plain-speaking, and the fact that she was a Francophile gave me an intimate feeling with her. As a journalist, she was good – direct, not scared, not impressed by authority. But I had the impression she was a colleague as well. She could team up with people in the British press, managing essential, vital contacts with colleagues.

"I had the impression she was old-fashioned in a way as a journalist, not looking for headlines. I always felt secure – it's not normal with modern journalists. She was a very civilized lady. Open, not respectful of authority, but at the same time, you could trust her. You are a bit scared of journalists. Sometimes they abuse you, but she did not.

"I found she had a good grasp and analysis of Europe, remarkably good. Not only contributing as a journalist, but in her own right. You could learn something from her. I learnt a lot from her."

POSTSCRIPT
AVE ATQUE VALE

On a squally, showery April day in the year 2000, I set off by train from Amsterdam to Rotterdam, excited and a little nervous, to visit Nel's island for the first time. I wanted to sniff the air she breathed and feel out the place where she grew up. I hoped this would be an inspiration as I went on trying to assemble the jigsaw of her exciting and sometimes tumultuous life. So many pieces were missing. I knew Nel for nearly twenty years, but I had never really been with her for more than odd hours or the odd evening. I learned Nel in very small slices, forced to reflect her world in broken fragments. But now at least I would have a glimpse of the island of which she was so proud. Something about an islander...

It was only a short metro ride from Rotterdam to Zuidplein to catch the bus to Goeree-Overflakkee, a very straightforward trip compared with Nel's epic outings to Rotterdam as a child. On the bus, I craned eagerly through the window like a child myself, looking out for the crossing to the island. Every detail of the trip became riveting, crying out for some significance, some meaning, some Nel association. As the bus reached the long bridge to the island, tall white wind turbines lined the mainland shore, one inexplicably immobile but the others briskly circling their skinny arms. Nel's island was just visible in the distance. On the other side, another line of turbines waved us onto the island. There, ponies and black cattle grazed between swathes of water, as if the land was reluctant to part from the sea. Then the heavens opened and blinding sheets of rain blotted everything out.

In Middelharnis, the rain abated. As I searched for the town hall, I was delighted to recognise Nel's old primary school from photos I'd seen. The town hall turned out to be at the previous bus stop and was closed for lunch. A group of some thirty teenagers clustered around a dark, barn-like café nearby. Did they perhaps have a distinctive Goeree-Overflakkee physiognomy? The girls were blonde, but seemed distinctively thin and wiry like Nel, not faintly bovine as they could sometimes be elsewhere. They looked a lively lot. The boys looked like boys anywhere.

The burley middle-aged café landlord said the place had changed since the first bridge was built, with people from Rotterdam settling here 'for the nature' and nobody speaking the old dialect anymore. Perhaps Nel spoke that dialect as a child.

When the town hall opened, the enthusiastic Mr Both had me enthralled for hours with his descriptions of early twentieth-century island life that have formed the basis of the first chapter of this book. Then there was just time to visit Middelharnis graveyard before catching the bus back. An imposing-looking group of Jewish gravestones faced the larger group of Protestant island dignitaries dominated by the Slis family. That Jewish community on the island reminded me of the only man Nel really loved: Dan Schorr. I wondered again whether the child Nel was perhaps a little fascinated by that community.

Here I came full circle and at last encountered the island of Nel's beginnings. Something about an islander... Back on the bus, I scrambled to do my daily translations via laptop; it ran out of battery in Rotterdam and I rushed into an Etos drugstore and borrowed some electricity to finish my work. So has it always been, always trying to do the Nel book along with too many other things. That's the story of *my* life.

From Rotterdam, I travelled on to The Hague's seaside suburb of Scheveningen to stay the night with Vera Vaughan Bowden, Nel's third successor as president of the Foreign Press Association. The next day, I talked on the phone to Nel's nephew Hans Nieuwenhuyzen, who was feeling terrible, as he was having chemotherapy, but still wanted to find an old photo of four generations of the Slis family including Nel, and to photocopy the Slis genealogy for me.

Later, Vera and I took the tram together to visit Nel. I was so happy Vera was coming too. On my last two visits on my own, Nel was sleepy and far away in some other world. I found it heartbreaking and could only bear to stay for a short while.

Her carers told us things were not too good and Nel was refusing to put in her teeth. I knew that she could be aggressive; I felt it must be the frustration of not remembering the end of any sentence you begin. The last I heard, from Friso, some old man in the home was convinced Nel was his wife and kept trying to hug her, but got a few kicks from Nel in return. "Tragic but humorous," said Friso. There was life in the old dog yet, I thought.

We started the usual hunt for Nel, who was inclined to wander into someone else's room and fall asleep. Then, at the end of the corridor near her room, we saw an unmistakable tiny figure silhouetted against the window and rushed to corral her into her room. She looked fragile and birdlike but still smart in a brown Chanel-type wool suit. Vera's soft Belgian chocolates were a big success; she could hardly wait for Vera to open the box and ate one after another. Now and again, she went and stood by the window and gazed out at the sky, far away somewhere else.

She was quite wide awake and several times attempted some sentences, but they died away unfinished, sometimes causing a flash of anger. The nearest to a coherent one was about some girl that disappeared; we wondered where that came from. She also walked companionably with us to the lift when we left, uttering more half-sentences; we could feel flashes of her old charm.

Vera and I talked later about how these kinds of sociable manners could persist. My mother, for instance, who was pretty much in a daze in her last few years, still invariably rallied to say: "Have you eaten yet?" Vera also reminded me of Nel's reluctance to part with us until Vera said we were going to see FPA member Frank de Jong, a name that produced a slight gleam of recognition.

While we were visiting, I talked determinedly at Nel about the book, optimistically told her it would be finished soon, and showed her photos from her archives and the ones of her father and mother that her nephew had given me. She gazed over my head for a while, but eventually started looking at the photos. She seemed interested in the ones of her father and Dan Schorr and then the ones with Prince Claus, Lubbers, Stravinsky and other famous people. For a moment, perhaps she was transported back in time to her days of power and glory, as the AP's Slis, La Slis of Brussels, Hellcat of The Hague…

We tiptoed away but she came friendly with us to the door…

'Rage, rage, how does that poem go?
I feel it so
So sad to see Nel now
Her battle almost done
A glorious fight, hacking
Through that grey male phalanx
Adding colour, illuminating
With sharp, clear eye for detail and what lies beneath
Her nose for news, her probing quest
Never flagging, unstoppable
Her iron Goeree constitution, tireless to the end.
And let's not forget, warm-hearted
Endless kindness
Empowering nervous newbies, women
A raucous laugh, a smoky voice, cutting through the cackle – or cackling!
We celebrate the life of Nel.'

Caroline Studdert

ACKNOWLEDGEMENTS

For the photos in the book, we are greatly indebted to the collection of The Netherlands Institute for Sound and Vision, which houses Nel's archives. And I would particularly like to thank conservator Jop Euwijk for all his enormous help and enthusiasm on this edition of the Nel Slis story.

Indeed, so many people helped me on the long road I have trodden in search of Nel that it is impossible to pay tribute properly to everybody. One thing is certain, though. Without Brad Gaiennie's patient piloting back in the day in Prague, *Hellcat of The Hague* would never have made it into print at all. Deepest thanks to Brad, sadly no longer with us.

Yolanda Frenkel Frank, Tyna Wynaendts and Piet Wackie Eysten, Friso Endt and Hans Nieuwenhuyzen, as mentioned previously, played key roles in the shaping of Nel's story, while going back to her beginnings, archivist Jan Both enthusiastically provided that picture of the island society of Goeree-Overflakkee in the early decades of the last century.

Special thanks are due to former Dutch Prime Minister Ruud Lubbers (RIP) for sitting on the steps of the Nieuwe Kerk with me and talking about Nel when the Dalai Lama was visiting Amsterdam back at the beginning of the millennium. Famous US journalist and commentator Daniel Schorr (RIP), one-time partner of Nel, and her old friend and *Financial Times* journalist Reginald Dale (RIP) both gave key telephone interviews from Washington. My own former AFX News colleagues Sarah Borchersen-Keto put me in touch with Schorr and John Buckley kept me informed on events including, sadly, Nel's demise after I left Holland.

Interviews and anecdotes came generously from Foreign Press Association former chairmen Helmut Hetzel and Friso Endt (RIP), former FPA president Vera Vaughan Bowden (RIP) and Nel's vice chairpeople David Post (RIP) and Laura Raun among many others. Members of the Prague Writers' Group gave me many suggestions when I was stuck, and in London, members of the Original Writers' Group had much good advice on making the tale more accessible. As I keep remembering more people from time to time, a special thank-you to those whose names the black hole I call my memory has yet to disgorge.

Fortunately, Nel's own voice can be heard joining in the conversation about her throughout the book thanks to the interviews she gave and her own writings. Her own battered filing cabinet yielded a wealth of source material on her own work, as well as masses of press cuttings on the various topics of the day. Any remaining deficiencies and errors despite all this help are all my own work and responsibility.

REFERENCES

Articles, typescripts and books consulted include:

1   1957 Slis typescripts on emigrant ship *Waterman*'s collision with Italian freighter, on trip to New York, articles written during her stint at the AP's New York and Washington offices
2   Slis typescript: Interview with Queen Fatima of Libya 1954
3   Foreign Press Association – Buitenlandse Persvereniging in Nederland thirtieth anniversary magazine, 1955. Forewords by Prime Minister Willem Drees and Prince Bernhard, articles by Henk Kersting and by Nel Slis ('*We – Women Correspondents – Want to be Taken Seriously*')
4   AP World Service item NEWSMEN AT WORK, on Common Market summit conference November 23–29, 1969
5   Slis typescripts on changes in the Netherlands in the 1960s and 1970s and on the den Uyl and Van Agt cabinets
6   Article on departure of Slis to Brussels, '*Hartelijk Afscheid van Nel Slis*' in *Het Parool*, 23 August 1963
7   Article by G. Toussaint on departure of Slis to Brussels in *De vrouw en haar huis* (*Woman and Home*), October 1963
8   Slis typescripts on trip around the United States
9   Slis typescripts on Staphorst story, November 1973
10 Miscellaneous Slis typescripts covering members of the royal family
11 Article on Slis in *The Bulletin* magazine, '*The Dutch in Belgium*', undated
12 Slis typescripts on Joseph Luns and Sicco Mansholt
13 Slis typescript for Kennemer Lyceum reunion, plus Schmal typescript, 1974
14 '*Het Europese journalistenwereldje*' ('*European Journalists' World*') in *Vrouwen en hun belangen* (*Women and their Interests*) Vol 39, no. 3, June 1974
15 Slis typescripts on hijacking, independence for Surinam, politics and politicians and other topics from 1974 onwards
16 Slis typescripts on Lockheed affair, 1976

17 AWCA (American Women's Club of Amsterdam) Guest speaker 2 March 1978, interview with Slis by Madeline Landau in November issue of AWCA *Bulletin.*

18 AP World item 'Nel Slis retires' by John Gale, Amsterdam Bureau Chief, 1979

19 *Vrij Nederland* interview with Robert Schouten, *'Nel Slis: "Geef me de kern van de zaak"'* (Give me the nub of the business), 1979

20 *Haagsche Courant*, *'De Franse ambassadeur Kemoularia reikt Nel Slis de onderscheiding uit'* (French ambassador Kemoularia presents Nel Slis with the decoration – La Croix d'Officier de l'Órdre National du Merit, 14 September 1982

21 *Vrij Nederland* interview by Igor Cornelissen (*'And on top of that I had the good fortune to have a nose for news'*), 1982

22 *Het Parool* item in Apropos round-up on women in a man's world, *'Een handvol luizen in een mannenpels'* (*'A handful of lice in a male hide'*), 11 October 1984

23 Article partly about Nel Slis by Jeanne Roos, 1983. Roos was a *Het Parool* journalist after the war and the first person seen on Dutch television's launch 2 October 1951, and she also appeared in Theo van Gogh films. She died 30 June 2001

24 *'Foreign Press Association celebrates 60th anniversary'*, Worldwide News, May 1985

25 *Haagsche Courant* interview, *'Ik viel erin al seen haar in de soep'* (*'I fell into it like a hair in the soup'*), 19 November 1988

26 *De Mediakrant* interview by Monique Smits, *'Als het om nieuws gaat, trap ik ze allemaal in de hoek'* (*'If it's about news, I trample them all into the corner'*), 1990

27 *Algemeen Dagblad* interview by Sjef van Woensel, *'Afscheid van een betrouwbare grote mond'* (*'Reception for a trustworthy big mouth'*), 3 September 1993

28 *Vrij Nederland* interview by Ageeth Scherphuis, *'Nel Slis' 80-year War: The Lady of the Press'*, 28 August 1993

29 NIEUWSPOORTNIEUWS interview by Ineke Geraerdts, *'Eighty-year old Nel Slis: "If Lubbers goes, I'll go too"'*, October 1993

30 Radio interview in 'Wie bent U eigentlijk' series 1990

31 NPnieuws, *'Invloed van de BPV sinds "Brussel" danig geslonken'* (*'Influence of the FPA much reduced since "Brussels"'*), September 2000

Books:

1 Nel Slis, journaliste Een levensschets door Piet Wackie Eysten, 2001

2 Harvest of Journeys by Hammond Innes, published 1960 by Knopf

3 Changing by Liv Ullman, first published in Great Britain 1977 by Weidenfeld and Nicholson

AUTHOR'S INTERVIEWS

Interviews include:

1   Jan Both, Middelharnis archivist (4 April 2001)
2   Randoll Coate, maze-maker, former diplomat and friend of Nel in The Hague and Brussels (21 March 2002)
3   Isabel Conway, journalist, former FPA vice president (sometime in 2000)
4   Reginald Dale, *Financial Times* journalist, friend (17 June 2001)
5   Friso Endt, journalist, friend and carer (3 August 2000)
6   Yolanda Frenkel Frank, theatre producer, friend and carer (29 March 2000)
7   Helmut Hetzel, journalist, former FPA president (23 April 2002)
8   Gonne Hollander, The Hague friend and travelling companion (2002)
9   Elizabeth de Jong van Beek en Donk, Nel and Gonne Hollander's beautician and friend in The Hague (February 2003)
10   Flora Lewis, renowned American journalist and columnist, friend of Nel and Daniel Schorr (20 January 2001)
11   Ruud Lubbers, former Dutch Prime Minister, World Wildlife chairman, UN High Commissioner for Refugees
12   Jan Nieuwenhuyzen, Nel's nephew (3 October 2000)
13   David Post, journalist, FPA vice chairman and friend of Nel and author
14   Daniel Schorr, renowned American print, TV and radio journalist (NBC, CNN) and the man Nel loved (19 December 1999)
15   Allan Tillier, journalist, friend of Reginald Dale (various)
16   Vera Vaughan Bowden, journalist, FPA president (2000)
17   Tyna Wynaendts, librarian, daughter of Nel's childhood friend Janneke (November 2002)
18   Piet Wackie Eysten, lawyer, brother of Tyna

Additionally, the author's first interview with Nel, published as '*Hellcat of The Hague*' in *Holland Life* magazine August 1981, plus several others with Nel at the end of the 1990s.

ABOUT THE AUTHOR

Irish writer, editor and translator Caroline Studdert has always made her living from some kind of writing and can even remember writing bits and pieces in childhood - though mostly reading omnivorously. Growing up happily with cats, dogs and ponies, home-schooled in an Anglo-Irish family in Waterford, Ireland, boarding school in England was a shock after her naval father died young.

She flourished at Trinity College Dublin, to her surprise doing well in economics and political science. Her first job, in market research, was in the London building where Dorothy Sayers set '*Murder must advertise*,' but she soon 'sidled into motivational research', then being pioneered in Ireland: 'Running away from economics into psychology.'

After years living abroad with her husband in Miami, Paris, London and Tobruk, Libya, came a move to Amsterdam and through Nel Slis, a new career. "The marriage didn't work out but the new career did. I really wanted to write, but as a single mum-of-two, I had to make a living. So friends said, you'd better be a journalist.' So she 'sidled back into economics' at AP-Dow Jones financial news service located in Nel's Associated Press office; her newborn daughter even slept in the AP dark room. Next came a stint at the Dutch financial newspaper, before winding up as bureau chief at Financial Times-AFP's AFX News.

Falling in love with Prague, she and her composer partner moved there in 2001. There she translated the Dutch news, worked on the first Hellcat version and became CEE Editor for Property Investor Europe. After the partner died, she settled in London near her son, leaving journalism to concentrate on her own writing, editing and translating. And to keep travelling: Montenegro, Macedonia, Kyrgyzstan, South America, Mongolia. She has three grandsons and one granddaughter, and is currently working on a children's book with one of her grandsons, as well as a novel and a short story collection.